After Universal Design

After Universal Design

The Disability Design Revolution

Edited by
Elizabeth Guffey

BLOOMSBURY VISUAL ARTS
LONDON · NEW YORK · OXFORD · NEW DELHI · SYDNEY

BLOOMSBURY VISUAL ARTS
Bloomsbury Publishing Plc
50 Bedford Square, London, WC1B 3DP, UK
1385 Broadway, New York, NY 10018, USA
29 Earlsfort Terrace, Dublin 2, Ireland

BLOOMSBURY, BLOOMSBURY VISUAL ARTS and the Diana logo are
trademarks of Bloomsbury Publishing Plc

First published in Great Britain 2023

Cover design by Louise Dugdale

A catalogue record for this book is available from the British Library.

A catalog record for this book is available from the Library of Congress.

ISBN: HB: 978-1-3502-4151-0
         PB: 978-1-3502-4150-3
         ePDF: 978-1-3502-4153-4
         eBook: 978-1-3502-4152-7

Typeset by Integra Software Services Pvt. Ltd.
Printed and bound in India

To find out more about our authors and books visit www.bloomsbury.com
and sign up for our newsletters.

Contents

Section 2 Equity

Section 3 Speculation

List of Figures

Acknowledgments

Books are very much like journeys where you begin the trip thinking you would go somewhere, only to discover serendipitous sidetracks, unexpected hold-ups, and always multiple changes of plan. This is the case with this text in particular. What started as a project centered on "design for one" and disability quickly took new shape and held unexpected twists as solicited manuscripts began to arrive. Conversations with colleagues shifted things still further. Supportive and discerning, the book's anonymous peer reviewers read the first iterations of this proposal with enthusiasm and vision, pushing the ambitions of this text even further by offering critical feedback and re-framing ideas. In all, the process has more than demonstrated the value of critique, allyship, and the collectivity of creative activities.

The Bard Graduate Center was the ideal environment for thinking about the implications of the historical and contemporary implications explored in this book. I thank Peter Miller, Catherine Whalen, Helen Polson, Frejya Hartzell, Meredith Linn, and Aaron Glass for their feedback and support. I have also benefited greatly from the intellectual engagement of colleagues at the Disability Studies Initiative at the University of California, Santa Barbara, including Catherine Nesci and Rachel Lambert, the History Department's History of Science workshop, including Brad Bouley and Patrick McCray, as well as Miroslava Chavez-Garcia. Many other people have taken time to read parts of this book or helped me along in the writing process, including Sarah Teasley, Carma Gorman, David Serlin, and Sara Hendren. I am especially indebted to Alison Adams for her invaluable assistance in assembling so many voices into one volume. Finally, my deepest gratitude is for my life partner, Matt Ferranto, whose support has continued to sustain me.

Glossary of Terms

Ableism (and ableist) is a term describing discrimination or prejudice against people with disabilities.

Allyship is the support, solidarity, and partnership between disabled people and/or with individuals who are nondisabled; this collaboration often involves advocacy for rights, access, and inclusion.

Assistive technology (AT) is used by people with disabilities in order to carry out tasks or functions that might in any other way be challenging or impossible.

Bespoke refers to a product designed and made specifically for one user, in consultation with that person.

Bodymind refers to the concept that the body and the mind are interconnected and should be seen as a single unit.

Crip refers to people who experience any form of disability; the term has been reclaimed, changing from a slur and becoming commonly used as an assertion of identity within the disability rights movement.

Crip time recognizes different experiences of the passing of time. Implicitly, it suggests an appreciation that disabled people can think, move, or speak at different pace.

Design for one focuses the design process on a single user, but implies a larger learning process that can be applied to future work.

Design for user empowerment not only centers a design on users' needs but enables them to solve their own accessibility problems.

Friction can refer to grinding, rubbing, or abrasion but also denotes anything that undermines goals or established plans. In disability design the term can suggest a form of critique, implying disrupted expectations of normal ways of being and moving through the world.

Impairment is a physical, mental, learning, and sensory difference. This can result from injury, illness, or a congenital condition that causes or is likely to cause a loss or variance of physiological or psychological function.

Interdependence posits a mutuality of trust, reliance, and aid between people. In disability studies this can also mean recognizing the joint work that people with disabilities and others do to make something accessible.

Medical model defines disability as an attribute of an individual. Seen as a personal characteristic, a disability means that each individual is treated separately with the ultimate goal of either fixing them or finding ways to adapt.

Neurodiversity refers to the human brain and forms of variation or difference (e.g., autism spectrum disorder, dyslexia, attention-deficit/hyperactivity disorder (ADHD), and Tourette syndrome).

Rehabilitation technology (RT) is a term describing aids that facilitate the recovery of function after illness or injury; it often invokes the medical model of disability.

Social model argues that disability is produced by interaction between a person and the features of society in which they live. In this way, disability is also a political terrain tied to social concerns and plays out in power relations.

Supercrip denotes an individual applauded publicly and often seen as inspiring for "overcoming" their disability.

User-initiated design emerges from lived experience, personalized to the needs of a specific individual, and often with the design process instigated by the user

A Universal Conundrum

ELIZABETH GUFFEY

Figure 1 Disability activists demonstrating in France, 2011. Image Frederick Florin / AFP via Getty Images.

This book is about human difference and how we deal with it. In one way or another, most people know and understand how it is to feel different to others. Less understood is one of the fundamental experiences of human experience: the feeling that the world was planned for somebody other than you. For people who experience disability, this is felt in the ways that we communicate, in the ways that we share information, in the ways that we move through space. Design—the making and shaping of this world—is behind much of this. Whether performed professionally, by architects and designers, or in daily practice, it is the decisions we make about how to order things and spaces. Whether in industry, schools, or the media, gatekeepers in design rarely allow voice nor hear disabled people's perspectives on this. The authors in this book argue for a more holistic approach to disability within design. Since the 1990s, disability activists globally have adopted the phrase "nothing about us without us." The slogan is as applicable to design as political action. But this also means making room for designers who identify as disabled and rethinking the spaces and practices of design for everyone.

Disability is pervasive in human experience. According to the World Health Organization, nearly one in seven people on earth are disabled (WHO 2021). Accounting for "invisible" disabilities as well as those physical, mental, or neurological conditions that are more evident, they define disability as occurring when these individuals interact "with personal and environmental factors including negative attitudes, inaccessible transportation and public buildings, and limited social support" (WHO 2021). But as much as this definition frames disability as a diverse range of experiences had by many, the WHO also notes that we are all of us only temporarily able-bodied. As Oedipus recognized in his response to the riddle of the sphinx, we humans pass in and out of states of disability throughout our lives, whether as infants, through sickness, or in old age. Despite the pervasive nature of disability, most design reflects neither the WHO nor Sophocles. Even as we understand and take into account the expansiveness of disability, the designed world is still shaped around nondisabled persons. Despite the last fifty years of legislation around the world, designers still have not done a good enough job investigating what kinds of humans inhabit the world and which of those bodies and minds are worthy of their attention. Many people—within the professional worlds of design and externally—continue to see this as a peripheral concern, best left to laws and guidelines. But perhaps design for disability could become more than interpreting a series of rules to accomplish a legal definition of accessibility. We might instead make a radical case for human difference—in body and mind—by reconceiving disability through design.

The emerging conversation around this new vision for disability and design is dynamic and varied, taking place in offices and nursing homes, in classrooms and studios, in labs and living rooms. The simultaneous rise of a sophisticated and lively do-it-yourself (DIY) movement and manufacturing processes that allow for unprecedented "mass customization" have given shape to newer strategies for design.[1] Popular explorations on social media platforms and more conventional academic research alike are bringing attention to both such innovations, particularly those of makers found outside the formal precincts of professional design and to the little told design histories that precede them. Another spur is the emergence of critical disability studies, a scholarly discipline developing in the past two decades, as well as disability activism in the wake of what is in the United States often called the ADA (Americans with Disabilities Act) generation (Forber-Pratt 2019). This body of critical thought draws its authority from the Civil Rights movement, as well as the rise of feminist and critical race studies and a fundamental rethinking of ideas of justice and power among activists. Whether they directly name design or not, all of these currents foreground human difference in body and mind as key to the design process.

This book documents the emergence of such ideas, attempting to bring the conversations around them together in one place. These currents rise from activism as well as design practice. They present a new recognition of the creativity that human difference in body and mind can bring to the design process. But the book also recognizes that designing for human difference does not yield a single voice or formulaic solution. Some of these ideas have been put to work productively. Others suggest challenges and provocations. This book does not provide a single voice or formulaic solution for disability design, nor does it attempt to engage in a zero-sum competition with other proposed approaches to design and designing. It suggests instead that a new iteration of many existing approaches can align with disability activism to create more effective, equitable design practices and outcomes. This means rethinking what is considered normal and clearing space for fuller insight into fundamental human needs. As a collection of reflections and articulations, the book aims to contextualize this paradigm shift in design practice, theory, and activism. We can learn much from difference and experience; these writings suggest what the world might gain from a disability point of view. Whether presented as schools of thought, lived experiences, artistic endeavors, calls for action, or life-work, the sometimes argumentative writings in this volume suggest that disability-led design can guide us all to dig deeper.

When Was Design Universal?

To understand these new approaches fully, it is necessary to pull back and gain a wider perspective. Arguments for barrier-free architecture had begun to take shape as early as the 1950s (Guffey 2017; Williamson 2019). In the US and Europe in the 1960s and 1970s, activists reconceptualized architectural access, linking it to broader questions of civil and human rights. But by the late 1970s, a group of US-based disabled and nondisabled people, architects, and other proponents began arguing that they could expand then-common understandings of design. Gradually they gave shape to "Universal Design," an idea that appeared to help designers cope with the burgeoning rights legislation and government oversight begun by the barrier-free architecture and disability rights movement. Both Universal Design and American civil rights law follow the social model of disability in suggesting that disability is produced by societal inaccessibility—in other words, by design that includes some people and excludes others, based on personal characteristics. Architect Ron Mace first brought widespread attention to the idea in the mid-1980s when he argued that accessible design could appeal to consumers while also planning for the greatest range of abilities possible.[2] While Universal Design originated in the practice of architecture, a much wider range of professionals have applied the principles of Universal Design in areas ranging from consumer technologies to public education. In 1997 the U.S. Department of Education National Institute on Disability and Rehabilitation Research (NIDRR) even funded research into this problem, ultimately leading to the publication of seven principles of Universal Design the next year (Story et al. 1998).

Impressive arguments support Universal Design. For example, when specialized designs are created solely for the use of disabled people, proponents of Universal Design rightly note that they tend to be expensive and hard to find (World Health Organization 2018). Furthermore, designs explicitly made for disabled people, such as canes, walkers, and wheelchairs, still often look more at home in hospitals than in domestic spaces (Pullin 2009; Shinohara and Wobbrock 2011). A second argument is that practicing Universal Design can benefit everyone. By encouraging nondisabled and disabled people to use the same spaces and products, Universal Designs can foster social cohesion (Persson *et al.* 2015). The innovative force of Universal Design is typically associated with several distinctive products and environments. Perhaps the best-known examples are the soft, nonslip handles of the OXO Good Grips kitchen products. Developed for an arthritic user, the line of cooking tools was introduced in the 1990s and quickly found a market far beyond disabled users. Universal Design is also often associated with the small sidewalk ramps commonly referred to as "curb cuts." Indeed, the term *curb cut effect* not only repeats the notion that designs for people with disabilities can benefit everyone but also demonstrates that they can become entirely normalized. Curb cuts on sidewalks made it easier for people pushing strollers, those rolling a suitcase, and cyclists and skateboarders.

Alongside Universal Design, some designers have further adapted its methods and goals to form an approach known as "Inclusive Design." To be sure, the latter is a fluid term, used more often in Europe and the UK. When construed as an entirely separate movement, proponents emphasize the inclusion of broader social groups in the design of products, services, and environments. Some aim for design outcomes that enable users' agency and effectiveness in the world; they try to reflect what others want. Other designers, as Susan Goltsman suggests, believe inclusive design also includes social considerations, "designing a diversity of ways to participate so that everyone has a sense of belonging" (Holmes 2017: 53).

Even as these definitions can be elusive and broad, some designers and activists argue that newer terms are needed to reflect the advent of both newer technologies and newer design strategies. Accessible design has gained particular resonance with the growth of the internet and, in particular, calls for Web Content Accessibility Guidelines (WCAG). In line with shifts within design toward design strategy and service design, advocates suggest that we are no longer focusing on products and the built environment but shifting attention to the design and provision of public services in the context of a barrier-free information society (Treviranus 2018). Kat Holmes associates inclusive design with large companies such as Microsoft and IDEO, proposing that they "consider disability to be an extreme but rich case that exists on a spectrum of broader human variation, and which can elicit insights that can be scaled into solutions for everyone" (Holmes 2017: 56). In this mode, design thinking strategies such as the creation of fictional or composite personas can become significant as ways to channel disabled people into the design process.

This heritage continues today, but increased scrutiny by activists, practitioners, and scholars has also led to a frank discussion of the "myth" of Universal Design and question the inclusiveness of inclusive design.[3] At issue is a range of assumptions and practices. Some arguments, for instance, complain that accessible design is too often an afterthought associated with box-checking that can fill guidelines but still prove unusable. These criticisms are grounded in practice, whereas others claim that Universal Design has been effective less "as a method of social justice activism, rather than as a marketing strategy" fit within broader economic and political critiques (Hamraie 2016). Even the broadly utopian aspects of Universal Design goals can seem challenging; presenting an almost impossible goal, it seems to suggest that we should be designing for absolutely everyone, everywhere, at all times (Chu 2021).

How relevant are these proposals and debates about approaches to designing to the ways we acknowledge difference in the designed world? We live in a moment of flux in many ways, but one push is moving us through Universal or inclusive design. Where the earliest efforts in Universal Design often focused on the needs of wheelchair users, notions—and legal definitions—of disability in the United States and many other countries have expanded to not only include neurodiversity but also bring increased attention to blindness and vision impairment, as well as deafness and hearing loss. As this unfolds, disability design and its more extended practices are changing. We might call this a newer, post—Universal Design practice (while also understanding that "post" is perhaps an academic convention). Like "post"-industrial or "post"-modern, the designation suggests we have not abandoned the past, but are instead building on—and moving beyond—what came before. In this case it indicates a conversation emerging from multiple perspectives, some now emerging from earlier traditions and others arriving from outside. As the contributions in this volume demonstrate, some of this dialogue is adjacent to Universal Design. Some of the conversation is productively opposed to it. And some of it extends from Universal Design's extended heritage.

Cripping Normal

A newer conversation about disability-led design is occurring. In the last half century, the American ADA, the UK's Equality Act, and a range of other human and civil rights—based legislation have asserted the right of disabled people to "live in the world" (*tenBroek* 1966). These laws prohibit discrimination but have been extended to design, leading to the introduction of a range of accommodations, most visibly including wheelchair ramps and specially designated parking areas. Even as similar rights-based frameworks for disability have burgeoned, as disability scholars Faye Ginsberg and Reyna Rapp note, they can "only go so far" (Ginsberg and Rapp 2017: 184). As with any ideal, implementation is often imperfect, confused, and inconsistent. But also, these goals have not fostered a sense of disability culture, individuality, and identity. In the American context, some of this stems from tensions within the early disability rights movement itself. Is disability a universal condition, or does it describe a minority group? And just how closely do we define and weigh the importance of "independence" itself (Basgentos 2009)? Also in the Anglo-American context some activists ask what role nondisabled people, particularly professionals, should play in this movement? To a greater or lesser extent, since the early 2000s these questions have been shaping new frameworks, fostering a more comprehensive sense of identity and nurturing a design culture that better reflects disability experience.

Such thinking envisages a world more capacious in its definition of normalcy. Influential cultural critics like arts activist Simi Linton have argued that disabled people should "claim" and take pride in a disability identity (Linton 1998), while disability theorist Alison Kafer turns to the word "crip" as a way of reclaiming an older stigmatizing term. Taking up an admittedly "harsh" term, she argues, can "shake things up ... jolt people out of their everyday understandings of bodies and minds, or normalcy and deviance" (Kafer 2013: 15). Scholar Lennard Davis suggests that disability studies should make it a goal "to help 'normal' people to see the quotation marks around their assumptions" (Davis 1995: xii). Looking more closely, he suggests, they might instead see "the connection between disability and the status quo in the way that many people now understand the connection between race and/or gender and contemporary structures of power" (Davis 1995). Cultural critics like Rosemarie Garland Thomson, whose recent writings build on the notion of disability as a social construct, tether these ideas to the material world. Effectively shifting discussion away from the specifics of individual cases, she directs our attention toward widespread misfits between bodies and a world that has not been constructed with them in mind (Garland-Thomson 2011). For Garland-Thomson, misfit is a "feminist materialist" concept with social implications, not a design methodology: she suggests that our focus is less on "fixing" the individual to fit the environment than vice versa. But since "misfit" mingles the political with the pragmatic, these ideas have been used to explicitly link social and political concepts with design itself.[4]

But these shifts in thinking must also be understood in relationship to contemporary activism, which positions itself as not against disability rights but rather suggests that we not stop just there. Highlighting the voices and life experiences of multiple types of people with disability experience can be a political act in itself. And by bringing more visibility to disabled people, activist Alice Wong argues, we may add "depth, range, and nuance to disability representation" (Wong 2020: xxi). Whereas activism in the 1970s was limited to sit-ins and demonstrations, more recent moves have expanded to posts online. Such activism makes a strong political statement, suggesting what we all might learn from the need for visibility, representation, and newer forms of collectivity. Taking part in these actions means reshaping who is considered disabled and who can and should be heard. Much of the early disability rights movement in Europe and North America was focused around the needs of white men, many of whom used wheelchairs. More recently, disability activists emphasize varieties of impairments in both body and mind, noting the diversity of disability voices and actively celebrating the range of human difference. Disability design justice means opening discussion to larger systems of racial oppression (Benjamin 2019) and exploring the work of disabled people of color as makers and innovators. Threaded throughout this edited volume is the design activism of disabled people of color; they note the whiteness of rights-based disability discourses in contexts like the United States and the United Kingdom by discussing how design can build on the intersectional strength of the disability justice movement (Sins Invalid 2019). In this way, disability activism can occur in design, speaking to both individuals who are disabled and otherwise marginalized because of race or class.

Not only does this discussion help create a new theoretical framework for disability politics and activism, it might also be seen as a part of the next progression of Universal Design. As activism, discussions around identity and demands for justice push the discussion still further, disabled designers, artists, and cultural producers are taking it in new directions within their practices and realms. Of course, the disability rights movement was never stable or monolithic, and has always contained within itself a series of tensions and debates. The same is true of approaches to disability within design. But a fundamental emphasis remains clear. As After Universal Design explores, it includes an embrace of ideas of agency, equity, and speculation as helping design to become a method for enacting greater change.

Dis/Ability-Led Design

We can all reap benefits if we pay more attention to disability design. This argument is one of the greatest strengths of Universal Design and inclusive design. Why not plan for extremes in ability, its supporters ask? This can only result in better, more useful design for everyone. That idea—of recasting disability into the realm of a productive difference that benefits all of us—has many merits. But could this idea be extended? What might we learn from the resilience, creativity, and wisdom of disabled people? Not only misguided, "designing for" disabled people is incompatible with the wider shift within design theory and practice toward equitable approaches, participatory methods, and reconceptualization of the designer as facilitator supporting others in determining outcomes. In other words, it's both wasteful and retrograde.

Disability design can sometimes be shaped by pressure and resentment, reduced to a kind of bureaucratic problem-solving that feels burdensome. How can we shift this perspective to fully incorporate the learning of long-standing practices, all the while understanding that we can do better? The chapters here attempt to show how design practice is aligning with a newer and vibrant conversation emerging from the shadows of laws, guidelines, and rules. There is much to be said for disabled people revealing their own life and design processes. Sometimes this is done in an ad hoc manner, as a tool for survival. Sometimes this occurs within professionally recognized practices, with disabled people reaching out to design for or to teach others. And some of this discussion means expanding our understanding of "design" to include nonprofessional activities and consider alternate practices like repair and adaptation.

In its most expansive mode, contemporary disability activism questions older modes of working, looking to design for new forms of "allyship." In so doing it is shifting the emphasis in such practices and suggesting new and alternative kinds of design processes. Richard Ladner, for example, urges us to consider disability design as a form of empowerment (Ladner 2015). Looking particularly at digital design, Ladner urges that rather than marginalizing people, designers engage users as active producers and innovators. As he notes, they might also add to and learn from the processes they are involved in. Benefiting from this approach, these users might turn around and apply their skills to solve new challenges. In this way, he asserts, disability-led practices might suggest a kind of "design for user empowerment" (Ladner 2015: 24).

Empowerment can combine what people like with what people need. In this way it informs another approach often implicitly touched on throughout this book, namely "user-initiated" design. Professional designers are often taught that they should subsume their own individuality so they might channel and serve the needs of the user. With user-initiated design this is taken further; the design process starts with the user and is shaped entirely around the needs, interests, and goals of the individual (Cole and Nolan 2019). In some ways these ideas align with other forms of design activism. For example, the communitarian approach resonates with other forms of design activism, bringing to mind, for instance, Ezio Manzini's call for rethinking the role of design and designers in contemporary society. But, whereas Manzini distinguishes between "diffuse design" that is practiced by everybody and "expert design" that is performed by those trained as designers, disability design shifts emphasis. The goal of such activism is to reframe disabled people—users of disability design—as "valuable knowers and experts" in their own right (Manzini 2015).

Disability design's activist leanings often mean reimaging design in more political terms. The emphasis on design empowerment and individual making aligns with a DIY philosophy. Here the goal is enabling people to design, build, and share their personalized solutions (Hunsinger and Schrock 2016; Kuznetsov and Paulos 2010) and therefore support self-determination (Ladner 2015). These ideas have been extended by technological innovation and diffusion such as the rise of digital proto-typing and production, allowing disability design to be tailored to an individual. Where "Universal Design" imagined flexible designs that might be usable by people of many abilities, it was always tied to the needs of mass production. The so-called "design for one" uses technology to create specially tailored or "bespoke" designs that reflect each person's needs and desires. By highlighting such individuation, these forms of designing and making echo the goals of recent disability activism. In these ways, the recognition of multiple forms of disability and the uniqueness of individual experience—what might in fact be called "disability for one"—makes a strong argument for "design for one."

This book constructs an outline around these ideas, clustering them around three propositions that include the power of agency, the significance of equity, and the expressive role of speculation in disability design. The following chapters approach these ideas in narrower but possibly more useful ways. Much of what follows draws from the authors' work in and engagement with disability culture, thought, and activism. The chapters are structured around three singular but reappearing ideas: agency, equity, and speculation. Each theme includes an introduction to the concept and several longer chapters that explore aspects of this idea in greater depth. They are followed by shorter "case studies" that outline actual designs, reflections, or other examples of this theme from real life. There is no single dominating voice, but rather a grouping of suggestions or communal responses. In the past, design has treated human difference as a conundrum. Combined, these writings offer a guide for thinking through the features and affordances of disability design. They are meant to be an invitation to designers of the future, disabled and nondisabled alike. We want your work. Let this be an invitation to help change the world.

Notes

1. See, for instance, Atkinson and Beegan 2008: 305–13 and Ratto and Boler 2014.
2. Focused on the needs of disabled users, Universal Design evolved as an imperative of socially inclusive design practices that developed from many directions in the 1960s and 1970s but the term was not coined until Mace 1985: 147–52.
3. See, for instance, Guffey 2021.
4. See, for example, Guffey 2018; Hamraie 2018.

References

Atkinson, P., and G. Beegan (2008), "Professionalism, Amateurism and the Boundaries of Design," *Journal of Design History* 21 (4): 305–13.

Bagenstos, S. R. (2009), *Law and the Contradictions of the Disability Rights Movement*, New Haven: Yale University Press.

Bellucci, A., J. Nolan, and A. Di Santo. (2018), "Research in the Wild(s): Opportunities, Affordances and Constraints Doing Assistive Technology Field Research in Underserved Areas," *Disability Studies Quarterly* 38 (4) https://dsq-sds.org/article/view/5934.

Benjamin, R. (2019), *Race after Technology: Abolitionist Tools for the New Jim Code, Cambridge*, UK: Wiley.

Carter-Long, L. (2019), "Where Have You Gone, Stephen Dwoskin? On Disability Film," *Film Quarterly* 73: 75–81.

Chu, A. (2021) "'Inclusive Design' Has Become so Widely Used That It's Meaningless," *Fast Company*, November 29, 2021. Available online: https://www.fastcompany.com/90697288/inclusive-design-has-become-so-widely-used-that-its-meaningless-that-has-to-change.

Cole, J. and J. Nolan J. (2019), "GimpGirl: Insider Perspectives on Technology and the Lives of Disabled Women," in B. Haller, G. Goggin and K. Ellis (eds), *Routledge Companion to Disability and Media*, 233–42, New York: Routledge.

Costanza-Chock, S. (2020), *Design Justice: Community-Led Practices to Build the Worlds We Need*, Cambridge, MA: MIT Press.

Davis, L. J. (1995), *Enforcing Normalcy: Disability, Deafness, and the Body*, New York: Verso.

Forber-Pratt, A. J. (2019), "(Re)Defining Disability Culture: Perspectives from the Americans with Disabilities Act Generation," *Culture and Psychology* 25 (2): 241–56.

Garland-Thomson, R. (2011), "Misfits: A Feminist Materialist Disability Concept," *Hypatia* 26 (3): 591–609.

Ginsburg, F., and R. Rapp (2017), "Cripping the New Normal: Making Disability Count," *ALTER - European Journal of Disability Research/Revue Européenne de Recherche Sur Le Handicap* 11: 179–92.

Guffey, E. (2017), *Designing Disability*, London: Bloomsbury.

Guffey, E. (2018), *Designing Disability: Symbols, Space, and Society*, London: Bloomsbury.

Guffey, E. (2021), "In the Wake of Universal Design: Mapping the Terrain," *Design Issues* 37 (1): 76–82.

Hamraie, A. (2016), "Universal Design and the Problem of 'Post-Disability' Ideology," *Design and Culture* 8 (3): 285–309.

Hamraie, A. (2018), *Building Access: Universal Design and the Politics of Disability,* Minneapolis: University of Minnesota Press.

Holmes, K. (2018), *Mismatch*, Cambridge, MA: The MIT Press.

Hunsinger, J. and A. Schrock. (2016), "The Democratization of Hacking and Making," *New Media & Society* 18 (4): 535–38.

Imrie, R., and P. Hall (2004), *Inclusive Design: Designing and Developing Accessible Environments*, New York: Routledge.

Jackson, L. (2018), "Opinion | We Are the Original Lifehackers," *The New York Times*, Opinion. Available online: https://www.nytimes.com/2018/05/30/opinion/disability-design-lifehacks.html.

Kafer, A. (2013), *Feminist, Queer, Crip*, Bloomington, IN: Indiana University Press.

Kuznetsov, S. and E. Paulos (2010), "Rise of the Expert Amateur: DIY Projects, Communities, and Cultures," in *Proceedings of the 6th Nordic Conference on Human-Computer Interaction: Extending Boundaries (NordiCHI '10). Association for Computing Machinery*, 295–304, New York, NY, USA.

Ladner, R. (2015), "Design for User Empowerment | ACM Interactions," *Interactions* 22 (2): 24–9.e.

Linton, S. (1998), *Claiming Disability*, New York: New York University Press.

Mace, R. (1985), "Universal Design: Barrier-free Environments for Everyone," *Designers West* 33 (1): 147–52.

Manzini, E. (2015), *Design, When Everybody Designs*. An Introduction to Design for Social Innovation (trans. r. Coad). Cambridge, MA: The MIT Press.

Mingus, M. (2017), "Access Intimacy, Interdependence and Disability Justice," *Leaving Evidence* (blog), April 12, 2017. Available online: https://leavingevidence.wordpress.com/2017/04/12/access-intimacy-interdependence-and-disability-justice/.

Persson, H., H. Åhman, A. A. Yngling, and J. Gulliksen. (2015), "Universal Design, Inclusive Design, Accessible Design, Design for All: Different Concepts – One Goal? On the Concept of Accessibility – Historical, Methodological and Philosophical Aspects," *Universal Access in the Information Society,* 14 (4): 505–26.

Pullin, G. (2009), *Design Meets Disability*, Cambridge, MA: MIT Press.

Ratto, M., and M. Boler (2014), *DIY Citizenship: Critical Making and Social Media*, Cambridge, MA: MIT Press.

Shinohara, K., and J. O. Wobbrock. (2011), "In the Shadow of Misperception: Assistive Technology Use and Social Interactions," in *Proceedings of the SIGCHI Conference on Human Factors in Computing Systems*, 705–14, Vancouver BC Canada: ACM.

Sins Invalid. 2019, *Skin, Tooth, and Bone: The Basis of Movement Is Our People, a Disability Justice Primer*. 2nd Edition. Primedia eLaunch LLC.

Story, M. F., J. Mueller, and R. L. Mace, (1998), *The Universal Design File: Designing for People of All Ages and Abilities. Revised Edition*. Raleigh, NC: Center for Universal Design, NC State University.

tenBroek, J. (1966), "*The Right to Live in the World: The Disabled in the Law of Torts*," *California Law Review* 54 (2): 841–919.

Treviranus, J. (2018). "The Three Dimensions of Inclusive Design: Part One **," *Fwd50* (blog), Available online: https://medium.com/fwd50/the-three-dimensions-of-inclusive-design-part-one-103cad1ffdc2.

Williamson, B. (2019), *Accessible America: A History of Disability and Design*, New York: NYU Press.

Wobbrock, J. O., S. K. Kane, K. Z. Gajos, S. Harada, and J. Froehlich (2011), "Ability-Based Design: Concept, Principles and Examples," *ACM Transactions on Accessible Computing* 3 (3) (April 1, 2011): 9:1–9:27.

Wong, A. (2020), *Disability Visibility: First-Person Stories from the Twenty-First Century*, New York: Knopf Doubleday Publishing Group.

World Health Organization (2018), Improving access to assistive technology, Pub. L. No. 12.5, WHA 71.8 Provisional agenda item 3.

World Health Organization (2021), "Disability and Health." https://www.who.int/news-room/fact-sheets/detail/disability-and-health (accessed October 15, 2021).

Section 1 Agency

Introduction

When the phrase "nothing about us without us" was first adopted by activists in the international disability rights movement, it announced a desire for self-determination in all aspects of life. Applied to design, the phrase still registers agency: a sense of control over one's life, even through moments of conflict or change. But more recent disability activism—in countries as diverse as Mexico and China—has so focused on giving voice and credibility to life experience and actions that the phrase bears new meaning. Above all, the embrace of the phrase suggests that now, more than ever, disabled people should be recognized as "needs knowers," or experts in their own wants, designers and makers, as well as users.

Politics and technology are often intertwined, and in this book Kelly Fritsch and Aimi Hamraie introduce a form of user-initiated design that they call "crip technoscience." This critical project centers the experiences of disabled people, many of whom may not be professionally trained but still engage in designing activities, but who modify, repurpose, and otherwise invent objects to get by in their everyday lives. Their arguments suggest that we expand our understanding of "design" to include nonprofessional activities and consider alternate practices like repair and adaptation. The "Four Commitments of Crip Technoscience" embrace such forms of agency as cripping, reclaiming, hacking, and tinkering not simply to create a more accessible world, but as part of a broader effort for disability justice.

There is much to be said for disability-led design examples, which present disability experience not as a deficit to be overcome nor a concern that revolves entirely around access but rather as a call to action that can inspire novel and even radical new approaches toward design. In "Fixing Meets Expressing: Design by Designers with Disability Experience," Natalia Pérez Liebergesell, Peter-Willem Vermeersch, and Ann Heylighen argue against the tendency to simplify lived firsthand knowledge of disability. Designers who choose to work *from* their own experience can make disability design empowering, they state, all the while making designs that are inclusive, aesthetically worthwhile, and poetically expressive.

Echoing broader, deeper tendencies within academic scholarship, design histories and research often ignore or overshadow embodied points of view. The implicit lack of focus on lived firsthand knowledge of disability within written scholarship, particularly, means that there's been little attention paid to fixing, adaptation, and other design-like activities. The shorter case studies in this section elaborate on these points, including historical instances as when Jaipret Virdi looks at user design of hearing aid carriers. While much attention has been paid to do-it-yourself (DIY), domestication, prosumption, end-user innovation, and hobbyist hacking, Virdi argues for something different. A close examination, she argues, can provide us with material insight into the everyday experience of wearing disability technologies. Not only do we learn how disability is tied to deep personal forms of aesthetics but also see it tied to an individual user's activities and various forms of performance.

Personal tinkering, adapting, and appropriating are all forms of making that engage design in a variety of ways. Beginning in the early 2000s, a wave of online DIY content began appearing on YouTube and other channels, many authored by disabled people offering informal design advice among peers. Hoping to derive insights for accessible design (Anthony et al. 2013), researchers have studied this activity. But, published online, these DIY approaches have also helped disabled people connect with one another. Among these online guides, Elizabeth Guffey highlights the nonprofessional design practices of Zebreda Dunham. In the online blog Zebreda makes it Work!, Dunham shows inventiveness but also negotiates implicit issues of access and power through her design solutions. A professionally trained designer like Jessica Ryan-Ndegwa might use their lived experience as a disabled person to augment her knowledge of the nature of disability; in "Privileging Agency," Ryan-Ndegwa speaks with Alison Kurdock Adamas about how she sees her platform Design for Disability as a way to advance user-initiated design, while also educating and advocating for the disability community.

Empowerment of the individual can be found in discourses about "designing with" rather than "designing for" disability. Looking at the activities of "disabled pioneers" who were both patients and assistants at a rehabilitation clinic in postwar New York, Bess Williamson examines "Rehabilitation Technology at the Self-Help Shop Then and Now." Where the conventions of the Self Help Shop complicate our understanding of design agency, Andrew Cook and Graham Pullin reimagine agency within the framework of bespoke or design for one today. They suggest that wearers or users of disability objects should be allowed the opportunity to take control of the stories that these objects tell about who they are. In "Beyond the Bespoke" they explore the opportunities—and challenges—inherent in designing economically viable disability-related design for one. In so doing they make an argument for designing these objects, so they are blend into everyday life, challenging narratives of triumph or tragedy and becoming remarkably unremarkable. And finally, on an institutional level, "Re-imagining Access and Its Pedagogies" describes a class-based project that merged participatory design with emerging technologies to study true access to archives for individuals with a broad spectrum of bodymind experiences, that is, visual, hearing, mobility, and cognitive disabilities.

Key Points

- Users design and adapt in ways that tell us much about their life experience and personal desires for functionality.
- Aesthetic customization can celebrate disability and encourage difference.
- Emphasizing access and needs challenges us to re-consider what aspects of living actually need assistance.
- Much access work has a collaborative and even collective nature that is overlooked in various design traditions.
- User-initiated disability design can be frictional, side-stepping engrained design cultures.
- "Maintenance" or the "fixing," updating, and regulating of technologies are often essential to users but ignored in narratives on design.
- If made a primary goal, disability-related design for one can be economically viable—and economically accessible.
- Increasing choices, including a range of options that encompass, for instance, shape or material, helps destigmatization.

1   Four Commitments of Crip Technoscience*

KELLY FRITSCH AND AIMI HAMRAIE

The following is excerpted from "The Crip Technoscience Manifesto" *Catalyst: Feminism, Theory, Technoscience* 5 (1): 1–33. Available online: https://catalystjournal. org/index.php/catalyst/article/view/29607.

As disabled people engaged in disability community, activism, and scholarship, our collective experiences and histories have taught us that we are effective agents of world-building and world-dismantling toward more socially just relations. The grounds for social justice and world-remaking, however, are frictioned; technologies, architectures, and infrastructures are often designed and implemented without committing to disability as a difference that matters. This manifesto calls attention to the powerful, messy, non-innocent, contradictory, and nevertheless crucial work of crip technoscience: practices of critique, alteration, and reinvention of our material-discursive world.

Disabled people are experts and designers of everyday life. But we also harness technoscience for political action, refusing to comply with demands to cure, fix, or eliminate disability. Attentive to the intersectional workings of power and privilege, we agitate against independence and productivity as requirements for existence. Building upon earlier work defining crip technoscience as politicized design activism (Hamraie 2015, 2017), we articulate four political commitments of crip technoscience as a field of critical scholarship, practice, and activism.[1] In framing crip technoscience as such, we follow feminist technoscience studies by describing both a realm of practice *and* a field of knowing that has emerged from it. Crip technoscience braids together two provocative concepts: "crip," the non-compliant, anti-assimilationist position that disability is a desirable part of the world, and "technoscience," the co-production of science, technology, and political life (Jasanoff 2004; Murphy 2012). Crip theory centers disability as a locus of resistance against "compulsory ablebodiedness" (McRuer 2006) and "ablenationalism" (Mitchell and Snyder 2015), agitating against liberal assimilation and inclusion practices by marking disability as a desirably generative and creative relational practice (Fritsch 2015a).

To struggle for a more accessible future in which disability is anticipated, welcomed, and in which disabled people thrive, we offer four commitments of crip technoscience as a field of critical scholarship, practice, and activism.

---

*The following is excerpted from "The Crip Technoscience Manifesto" *Catalyst: Feminism, Theory, Technoscience* 5 (1): 1–33. Available online: https://catalystjournal. org/index.php/catalyst/article/view/29607.

Crip technoscience centers the work of disabled people as knowers and makers. Crip technoscience privileges disabled people as designers and world-builders, as knowing what will work best and developing the skills, capacities, and relationships to make something from our knowledge. Unlike typical approaches to disability that objectify disabled people and situate expertise in medical professionals and non-disabled designers or engineers, crip technoscience posits that disabled people are active participants in the design of everyday life. Not only do disabled people make access in our everyday lives in ways that do not get recognized as design but the lived experience of disability, and the shared experience of the disability community, creates specific expertise and knowledge that informs technoscientific practices.

We call for greater acknowledgment of the lived experiences and material design practices of disabled people in the work of technoscientific intervention. There is a widespread perception that access technologies are made for us by nondisabled experts, but there is little recognition of our own practices of remaking the material world. Yet the field of disability scholarship grew out of activism against rehabilitative models of medical expertise and intervention (UPIAS 1976), crafting a materialist politics with anti-capitalism at its center (Oliver 1990; Russel 1998), and continues to struggle against "compulsory ablebodiedness" (McRuer 2006). Crip knowing-making forms the basis of political slogans such as "Nothing About Us Without Us" (Charlton 2000), framing disabled people not just as design experts but also as epistemic activists whose politicized ways of knowing the material world also situate us to produce the material conditions that allow disability to thrive, in addition to remaking how disability is known and experienced. Without glorifying do-it-yourself design practices, crip technoscience recognizes that disabled peoples' world-dismantling and world-building labors stem from situated experiences of "misfitting" in the world (Garland-Thomson 2011). Crips are not merely formed or acted on by the world, we are engaged agents of remaking.

In centering the expertise of disabled knowers and makers, crip technoscience involves the use of materials and technologies to produce forms of access otherwise unavailable—or economically inaccessible—via mainstream assistive technology channels. There are many examples of disability experience as knowing-making, so many creative and ingenious ways of living in the world. For example, historian Bess Williamson (2012a) has traced the ways that disabled people in the American postwar period documented their work as "tinkerers" in community periodicals, retrospective memoirs, and oral histories. They adapted specialized medical and assistive equipment, altered their houses, and repurposed everyday household tools. Disabled people turned away from medical supply companies to hardware stores to alter objects to their own advantage, asserting their "presence in a world that largely ignored them" (Williamson 2012a: 12). Disabled designers such as Alice Loomer, a wheelchair user, described her crip maker practices of repurposing household items for wheelchair maintenance or for ad hoc assistive technologies as "hanging onto the coattails of science" (1982: 30). Loomer argued that her own tinkering and maintenance practices "kept [her] away from nursing homes and attendants": "I made it. So

I know how to fix it … I may have failed as often as I succeeded, but I have equipment that fits me" (30–1). Loomer's work complicates the typical association of the disabled cyborg with a desire for innovation, instead turning to maintenance practices as sites for examining the "frictions, limitations, and failures inherent to technoscientific design processes" (Hamraie 2017: 107).

Similarly, in the 1960s, disabled engineer Ralf Hotchkiss hacked his wheelchair to plow snow off sidewalks while attending Oberlin College, and in the 1980s began the Whirlwind Wheelchair International, when his global travels to find better designs for wheelchairs took him to Nicaragua:

> I met these four young fellows sharing one wheelchair, and they had already redesigned that wheelchair. They had ridden it so hard that it had broken in 20 different places. They had reinforced it, welded it all back together, and made it much stronger than it had been. And they knew so much about good wheelchair design. It was clear they were the people I was looking for to help me, and I could help them as well, so we've been working together ever since.
>
> (Hotchkiss 2011)

While wheelchair users are not often treated as engineers, the four disabled designers had become experts in wheelchair engineering through trial and error and ingenuity, an ethos that continues in Whirlwind Wheelchair International's low-cost, open-source wheelchairs, which are intended to be maintainable for a lifetime, enabling a broader range of people to access them.

More recently, designer Sara Hendren and anthropologist Caitrin Lynch's (2016) project Engineering at Home has called attention to the ad hoc design practices of "Cindy," a recently disabled woman with several amputations. While Cindy "received the best available 'rehabilitation engineering' technology that money can buy," she nevertheless "found she had little use for it," opting instead to use tools of her own design (Hendren and Lynch 2016). Hendren and Lynch frame Cindy's work as "user-*initiated* design," which can "yield a powerful course correction to the top-down modes of manufacturing." Another disabled designer, Sarah Welner, began her career as an obstetric surgeon before focusing on gynecological health for disabled people. Recognizing that "conventional examining tables are too high and narrow" for disabled women, particularly wheelchair users, Welner designed a table with a button-operated "hydraulic lift" and more comfortable foot rests (Waldman 1998). While the engineering and design professions have historically excluded women, Welner, Loomer, and Cindy's work are clear examples of the places where crip technoscience and feminist design practices meet. Gender and disability expertise diffract through one another to question dominant modes of knowing and making.

Disabled parents have also been agents of crip knowing-making. Disabled parents hack baby cribs and change tables, sew bells on children's clothing to enable blind parents to keep track of their children when moving through public spaces, and mount car seats on portable luggage carriers to enable blind parents who use white canes or have a guide dog to pull their child behind them with their free hand (Fritsch 2017). Wheelchair users adapt slings, wraps, and nursing pillows to carry babies and toddlers on their laps. Other parents invent various tools to help feed and bathe their children, get them dressed, do their laundry, put on shoes, zip up coats, and engage in play. Queer, gender non-conforming, and trans disabled people also hack and tinker with reproductive technologies and kin formation to become pregnant, gestate, chest feed, and share responsibilities. All these forms of knowing-making are shared on social media—such as with the Disabled Parenting Project's website, blog, Twitter feeds, and related video projects—through disability community publications and events, and during conversations at parks and playgrounds. While disabled people face a multitude of barriers to becoming parents, disabled parents hack, tinker, and alter our material-discursive world, creating crip communities of knowing and making that challenge normative assumptions about parenting as a non-expert consumer activity.

Crip technoscience is committed to access as friction. Emerging out of historical fights for disability rights, the terms *accessibility* and *access* are usually taken to mean disabled inclusion and assimilation into normative able-bodied relations and built environments. When viewed as synonymous with inclusion and assimilation, access and accessibility are treated as self-evident goods.[2] As Kelly Fritsch explains, however, the etymology of the word *access* reveals two frictional meanings: access as "an opportunity enabling contact," as well as "a kind of attack" (2016: 23). Taking access as a kind of attack reveals access-making as a site of political friction and contestation. While historically central to the fights for disability access, crip technoscience is nevertheless committed to pushing beyond liberal and assimilation-based approaches to accessibility, which emphasize inclusion in mainstream society, to pursue access as friction, particularly paying attention to access-making as disabled peoples' acts of non-compliance and protest. For example, before enforceable disability rights laws in the United States, disabled people took direct action to create ramps and curb cuts, making obvious the inaccessibility of the built environment. Disability activists have taken sledgehammers to sidewalks in acts of protest, using bags of cement to pour curb cuts, and have used the design of curb cuts and ramps—conceived as levers for facilitating participation—as sites of productive friction through which interdependence-based disability politics could arise (Hamraie 2017: 99–102).

The Independent Living movement has also used material experimentation to enact crip technoscience and access friction. While the movement was critical of rehabilitation as a field of expert knowledge, it did not refuse the language or tools of rehabilitation outright. In addition to appropriating the term "Independent Living" to promote a disability politics of interdependence, the movement understood technoscience as a site of politicized resistance and regularly used hacking and tinkering practices as the basis of disability organizing. Many of their methods are captured in designers Ray Lifchez and Barbara Winslow's book *Design for Independent Living*, produced in collaboration with the movement. The book reveals the everyday technological hacks that disabled people in Berkeley in the 1960s and 1970s developed to thrive in an inaccessible city. Emblematic of the movement's crip technoscience ethos, Lifchez and Winslow offer the concept of "non-compliant users," illustrating this with an image of a powerchair user wheeling against traffic on a street without curb cuts (1979: 153). This technology-enabled movement against the flow of traffic marks anti-assimilationist crip mobility: not an attempt to integrate—as in the liberal approach to disability rights—but rather to use technology as a friction against an inaccessible environment.

More recently, Toronto resident Luke Anderson was frustrated by the lack of wheelchair access he experienced on a daily basis. Trained as a structural engineer, Anderson designed a simple portable wooden ramp in 2011 stenciled with the URL "stopgap.ca" and gifted thirteen of these ramps to businesses in his neighborhood. Built as a temporary "stop gap" measure to improve accessibility, the ramps are a non-compliant technology; they are not intended to be a permanent solution or structure, do not have to follow building codes, and do not require a city building permit or variance, all of which can be expensive and difficult to obtain. Anderson's experiment took off, leading to the formation of the StopGap Foundation and the Community Ramp project, which has now distributed over 1,200 portable wooden ramps worldwide (Fritsch 2019).

In another contemporary example of access as friction, Collin Kennedy, a cancer patient in Winnipeg, Manitoba, protested hospital parking prices by filling the pay-slot on a parking meter with spray foam, telling the local news that he planned to continue doing so "until changes are made" (Canadian Broadcasting Corporation (CBC) 2016). When crip time came into friction with the hospital's parking meter time, Kennedy challenged health capitalism, "You should be able to come here, park, get your treatment, however long that treatment takes … This is a medical facility where people are not going for entertainment. They're not going for productivity and commerce. We're here because of life and death" (CBC 2016). Kennedy's activism—the use of spray foam to obstruct the parking meter—creates frictional access through attacking a technology of capitalist time and contests the commercialization of health care.

Crip technoscience is committed to interdependence as political technology. We position the crip politics of interdependence as a technoscientific phenomenon, the weaving of relational circuits between bodies, environments, and tools to create non-innocent, frictional access. Mainstream disability technoscience presumes disability as an individual experience of impairment rather than a collective political experience of world-building and dismantling. This perception has two primary consequences. First, disabled people are perceived as dependent and the goal of technoscience becomes to encourage independence. Second, disability and technology are both perceived as *apolitical* and stable phenomena, rather than material-discursive entanglements that take shape through struggle, negotiation, and creativity.

The crip analytic of interdependence helps us understand how technoscience can simultaneously be entangled with global networks of domination and also provide opportunities for kinship and connection. Donna Haraway's (1991) cyborg figure, for instance, is a material metaphor for the entanglement of nature and techno-cultures. This figure shaped the critical concept of technoscience by showing the networks of knowledge and material production that comprise global capitalism as a force organizing relations between bodies, technologies, and environments. Disability critics of the cyborg figure, however, argue that Haraway's approach to the cyborg takes for granted that disabled people easily meld into technological circuits, an assumption shaped by imperatives for rehabilitation, cure, independence, and productivity. As Alison Kafer (2013) demonstrates, the imagination of disability in feminist technoscience is often limited to either eugenicist ideals of a disability-free future or "depoliticized" ideals of the cyborg hybrid body (8–10); disability is either a "master trope of human disqualification" (Snyder and Mitchell 2006: 125) or a "seamless" integration of body and machine (Kafer 2013: 05). Frequently, feminist technoscience conflates "'cyborg' and 'physically disabled person'" (105), treating disabled people as "post-human paragons" (Allan 2013: 11). Even when taken up critically, the cyborg figure in feminist technoscience reinforces ideas about disability as lack and disqualification (Bailey 2012).

If, as Kafer argues, disabled people have often uneasy or "ambivalent relationship[s] to technology" (2013:119), our practices of interdependence, access intimacy, and collective access can be understood as alternative political technologies: "disabled people," she writes, "[are not] cyborgs … because of our bodies (e.g., our use of prosthetics, ventilators, or attendants), but because of our political practices" (120). Crip technoscience offers interdependence as a central analytic for disability—technology relations, recognizing that in disability culture, community, and knower-maker practices, interdependence acts as a political technology for materializing better worlds. In alliance with Moya Bailey and Whitney Peoples's call for "black feminist health science studies," crip technoscience is "suspicious of the individualism and siloing practices rewarded in the academy and see[s] collaboration and interdisciplinary as core" values that ought to guide intellectual and material production (2017: 18). These values extend beyond the academy, however. As disability justice activist Mia Mingus writes, interdependence offers a politics of crip alliance and solidarity: "It is truly moving together in an oppressive world towards liberation ….It is working in coalition and collaboration" (2010a). We call for crip technoscience to design for collective access and disability justice.

We find interdependence as a political technology throughout the history of disability activism. For example, in North American disability activist histories, the most frequently narrated of these is the story of the "504 protest," which took place in 1977 when disability activists in Berkeley, California, occupied the Department of Health, Education, and Welfare to protest for the enforcement of section 504 of the Federal Rehabilitation Act, a law that mandated accessible federal programs, spaces, and services. Activists in the Independent Living movement had sought to foster a "cross-disability consciousness" across mobility-disabled, blind, and Deaf people (Zukas 2000: 141). At the protest, they transformed this consciousness into a political technology, using American Sign Language (ASL) to communicate with the outside when phone lines were cut off, rigging an air conditioner from other mechanical parts in the building, and establishing networks of care (O'Toole 2000: 47). Similar narratives have been told about the birth of Autistic community through organizing made possible by the internet and Autistic-accessible conference spaces (Sinclair 2010) and are currently being written through new crip technoscience projects. These and other material practices describe a crip technoscientific sensibility wherein disabled interdependence also enables what Mingus (2017) calls "access intimacy," a crip relational practice produced when interdependence informs the making of access.

Crip technoscience also plays with the boundaries of trust, interdependence, and crip relations. Blind artist Carmen Papalia, for instance, stages crip uses of technology in public space. In one practice, Papalia uses a twenty-foot white cane on busy streets to create a sense of antagonism with other pedestrians, which renders access as a frictioned practice; in his work *Blind Field Shuttle*, Papalia leads groups of (sighted) people on walks with their eyes closed. Both practices make use of a technology—Papalia's white cane—to stage social interactions in public space that put ideas of independence into question (Papalia 2013).

Also drawing on crip political interdependence, Georgina Kleege and Scott Wallin's practice of "participatory description" compels narrated visual content through group-based methods. Unlike the traditional role of audio description "as a detached, neutral act of translation that functions only as an enabling accommodation," participatory description uses technoscientific modes, including internet video databases, to "explore the aesthetic, ideological, political and ethical underpinnings of this work of representation and its described object or event" (Kleege and Wallin 2015).

Participatory audio description has also influenced the emergence of new technoscientific tools for accessibility mapping projects. Blind designer Josh Miele, for instance, worked with Touch Graphics, Inc. to design tactile and audio maps of the Bay Area Rapid Transit system. Other projects use mapping for collective access. Unlike mainstream disability technoscience crowdsourcing projects, which invoke a charity model of disability wherein non-disabled people collect data but do not engage in disability culture or politics, emerging projects such as Mapping Access are making participatory access-making the basis of a kind of technoscientific "access intimacy" (Mingus 2017) through practices such as "critical crowdsourcing" of accessibility data (Hamraie 2018). Rather than simply creating functional maps, Mapping Access focuses on mapping as a tool for producing critical relations between bodies, environments, and technologies. At collective map-a-thons, the project enrolls disabled and non-disabled data collectors in the process of interrogating the messiness of access-making in institutional conditions and describing these conditions collectively. Critical crowdsourcing practices include enrolling large numbers of both disabled and nondisabled people to collaborate on surveying and describing building accessibility while simultaneously identifying the aspects of the Americans with Disabilities Act compliance that fail to consider the lived experience of accessibility. Collaborative mapping visualizes the evidence of inaccessibility while creating opportunities for collective response. Crip cartographic technoscience thus enables more critical design, and interrogation of the everyday built environment.

Our call for crip technoscience theory and practice holds in tension Kafer's crip politics of interdependence with the crip ambivalence toward technology. We follow Kafer by calling on the usefulness of the cyborg—and the technoscientific circuits it embodies—not as a disabled figure per se, but as a tool for "stag[ing] our own blasphemous interventions in feminist theory" (Kafer 2013: 106). Crip technoscience borrows the tools of feminist hacking and coding to blaspheme against liberal theories of disability rights and rehabilitation imperatives, as well as against the technological essentialisms of disability scholarship. While disability technoscience is often deployed for unwanted cures or enhancements, we contend that it can also be cripped, reclaimed, hacked, and tinkered with to create a more accessible world.

Crip technoscience is committed to disability justice. Crip technoscience aligns with the disability justice movement, with its critique of mainstream disability rights concepts, and its focus on intersectionality, collective liberation, and wholeness. Crip technoscience emphasizes that disabled people are not mere consumers of, or objects for, assimilationist technologies, but instead have agential, politicized, and transformative relationships to technoscience. We note that—as a matter of disability justice—disabled people often reject devices that cause pain or lead to infections, refuse pharmaceutical drugs with undesirable effects, discard technologies produced solely to make non-disabled people more comfortable rather than to make life easier for disabled people, problematize expensive tools crafted by the medical and military-industrial complex, and instead demand more public, widespread forms of access. These critiques and practices align crip technoscience with impurity (Shotwell 2016), embracing the ugly (Mingus 2011), and staying with the trouble (Haraway 2016).

While we write from our position as English-speaking, North American, settler and immigrant scholars and makers, we commit to crip technoscience that centers the leadership of those most impacted, including the expertise of black, brown, and Indigenous disabled people. We call for a crip technoscience that disrupts the entitlements of whiteness and colonialism in designed spaces and highlights access as a frictioned project requiring decolonization and racial justice. We imagine disability justice-informed crip technoscience as building upon projects such as "Open in Case of Emergency," a 2017 issue of the *Asian American Literary Review* edited by Mimi Khuc, which uses print culture, images, and symbolic imaginaries to hack the *Diagnostic and Statistical Manual (DSM)*. This interactive project draws upon familiar technoscientific objects (such as the *DSM*), as well as poetry, tarot, and hacked science, to work through Asian American intergenerational trauma and displacement. We also imagine crip technoscience allying with emerging work in feminist of color technoscience, such as a recent *Catalyst* "Lab Meeting" on Black Lives Matter and pedagogy that describes possibilities for extending critical ideas about race, intersectionality, and the environmental construction of health to rehabilitation, immunology, and mental disability (Pollock and Roy 2017). Crip technoscience is not only in alliance with these projects, but takes the position that they ought to be central to how we imagine accessible futures.

In committing to disability justice, crip technoscience explicitly engages the tensions that arise out of taking disabled bodies to be whole, railing against the ways that we are assumed to be damaged, tragic, or in need of cure. To approach disabled bodies by way of wholeness marks the importance of collective, relational, and inter-dependent approaches to disability. Following Eli Clare, we crip wholeness to include "that which is collapsed, crushed, or shattered" (2017: 58), emphasizing that whole and broken are not opposites but rather can be held in productive tension. Following a disability justice framework, marking disabled people as whole is to "value our people as they are, for who they are, and understand that people have inherent worth outside of capitalist notions of productivity" (Berne and Sins Invalid 2016: 17). Taking up wholeness in this way also addresses the complexity of wanting to both accept disabled bodies as they are while simultaneously desiring to hack, tweak, and otherwise engage and alter our relationships to our bodies and technology. As Clare asks, "How can I reconcile my lifelong struggle to love my disabled self exactly as it is with my use of medical technology to reshape my gendered and sexed body-mind?" (2017: 175). Crip technoscience embraces this contradiction, making space for crit-ically engaging technological intervention while maintaining that such interventions are not compulsory.

We find inspiration for crip technoscience and disability justice within what Alice Sheppard (2019) calls "cultural-aesthetic technoscience," particularly the ways that disability artistry, performance, and media explore the complexities of wholeness, seeking neither to overcome disability nor lapsing into a celebration of individual difference in and of itself. For example, Sins Invalid, a performance collective led by queer and disabled people of color, uses live and video performances, along with publications, to convey alternatives to disability rights perspectives centered on assimilation. In their performances, which feature people who use assistive devices such as canes, power wheelchairs, and crutches, deaf people, amputees, and people with non-apparent disabilities, "normative paradigms of 'normal' and 'sexy' are challenged, offering instead a vision of beauty and sexuality inclusive of all individuals and communities" (Sins Invalid 2018). In their publication *Skin, Tooth, and Bone* (2016), the collective outlines a framework for disability justice organizing that draws on performance and activist work made possible through technology.

Similarly, the Canadian disability arts organization Collaborative Radically Integrated Performers Society in Edmonton (CRIPSiE) challenges "dominant stories of disability and other forms of oppression, through high-quality crip and mad perfor-mance art, video art, and public education and outreach programs" that "celebrate the generative possibilities of 'disability' and 'mental illness,' in terms of how these experiences can offer important alternative perspectives" (2018). In the dance-based video-art project *Other-wise*, Danielle Peers and Lindsey Eales (2013) explore themes of interdependency, access, and wholeness, speaking the movements of their dance as Peers's and Eales's bodies move toward and away from each other, limbs entan-gling over and around Peers's wheelchair: "Lifts. Supports. Draws me out and pulls me in. Connects … We are the chair … We will not overcome, but we are becoming." Performative uses of technology transform the meaning of functional technology from rehabilitative or adaptive to cultural.

Another site of crip technoscience world-remaking is disability fashion. For example, Chun-Shan Sandie Yi's *Crip Couture* project (2017) creates wearable art, tailor-made prosthetics, and orthotics to highlight difference and disability. Yi works with unconventional materials, including skin and hair, to engage the contradictions of disability wholeness. Designer James Shutt's Myostomy project likewise offers lingerie-inspired stoma plugs for colostomy bag users, as well as body art products that aestheticize the stoma (London 2012). Like Yi's work, these interventions transform the typical understanding of assistive technology, rendering it as crip fashion, art, and culture.

Crip media production is also a tool for producing new representations of disability that challenge disability technoscience discourses. For example, disabled artist Sue Austin developed a wheelchair that allows her to dive underwater. Documenting these experiences in the ocean's depths, surrounded by blue water and oceanic creatures, Austin highlights the joy and freedom of "revisioning the familiar" (2012) by using a wheelchair to negotiate unexpected worlds. Appearing in the disability and technology documentary *Fixed* (2014) directed by Regan Brashear, Austin's work offers ways of "seeing, being, and knowing" *with* disability that affirms crip world-remaking (Austin 2012).

In the digital age, YouTube and other online services have become tools for distributing disability justice content. Autistic activist Mel Baggs's manifesto, "In My Language"—viewed over 1.5 million times as of this writing—uses video and sound to make a strong case for the dignity and personhood of Autistic people (2007). In a series of clips, Baggs makes sounds, touches objects, and uses their body to move through space. Later, Baggs shows the same clips with a computer-generated voiceover explaining that moving and feeling are a language. Because "the way [Baggs] naturally thinks and responds to things looks and feels so different from standard concepts, some people do not consider it thought at all, but it is a way of thinking in its own right" (Baggs 2007). Instead, Baggs advocates for the agency and power of Autistic people, particularly non-speaking people, who are often excluded from mainstream disability narratives.

While recognizing the inequitable ways in which many people come to disability, crip technoscience claims disabled life as desirable life, as life worth living, and as a difference that matters. Disability rights often foreground a pride-centered framework without acknowledging the relationships between pride and "the violence of social/economic conditions of capitalism" (Erevelles 2011: 17). Crip technoscience acknowledges that that pride-centric frameworks may make it "difficult to acknowledge the overwhelming suffering that results from colonization, war, famine, and poverty" (Meekosha 2011: 677), such that it becomes crucial to reject "the ways in which disability is presently employed as a mechanism for oppression in the global context" (Jaffee 2016: 118). Within such contexts, "positive re-envisionings of disability" are not always politically salient (Puar 2017: xix). Building on disability justice, however, crip technoscience centers the transformative role of disabled people in both technoscientific and activist conditions to both build and dismantle the world toward more just social relations, which includes engaging the "specific sensibilities and discourses" (Ben-Moshe 2018) that disability culture offers to refute disability "as a vector of social control" or "a weapon of debilitation" (Fritsch and McGuire 2019: 48). Following Clare, we ask, "how do we witness, name, and resist the injustices that reshape and damage all kinds of body-minds—plant and animal, organic and inorganic, nonhuman and human—while not equating disability with injustice?" (2017: 56). This question acknowledges the messiness of access-making in conditions shaped by colonialism, militarism, and injustice, but also asks us to go further and locate the conditions and transformative power of crip knowing-making under these systems.

Disabled people use technoscience to survive and alter the very systems that produce disability or attempt to render us as broken. Take the example of Safwan Harb, a disabled Syrian refugee with two disabled family members (British Broadcasting Corporation 2016). While living in a refugee camp, Harb designed an accessible scooter using found materials, which enabled him and other family members to navigate the camp's unpaved streets. Harb's invention signifies crip knowing-making in spaces produced through war and displacement. Mobility, in this context, is not a tool for reinforcing ablenationalism, productivity, or even rights. But Harb's invention *is* an outcome of a design process enacted through crip experience. Crip technoscience recognizes the non-innocent contexts in which knowledge and access emerge. In some cases, crip technoscience may be an individual knowing and making that reorients the material world. In others, it may be collective, politicized work toward interdependence and justice. Building on Haraway, we offer crip technoscience as a critical project that holds in tension the unjust imperatives of technoscientific innovation with the transformative capacities to shape matter and meaning through praxis. The point is not to achieve ideological purity outside of mainstream disability technoscience, militarism, or capitalism but to locate and center threads of resistance already occurring within and against these systems.

As technoscience expands beyond Cold War-era emphases on militarism to include conditions often deemed innocent or uncontroversial, such as sustainability, disabled people are often caught between imperatives to save resources and enable access. But crip technoscience can offer us a sensibility and set of practices for responding to collective problems such as climate change and pollution. Not only do disabled people act as experts and designers in matters of how to reduce single-use plastics such as straws, but we can also draw on our community-generated accessibility and Universal Design practices to shape responses to the Anthropocene. For example, recent studies estimate that volatile organic chemicals (VOCs) in fragranced beauty products and aerosol sprays produce more CO_2 emissions than cars (McDonald et al. 2018). Disabled people with chemical sensitivities or injuries have long advocated for fragrance-free spaces to avoid migraines, brain fog, and illness, in addition to calling for reduced industrial pollution. Activists such as Piepzna-Samarasinha (2018) have not only offered education about fragrance accessibility but also hacked the production of fragrance-free products. Following

Piepzna-Samarasinha, who describes accessibility as an "act of love" (2018: 74), crip technoscience imagines the hacking of non-harmful resource use as an act of planetary love through which accessibility for marginalized disabled and chemically injured people can also mitigate chemical harm toward the atmosphere and oceans. These opportunities for hacking and tinkering with pervasive practices such as VOC use also show us that crip expertise and ingenuity need not rely on disability pride narratives to challenge global conditions harming human and non-human life. In drawing on disability justice principles, crip technoscience agitates against compulsory able-bodiedness and ablenationalism, and mandates for independence and productivity. It works on multiple scales—from the most basic everyday hacks to organized efforts toward collective access—to materialize accessible futures as those in which bodies need not be perceived as productive, legible, articulate, or beautiful to be understood as important agents of world remaking.

Conclusion

Crip technoscience spans historical and contemporary design practices, political activism, scholarly alliances, global systems, and micro-scale resistances. We call for crip technoscience practices that challenge the political economy of technology, particularly as it is ensnared within injustices perpetrated by imperatives to fix, cure, or eliminate disability.

Crip technoscience struggles for futures in which disability is anticipated and welcomed, and in which all disabled people thrive, regardless of their productivity. By endorsing accessible futures, we refuse to treat access as an issue of technical compliance or rehabilitation, as a simple technological fix, or a checklist. Instead, we define access as collective, messy, experimental, frictional, and generative. Accessible futures require our interdependence.

We center technoscientific activism and critical design practices rooted in disability justice, collective access, and collective transformation toward more socially just disability relations. We call for activists, scholars, and makers to expand possible futures for disabled people. We find crip knowing-making in the design and implementation of architectures, technologies, and infrastructures. We seek broad recognition for, and engagement with, the world-building and world-dismantling force of crip technoscience.

Notes

1. Earlier work defined crip technoscience as "experimental practices of knowing-making [that] challenged hierarchies and power relations ... by shifting expertise to those with lived experiences of disability and away from the outside experts often designing in their name" (Hamraie 2017: 99) and "technoscientific practices ... that politicize disabled people's relationships to technologies produced by the military or pharmaceutical

companies, while valuing the technoscientific activism that has characterized disability rights history" (Hamraie 2015: 309). Available online: https://catalystjournal.org/index.php/catalyst/article/download/29607/24772?inline=1#body1.

2. As disability justice activists point out, disability rights approaches are often focused on assimilation into middle-class, white, productive, heteronormative norms. Additionally, disability rights are often enforced through "accommodations" that integrate disabled people into mainstream society using standardized formulas and checklists. We find this focus on accommodation to be depoliticizing. Crip technoscience pivots instead on friction and protest as accessible world-making.

References

Allan, K. (2013), "Introduction," in K. Allan (ed.), *Disability in Science Fiction: Representations of Technology as Cure*, 1–15, New York, NY: Palgrave Macmillan.

Austin, S. (2012, December), "Deep Sea Diving … in a Wheelchair [Video file]," *TedxWomen*. Available online https://www.ted.com/talks/sue_austin_deep_sea_diving_in_a_wheelchair?language=en-t-266710.

Baggs, M. (2007), "In My Language," YouTube video, 8: 36. Posted January 14. Available online: https://www.youtube.com/watch?v=JnylM1hl2jc.

Bailey, M. (2012), "Vampires and Cyborgs: Transhuman Ability and Ableism in the work of Octavia Butler and Janelle Monáe," *Social Text Online*, January 4. Available online: fhttps://socialtextjournal.org/periscope_article/vampires_and_cyborgs_transhuman_ability_and_ableism_in_the_work_of_octavia_butler_and_janelle_monae (accessed December 6, 2018).

Bailey, M., and W. Peoples (2017), "Towards a Black Feminist Health Science Studies," *Catalyst: Feminism, Theory, Technoscience* 3 (2). Available online: http://catalystjournal.org/ojs/index.php/catalyst/article/view/120/html_17 (accessed December 6, 2018).

BBC News (2016), "The Disabled Refugee Inventor Who Built an Electric Bike," [TV program] *BBC*, March 26. *Available online:* http://www.bbc.com/news/av/technology-35871803/the-disabled-refugee-inventor-who-built-an-electric-bike.

Ben-Moshe, L. (2018), "Weaponizing Disability," *SocialText Online*. Available online: https://socialtextjournal.org/periscope_article/weaponizing-disability/.

Berne, P., and Sins Invalid (2016), "10 Principles of Disability Justice," in Sins Invalid (ed.), *Skin, Tooth, and Bone—The Basis of Movement Is Our People: A Disability Justice Primer*, 16–20, San Francisco, CA: Sins Invalid.

Blume, S., V. Galis, and A. Valderrama Pineda (2013), "Introduction: STS and Disability," *Science, Technology, & Human Values* 39 (1): 98–104.

Brashear, R., dir. (2014), *Fixed: The Science/Fiction of Human Enhancement*, United States: Making Change Media.

Casper, M. J., and B. A. Koenig (1996), "Reconfiguring Nature and Culture: Intersections of Medical Anthropology and Technoscience Studies," *Medical Anthropology Quarterly* 10 (4): 523–6.

CBC News (2016), "Cancer Patient Fed up with High Parking Fees at Health Sciences Center," [TV program], *CBC*, May 31. Available online: http://www.cbc.ca/news/canada/manitoba/cancer-patient-fed-up-with-high-parking-fees-at-health-sciences-centre-1.3608227.

Charlton, J. (2000), *Nothing about Us without Us: Disability Oppression and Empowerment*, Berkeley, CA: University of California Press.

Clare, E. (2017), *Brilliant Imperfection: Grappling with Cure*, Durham, NC: Duke University Press.

Collaborative Radically Integrated Performers Society in Edmonton (CRIPSiE) (2018), "About Us," *CRIPSiE*. Available online: http://www.cripsie.ca/about-us.htm.

Da Costa, B., and K. Phillip (2008), *Tactical Biopolitics: Art, Activism, and Technoscience*, Durham, NC: Duke University Press.

Epstein, S. (1996), *Impure Science: AIDS, Activism, and the Politics of Knowledge*, Berkeley, CA: University of California Press.

Erevelles, N. (2011), *Disability and Difference in Global Contexts: Enabling a Transformative Body Politic*, New York, NY: Palgrave Macmillan.

Fritsch, K. (2015a), "Desiring Disability Differently: Neoliberalism, Heterotopic Imagination and Intracorporeal Reconfigurations," *Foucault Studies* 19: 43–66.

Fritsch, K. (2015b), "Gradations of Debility and Capacity: Biocapitalism and the Neoliberalization of Disability Relations," *Canadian Journal of Disability Studies* 4 (2): 12–48.

Fritsch, K. (2016), "Accessible," in K. Fritsch, C. O'Connor, and A. K. Thompson (eds), *Keywords for Radicals: The Contested Vocabulary of Late Capitalist Struggle*, 23–8, Chico, CA: AK Press.

Fritsch, K. (2017), "Contesting the Neoliberal Affects of Disabled Parenting: Towards a Relational Emergence of Disability," in M. Rembis (ed.), *Disabling Domesticity*, 243–68, New York, NY: Palgrave Macmillan.

Fritsch, K. (2019), "Ramping up Canadian Disability Culture," in V. Kannen, and N. Shyminsky (eds), *The Spaces and Places of Canadian Popular Culture*, 265–72, Toronto, ON: Canadian Scholars.

Fritsch, K., and A. McGuire (2019), "Risk and the Spectral Politics of Disability," *Body & Society* 25 (4): 29–54.

Garland-Thomson, R. (2011), "Misfits: A Feminist Disability Materialist Concept," *Hypatia: A Journal of Feminist Philosophy* 26 (3): 591–609.

Giordano, A. (2013), "Nelia's Story—and Yours—in an Oral History of the No Nukes Movement," *The Narcosphere, July 22*. Available online: https://narcosphere.narconews.com/thefield/4945/nelias-story-and-yours-oral-history-no-nukes-movement (accessed December 6, 2018).

Hamraie, A. (2012), "Universal Design Research as a New Materialist Practice," *Disability Studies Quarterly* 32 (4). Available online: http://dsq-sds.org/article/view/324 (accessed December 6, 2018).

Hamraie, A. (2015), "Cripping Feminist Technoscience," *Hypatia: A Journal of Feminist Philosophy* 30 (1): 307–13.

Hamraie, A. (2017), *Building Access: Universal Design and the Politics of Disability*, Minneapolis, MN: University of Minnesota Press.

Hamraie, A. (2018), "Mapping Access: Digital Humanities, Disability Justice, and Socio-spatial Practice," *American Quarterly* 70 (3): 455–82.

Haraway, D. (1991), *Simians, Cyborgs, and Women: The Reinvention of Women*, New York, NY: Routledge.

Haraway, D. (1997), *Modest_Witness@Second_Millennium. FemaleMan©_Meets_OncoMouse™: Feminism and Technoscience*, New York, NY: Routledge.

Haraway, D. (2016), *Staying with the Trouble: Making Kin in the Chthulucene*, Durham, NC: Duke University Press.

Hendren, S., and C. Lynch (2016), "This Counts Too: Engineering at Home," *Engineering at Home*, January 17. Available online: http://engineeringathome.org/manifesto (accessed December 6, 2018).

Hotchkiss, R. (2011), "Extended Interview: Ralf Hotchkiss," *Frontline/World*. Available online: http://www.pbs.org/frontlineworld/stories/vietnam804/interview/extended.html (accessed December 6, 2018).

Jaffee, L. J. (2016), "Disrupting Global Disability Frameworks: Settler-Colonialism and the Geopolitics of Disability in Palestine/Israel," *Disability & Society* 31 (1): 116–30.

Jasanoff, S. (2004), *States of Knowledge: The Co-Production of Science and Social Order*, London: Routledge.

Kafer, A. (2013), *Feminist, Queer, Crip*, Bloomington, IN: Indiana University Press.

Khuc, M., ed. (2017), "Open in Emergency: A special issue on Asian American Mental Health," Special issue, *Asian American Literary Review*. Available online: https://aalr.binghamton.edu/special-issue-on-asian-american-mental-health/ (accessed December 6, 2018).

Kleege, G., and S.Wallin (2015), "Audio Description as a Pedagogical Tool," *Disability Studies Quarterly* 35 (2). Available online: http://dsq-sds.org/article/view/4622/3945 (accessed December 6, 2018).

Lifchez, R., and B. Winslow, (1979), *Design for Independent Living: The Environment and Physically Disabled People*, New York, NY: Whitney Library of Design.

Linton, S. (2007), "'Coming Home' to 'Music Within': Going Backwards or Forwards?" *Disability Culture Watch*, November 6. Available online: http://similinton.com/blog/?p=83 (accessed December 6, 2018).

London, B. (2012), "Victoria's OTHER Secret: Designer Creates World's First Lingerie Colostomy Bags as They Often Put Partners Off," *Daily Mail*, July 20. Available online: http://www.dailymail.co.uk/femail/article-2176425/Victoria-s-OTHER-Secret-Designer-creates-world-s-lingerie-colostomy-bags-partners-off.html (accessed December 6, 2018).

Longmore, P. (2015), *Telethons: Spectacle, Disability, and the Business of Charity*, Oxford: Oxford University Press.

Loomer, A. (1982), "Hanging onto the Coattails of Science," *Rehabilitation Gazette* 25: 30–1. Available online: http://www.polioplace.org/sites/default/files/files/Rehabilitation_Gazette_1982_OCR.pdf (accessed December 6, 2018).

Lorde, A. (1997), *The Cancer Journals*, San Francisco, CA: Aunt Lute Books.

McBride, S. (2017), "ADAPT Activists Arrested at Senate Health Care Protest," *New Mobility Magazine*, June 27. Available online: http://www.newmobility.com/2017/06/adapt-activists-arrested-senate-health-care-protest/ (accessed December 6, 2018).

McDonald, B. C., et al. (2018), "Volatile Chemical Products Emerging as Largest Petrochemical Source of Urban Organic Emissions," *Science* 359 (6377): 760–4.

McRuer, R. (2006), *Crip Theory: Cultural Signs of Queerness and Disability*, New York, NY: NYU Press.

Meekosha, H. (2011), "Decolonising Disability: Thinking and Acting Globally," *Disability and Society* 26 (6): 667–82.

Mills, M. (2011), "On Disability and Cybernetics: Helen Keller, Norbert Wiener, and the Hearing Glove," *Differences* 22 (2–3): 74–111.

Mingus, M. (2010a), "Interdependency (Excerpts from Several Talks)," *Leaving Evidence* (blog), January 22. Available online: https://leavingevidence.wordpress.com/2010/01/22/interdependency-exerpts-from-several-talks/ (accessed December 6, 2018).

Mingus, M. (2010b), "Reflections on an Opening: Disability Justice and Creating Collective Access in Detroit," *Leaving Evidence* (blog), August 23. Available online: https://leavingevidence.wordpress.com/2010/08/23/reflections-on-an-opening-disability-justice-and-creating-collective-access-in-detroit/ (accessed December 6, 2018).

Mingus, M. (2011), "Moving Toward the Ugly: A Politic beyond Desirability," *Leaving Evidence* (blog), August 22. Available online: https://leavingevidence.wordpress.com/2011/08/22/moving-toward-the-ugly-a-politic-beyond-desirability/ (accessed December 6, 2018).

Mingus, M. (2017), "Access Intimacy, Interdependence, and Disability Justice," *Leaving Evidence* (blog), April 12. Available online: https://leavingevidence.wordpress.com/2017/04/12/access-intimacy-interdependence-and-disability-justice/ (accessed December 6, 2018).

Mitchell, D., and S. Snyder (2015), *The Biopolitics of Disability: Neoliberalism, Ablenationalism, and Peripheral embodiment*, Ann Arbor, MI: University of Michigan Press.

Murphy, M. (2012), *Seizing the Means of Reproduction: Entanglements of Feminism, Health, and Technoscience*, Durham, NC: Duke University Press.

Nelson, A. (2013), *Body and Soul: The Black Panther Party and the Fight against Medical Discrimination*, Minneapolis, MN: University of Minnesota Press.

O'Toole, C. (2000), *Advocate for Disabled Women's Rights and Health Issues*, Berkeley, CA: The Bancroft Library, University of California–Berkeley.

Oliver, M. (1990), *The Politics of Disablement: A Sociological Approach*, New York, NY: Palgrave MacMillan.

Ollis, T. (2012), *A Critical Pedagogy of Embodied Education: Learning to Become an Activist*, New York, NY: Palgrave MacMillan.

Ott, K., D. Serlin, and S. Mihmeds (2002), *Artificial Parts, Practical Lives: Modern Histories of Prosthetics*, New York, NY: NYU Press.

Papalia, C. (2013), "A New Model for Access in the Museum," *Disability Studies Quarterly* 33 (3). Available online: http://dsq-sds.org/article/view/3757/3280 (accessed December 6, 2018).

Peers, D., and L. Eales (2013), *Other-wise*. Available online: http://www.cripsie.ca/film–video-art.html.

Piepzna-Samarasinha, L. L. (2018), *Care Work: Dreaming Disability Justice*, Vancouver, BC: Arsenal Pulp Press.

Pollock, A. and D. Roy (2017), "Lab Meeting: How Do Black Lives Matter in Teaching, Lab Practices, and Research?" *Catalyst: Feminism, Theory, Technoscience* 3 (1). Available online: http://catalystjournal.org/ojs/index.php/catalyst/article/view/220/html_7 (accessed December 6, 2018).

Puar, J. (2017), *The Right to Maim: Debility, Capacity, Disability*, Durham, NC: Duke University Press.

Ratto, M., and M. Boler, eds (2014), *DIY Citizenship: Critical Making and Social Media*, Cambridge, MA: MIT Press.

Russell, M. (1998), *Beyond Ramps: Disability at the End of the Social Contract*, Monroe, ME: Common Courage Press.

Sayers, J. (2018), *Making Things and Drawing Boundaries: Experiments in the Digital Humanities*, Minneapolis, MN: University of Minnesota Press.

Sheppard, A. (2019), "Staging Bodies, Performing Ramps: Cultural, Aesthetic Disability Technoscience," *Catalyst: Feminism, Theory, Technoscience* 5 (1): 1–12.

Shotwell, A. (2016), *Against Purity: Living Ethically in Compromised Times*, Minneapolis, MN: University of Minnesota Press.

Sinclair, J. (2010), "Being Autistic Together," *Disability Studies Quarterly* 30 (1). Available online: http://dsq-sds.org/article/view/1075/1248 (accessed December 6, 2018).

Sins Invalid, ed. (2016), *Skin, Tooth, and Bone—The Basis of Movement Is Our People: A Disability Justice Primer*, San Francisco, CA: Sins Invalid.

Sins Invalid (2018), "About Us," *Sins Invalid*, last modified 2018. Available online: https://www.sinsinvalid.org/mission.html.

Snyder, S., and D. Mitchell (2006), *Cultural Locations of Disability*, Chicago, IL: University of Chicago Press.

Sobchack, V. (2006), "A Leg to Stand On: Prosthetics, Metaphor, and Materiality," in M. Smith, and J. Morra (eds), *The Prosthetic Impulse: From a Posthuman Present to a Biocultural Future*, 17–41, Cambridge, MA: MIT Press.

Sterne, J. (2001), "A Machine to Hear for Them: On the Very Possibility of Sound's Reproduction," *Cultural Studies* 15 (2): 259–94.

Thompson, V. (2019), "How Technology Is Forcing the Disability Rights Movement into the Twenty-first Century," *Catalyst: Feminism, Theory, Technoscience* 5 (1): 1–5.

UPIAS (1976), *Fundamental Principles of Disability*, London: Union of the Physically Impaired Against Segregation.

Waldman, H. (1998), "New Equipment, New Outlook: Providing Reproductive Health Care for Women with Disabilities," *Hartford Courant*, 5 March.

Williamson, B. (2012a), "Electric Moms and Quad Drivers: People with Disabilities Buying, Making, and Using Technology in Postwar America," *American Studies* 52 (1): 5–29.

Williamson, B. (2012b), "The People's Sidewalks: Designing Berkeley's Wheelchair Route," *Boom California* 2 (1). Available online: https://boomcalifornia.com/2012/06/26/the-peoples-sidewalks/

Wolfson, P. (2014), "Enwheeled: Two Centuries of Wheelchair Design, from Furniture to Film," MA diss., Parsons School of Design, New York, NY.

Wong, A. (2015a), "Assistive Technology by People with Disabilities, Part I: Introducing Team Free To Pee," *Model View Culture* 29. Available online: https://modelviewculture.com/pieces/assistive-technology-by-people-with-disabilities-part-i-introducing-team-free-to-pee (accessed December 6, 2018).

Wong, A. (2015b), "Assistive Technology by People with Disabilities, Part II: Designing Better Makeathons," *Model View Culture* 29. Available online: https://modelviewculture.com/pieces/assistive-technology-by-people-with-disabilities-part-ii-designing-better-makeathons (accessed December 6, 2018).

Wong, A. (2019), "The Rise and Fall of the Plastic Straw: Sucking in Crip Defiance," *Catalyst: Feminism, Theory, Technoscience* 5 (1): 1–12.

Yergeau, M. (2014), "Disability Hacktivism," Computers and Composition Online. Available online: http://www2.bgsu.edu/departments/english/cconline/hacking (accessed December 6, 2018).

Yi, C. S. (2017), *Crip Couture*. Available online: https://www.cripcouture.org.

Zukas, H. (2000), "National Disability Activist: Architectural and Transit Accessibility, Personal Assistance Services," in an oral history conducted by Sharon Bonney, *Volume III of Builders and Sustainers of the Independent Living Movement in Berkeley*, 93–197, Berkeley, CA: Regional Oral.

2 Fixing Meets Expressing: Design by Designers with Disability Experience

NATALIA PÉREZ LIEBERGESELL, PETER-WILLEM VERMEERSCH, ANN HEYLIGHEN

The inside, our inside, has to come out and be an inspiration for design, rather than design imposing outsides that people have to fit into … The future of architecture, and of ourselves, seems to be in finding out what we need and enjoy and who we are, rather than in making something that we have to adapt to and in being what we are forced to be.

—Franck and Lepori 2000: 8

Design not only responds to different people and accommodates diverse human bodies; bodies and embodied experiences can also *inspire* design. The future of architectural design, Karen Franck and Bianca Lepori (2000) point out, seems to be in finding out what we need (e.g., functionality), what we enjoy (e.g., aesthetics/poetics), and who we are (identity), and design engaging with all three domains. However, design for "the disabled" has been stuck in associations with solving functional aspects of accessibility (e.g., Gray, Gould, and Bickenbach 2003; Rieger and Strickfaden 2016). Sara Hendren (in Kolson Hurley 2016) mentions that while we tend to think that disability is about ramps and elevators, it is not "ticking off a laundry list of compliance-based rules to avoid being sued, but actually thinking: what could architecture do?" Designers generally design *for* "the disabled," but rarely with, or *from*, their experiences.

Not only has the added value of the rich and multifaceted embodied experiences of many disabled people begun to be acknowledged, some studies also examine how their experiences and derived knowledge could inform, and further benefit, design practice at large (e.g., see Butler and Bowlby 1997; Cassim 2007; Edwards and Harold 2014; Guffey 2018; Heylighen, Devlieger, and Strickfaden 2009; Lifchez 1986; Titchkosky 2011; Vermeersch and Heylighen 2010; 2013). Specific architectural (e.g., sensory) qualities some disabled people are particularly attentive to can invite designers to understand socio-material configurations in novel, human-oriented ways, and potentially be a resource for expanding their understanding of spaces. But even if disabled people are involved in the design process, some kind of translation is needed as designers cannot gain direct access to their embodied experiences.

What if disabled/impaired people were the actual designers of buildings? Within literature around the topic of disability (experience) and (architectural) design few studies can be found on, what we consider, the closest relation between architecture and disability, namely, design by designers who experience feeling disabled themselves. In our research, we investigate the perspectives of practicing architects with disability experience and explore diverse relationships between the ways in which they feel disabled and their interpretation in design. A tendency exists to simplify disability experience, rather than grasp and use its full complexity. But two core themes that capture the experience of designing with disability are clear. For several of the designers whose perspectives we studied, a crucial component among the features that characterize accessibility seems to be fixing barriers. However, designing entails more than fixing mismatches between bodies and built environments. Most recognize that stigma and othering in design can be generated by use, such as secondary entrances, or appearance—ugly-/institutional-/different-looking design—sometimes experienced simultaneously. In their designs, they aim to silence the commonly encountered depreciation of disability by being attentive to usability and aesthetic components as a form of expression.

At the same time, some of the designers whose perspectives we studied find in design a way of making sense of and using their experiences, thus elevating their work and changing their status within the profession. It also helps them gain control and agency over their lives—or ways to live—and well-being: a way to re-discover and empower themselves. Ultimately, our research suggests that practitioners who have first-hand experience of being disabled are in a privileged position to reconcile design and disability. Integrating disability (experience) in design can be inclusive, aesthetically worthwhile, and poetic/expressive.

Context

In the last two decades a phenomenological orientation in architecture has turned away from addressing architectural design merely from a functional, measurement-oriented angle toward looking into the feeling and meaning of spaces (Holl, Pallasmaa, and Pérez-Gómez 2006; Zumthor 2006; 2010). However, it has done so for a nondisabled majority. Architectural design for disabled people largely remains disconnected from any creative, poetic, meaningful, and aesthetic-emotional dimension beyond minimal code compliance (Boys 2014; 2017; Hall and Imrie 1999; Hamraie 2016; Pereira, Heitor, and Heylighen 2018). Some so-called architectural "solutions" aimed at fixing disability-related "problems" are often rejected—by disabled and nondisabled people alike—due to an imbalance between functional and aesthetic aspects, the former receiving most attention. Design for "the disabled" is associated with a belief that features needed to make buildings usable for disabled people are unaesthetic and thus detract from, rather than enhance, their quality and appearance (Fitzsimons 2017; Manley, de Graft-Johnson, and Lucking 2011; Pallasmaa 2000; Stilgoe 1998).

Moreover, several authors argue that the design of built environments is shaped by a discourse which disregards the complexity of the human body and the manifold ways in which it interacts with material objects (e.g., see Boys 2014; Imrie 1998; 2015; Pullin 2009). In architecture, the disabled body and its phenomenological existence are often considered, if at all, through notions of bodiliness; it has been reduced to anatomical physical properties—generalized, imprecise, and stereotypical abstractions—at the expense of its relational and inner-felt experiential aspects (Leder 1990; Reid-Cunningham 2009; Verhulst, Elsen, and Heylighen 2016). Wanda Liebermann stresses—and Juan Toro et al. (2020) corroborate—that "the hegemony of an abstract body suppresses atypical embodiment, whose accommodation is seen to pollute aesthetic purity and hinder creative expression" (Liebermann 2019: 803).

Parallels can be drawn to how scholars criticize the social model of disability (Oliver 1983; 2013) for underestimating the importance of the individual's embodied experiences and multiple identities, including the manifold effects and meanings of impairment (e.g., see Butler and Bowlby 1997; Heylighen 2015; Hughes and Paterson 1997; Owens 2015; Winance 2014). Jenny Morris, for instance, mentions that, in focusing on external (e.g. architectural) barriers, "we have tended to push to one side the experience of our bodies" (1998: 13). Some critics express concern insofar as addressing disability in architecture through legislation alone—as often happens—holds the risk to universalize the category of "the disabled" (e.g., see Hamraie 2016; Ingstad and Whyte 1995).

In what follows we zoom in on multiple and diverse bodily, material, and social experiences of four architects who experience feeling disabled,[1] and link them with their design practices and outcomes. Details on how this research was carried out, including approach, methods, and ethical considerations, can be consulted in the first author's PhD thesis *The Difference Disability Makes* (Pérez Liebergesell 2020).

To Fix and Express

In recent years society has moved its focus from fixing impairment through medical interventions to fixing, e.g., physical barriers through architectural ones. In both scenarios the emphasis lies on *fixing*. The dominant culture is one around solving disability-related "problems" (Pullin 2009). However, our analysis has shown that architects with disability experience have attended to fixing, and offer a richer understanding of it, balancing between functional components of access and expressive ones.

And yet fixing means slightly different things to the different designers whose perspectives we studied. Marta Bordas Eddy, a Barcelona-based architect and consultant who became a wheelchair-user as a teenager, refers to her embodied knowledge in designing her 53-square-meter house (Pérez Liebergesell, Vermeersch, and Heylighen 2018). Marta wishes to fix negative encounters with built environments in her practice and design of her house almost one-on-one. In her role as an accessibility consultant, she tries to point at, and propose solutions for, design elements that seem to hinder her during site visits. As a wheelchair-user, Marta's very presence makes design problems explicit as her experience unfolds. But in her house, she mentions, she feels hindered by neither material nor bodily features. Experiences of feeling disabled dissolve in built environments tailored for her body: "in my house … where I have designed everything according to my needs and where I do not have any problem in performing any task." In this context, she notes, "I am not disabled at any moment" (Bordas Eddy 2013: 12).

Although architect Stéphane Beel mentions encountering physical barriers to a lesser degree, he too aims to eliminate potential barriers wheelchair-users encounter. As a Belgian architect based in Gent who was diagnosed with multiple sclerosis, he expresses having become more sensitive to others as a consequence (De Standaard 2011; Plets 2011; Pérez Liebergesell, Vermeersch, and Heylighen 2021a). Stéphane considers functionality as basic in architectural design: "for me a good architect has to be functional. [A building] has to function anyway. That's the least you can ask."[2] Stéphane inscribes wheelchair-accessibility within the basic functional requirements any built environment needs to accomplish. In his design of the AtricaMuseum in Tervuren, for instance, some steps were converted into ramps, elevators were introduced at strategic points, and platform elevators that can be operated autonomously give access to formerly wheelchair-inaccessible areas. Among the features that characterize accessibility, fixing barriers seems to be crucial for both Marta and Stéphane. However, for both architects, good design entails more than fixing mismatches between bodies and built environments.

An absence of architectural barriers needs to be combined with the presence of other design considerations; expression also plays a key role here. Stéphane points out accessibility has no value in itself, but needs to relate to the overall design. To become fully integrated, it should serve multiple purposes and be—physically and aesthetically—connected with other design features. Otherwise, "you make accessibility a special thing and it's only for [disabled] people."[3] Marta, too, expresses a need to think of accessibility from the outset and counter the perceived physical, and by extension social, fragmentation deriving from designing "for the whole community (us), and then add[ing] solutions for the disabled minority (them)" (Bordas Eddy 2017: 3).

Accessibility features that Marta and Stéphane have encountered speak a particular language to them. Both recognize that stigma and othering in design can be generated by functionality (e.g., secondary entrances) or appearance (e.g., ugly-/institutional-/different-looking design). This problem is sometimes experienced simultaneously. In their designs, they aim to silence the commonly encountered depreciation of disability by being attentive to aesthetics and functionality "as one." Marta and Stéphane refer to attractiveness as fundamental to destigmatizing design for "the disabled." Marta mentions that aesthetic appeal is key to reducing the perceived difference between disabled design and nondisabled design. Moreover, Stéphane emphasizes that good design—which includes accessibility features—is not the sum of many beautiful things put together but a result of several functional and other-than-functional aspects *relating* to each other.

These designers actively avoid designs that look like they are intended only for disabled people. Marta, for instance, thinks of platform elevators not as architectural design but as stigmatizing assistive devices; they often look like clinical add-ons, are usually operated by key (producing dependence and/or selecting people entitled to use them), are slow, and are exclusively associated with disability. As such, they are unlikely to be used by nondisabled people. Nevertheless, Marta introduced a platform lift in her own house, gapping a one-floor height difference and addressing functionality. The platform lift has a considerable size, but "disappears" into the floor by blending in with the adjacent floor material. Thus it gives the impression of being not an add-on but an element integrated in its context and contravening issues of appearance and stigma. Marta describes her experience of using the platform as joyful; unlike a boxed elevator, she enjoys having an unobstructed view as her perspective changes and brings an aesthetic element into the feature. In addition, the platform lift is the *only* way for people to go up or down, and thus circumvents the disabled/nondisabled split, both addressing functionality and avoiding stigma.

Indicating an additional strategy to de-stigmatize design for "the disabled," both draw on the concept of "signifying," i.e., how possible actions—affordances—are communicated or implied by objects or built environments. Marta and Stéphane each recognize how designing signifiers communicating affordances diminish the need for disability-related signage (e.g., the use of a wheelchair-symbol) and overly steering elements they consider as contributing to separating people based on their bodily differences. In the AfricaMuseum, for instance, wayfinding is frequently communicated through signifiers, e.g., the vertical circulation core of the extension is located in a "black box" where stairs and elevators are positioned close to each other; natural light is used to capture visitors' attention in the ascending path and to signal which way to go; the first step of a stairwell is extended to be seen by visitors from afar even when the stairwell remains hidden, and several passages next to stairwells signal the entrance to elevators.

Communicating through signifiers could potentially counter disability stigma in architecture. Marta, for example, raises concern over how spaces for "the disabled" are communicated largely through wheelchair-signs. With regard to toilets for "the disabled," for instance, she advises to communicate differences of spaces and what they afford (e.g., big or small bathrooms affording certain actions), rather than differences between people (bathrooms for "the disabled" or nondisabled). Architect George Balsley questions the use of wheelchair-signs in accessible buildings altogether: "why should we put up a wheelchair-logo on bathroom doors, if the whole building is accessible?"[4]

If Marta and Stéphane seem to be mindful of architecture's expressive features, especially, but not limited to, how they depict disabled people, others believe design can act as a medium for expressing their experiences and giving voice to their particular narratives. George Balsley's Deaf ways of seeing inform the design process of a university building, the Sorenson Language and Communication Center (SLCC) in Washington DC (Pérez Liebergesell, Vermeersch, and Heylighen 2019). It was the first building to be built with a set of design principles aimed for deaf people—developed into what are nowadays known as the DeafSpace guidelines. They were drawn up by deaf students and scholars in a visionary workshop in 2005 at Gallaudet University. The design process and outcome of the SLCC seem to have boosted awareness among the Deaf community of architecture's expressive potential. Hansel Bauman,[5] credited for the DeafSpace guidelines that were developed from the abovementioned workshop, and also interviewed in the context of our research, points out: "the strength and the euphoria in the early years around the idea of [DeafSpace] had to do with 'we have a voice, here's a new medium for our voice.'"[6]

George explains how the design process of the SLCC felt empowering for the Deaf community: "it was really time for us deaf people to drive the architecture instead of the hearing majority."[4] The SLCC represents a paradigm shift insofar as its initiators set out to fix neither deafness nor the environment, but rather to find ways for the latter to respond to and express Deaf culture.

George was keenly interested in design that is visually appropriate and enjoyable, not only in the realm of appearance, aesthetics, and well-being but also with regard to the sociality of architecture; visual affordances conductive of (deaf) interpersonal communication were carefully designed. The feeling of coming together, and ultimately belonging to a place, took a prominent role in the design. George points at the atrium as a central element and stresses the importance for deaf people to have an open and welcoming space to be in:

> We need some kind of atrium, some kind of space for people to gather, to mingle, to see each other. The thing about the other buildings on campus, you know, you come in [to] a very narrow, tight hallway. It's not a welcoming thing. I wanted deaf people to experience what people at other colleges and universities have, you know, big, nice gathering spaces … Just to come in and be welcomed in that space, made such a difference.[4]

The design team seemed to also play with the symbolic-expressive quality of the atrium: "it represents that being deaf is not limiting, it's expansive … It's intentional to remove that oppression … We wanted to represent that Deafness is not a disability, it's natural, it's organic. And [the atrium] is an attempt to project that image."[4]

William Feuerman, an American architect, writer, and academic based in Sydney, taps into a different realm of expressing experiences of vision impairment in his design practice (Pérez Liebergesell, Vermeersch, and Heylighen 2021b). For him, architecture and architecture drawings and photographs seem to serve as something akin to a therapeutic outlet, allowing him to express his overwhelming experience of becoming vision impaired:

> To be able to kind of tie my own experience to a way of thinking about architecture, it was incredibly therapeutic … It just kind of evolved through a series of projects that we've been doing. We're exploring the role that architecture can play if we're inducing architectural awareness by intensifying the real. [It] puts us back to ideas [of] my own experience, where I was blind, but I was actually more aware of the space around me.[7]

Figure 2 Atrium of the Sorenson Language and Communication Center as seen from the first floor. The atrium consists of an open space connecting three floors. © Prakash Patel.

Marta and George do not mention explicitly feeling impacted by their impaired bodies—being unable to walk or hear—but refer to how their impairments play a role in specific built and social contexts and interactions. For Stéphane and William, however, the direct impact of impairment itself seems to take a more prominent role. William, for instance, explains that his vision impairment disrupted his habitual functioning and perception. Its effects, however, also brought about an attention to his surroundings that he felt he benefited from: "my partial blindness led me to a much more clear awareness of the space I was in. I was noticing things that I hadn't really noticed before; I was paying attention to things that I had never paid attention to, and I just became *way* more aware of my environment."[7] His experiences motivated him to make them explicit and available—first to himself, then to others—through material expressions; his experiences affect the design of spaces, while, at the same time, he sets out to design spaces that affect experiences (of others).

Just as Marta and Stéphane wish to fix built environments and simultaneously pay attention to expression, George and William aim to express experiences through architecture; at the same time, they hope to address functional needs, albeit with a different emphasis. William does not wish to express his experiences for the sake of it, and George understands that expressing cultural aspects of being deaf goes along with fixing environments in order to accommodate Deaf ways of being. Hence all four architects whose perspectives we studied seem to cohere, in one way or another, with Stéphane's design principle of "doing something for more than one reason."

In the design of *Urban Chandelier*, an installation hung above an alleyway in Chattanooga, William's experiences inspired the design team to develop a chandelier made out of triangles attached to rods that throw light patterns onto the brick walls of a formerly underused alleyway. Besides pursuing visual enjoyment through their intervention, the design team aims for passers-by to engage with that space, generate activity, enhance social relations, and promote community building. Ultimately, William wishes to fix what he recognizes as a broader social problem, i.e., people being unaware of and disconnected from their built, and by extension social, environments due to an excessive use of technological devices. People's attention, William mentions, is continuously disrupted by electronic appendages, making most of them unaware of their immediate socio-material surroundings. Ultimately, he considers benefiting from interpreting his experiences in design by finding ways to bring people in closer touch with their environments.

Not Absence, but Presence

To some extent, our analysis reflects a shift in perspective toward disability (in architecture) that some scholars in the last decade have been hinting toward (e.g., see Bauman and Murray 2014; Edwards and Harold 2014): a shift from the medically oriented inclination to fix problems caused by impairment to seeing disability as an experience and/or way of being. Extended still further, there has been a shift from seeing the built environment as a problem (akin to the social model of disability) to using it as a conduit for (e.g., cultural or perceptual) expression. The designers whose perspectives we have analyzed confirm an understanding of disability experience as being more than having a body that does not function efficiently, and/or encountering practical challenges in one's environment. The designs we studied show potential in reflecting this shift. In 2014 Dirksen Bauman and Joseph Murray claimed that the biological, social, and cultural implications of experiencing disability may be defined, not automatically as a loss or lack, but simply as a difference, and, in some significant instances, as gain (2014: xv). We found that the designers whose perspectives we studied understand their experiences not as "absence" (something lost or lacking) but rather as "presence" (something being done or gained).

Neither Marta nor George explain their experiences on the basis of *not* walking or *not* hearing—where mainstream thinking often assumes the problem lies. Rather, they explain what they do, pay attention to, and value as a wheelchair-user and a person born deaf. Likewise, William and Stéphane express how their bodily and/or spatial awareness has been sharpened, and how they have gained relevant insight they apply in their practices as a consequence of the disruptions they experienced.

On a second level, and relating these designers' experiences to their design practices and outcomes, we found that their approaches are focused less on eradicating the experience of having an impairment and/or providing solutions to living without "*x*" (absence), but on designing places that allow for their diverse ways of being to be expressed (presence). The designers whose perspectives we studied make use of the rich lexicon of architecture at their disposal to fix some of the negative aspects encountered in their lives, take into consideration sociocultural aspects (e.g., related to depiction of difference), and explore ways to creatively express their ways of being. Marta, George, William, and Stéphane indicate the importance of functionality (in which they inscribe multiple facets of access). Nevertheless, this can be combined with one or several other design qualities—to do something for more than one reason. Fixing design problems, ensuring built environments perform correctly, and finding a right fit between their bodies and built environments are only a few aspects of how they understand and practice design. George and William especially extract perceptual components from their experiences of space and translate them in their designs.

Including disabled people into mainstream society often supposes removing the differences that make up impairment and remain close to the ideology behind the medical model of disability. Design for, or with, disabled people is not about making them feel "more normal" but about affording belonging to someone and someplace while respecting their differences. Hence, the architecture presented here is not about removing the differences that make up impairment—some impairments cannot be approached by changes in either the environment or their bodies. Instead, it is about being attentive to, and countering, design features reproducing the idea that living with an impairment is inherently negative and/or has a markedly negative impact in architectural design.

Design for "the disabled" has long been associated with access, and predominantly thought of in static, functional terms; a property that built environments either do or do not have (Boys 2014; Fitzsimons 2012; Morrow 2000; Morrow and Moore 2004). This way of operating mirrors a binary way of thinking about bodies being either in or out of line with their built environments; it is rarely questioned what access means, how it is experienced and made sense of, or how it may relate people with places (Dokumaci 2018; Titchkosky 2011).

In our research, we learned to see access as a necessary subset of a well-functioning design, but it is insufficient to stand on its own. The designers whose perspectives we studied think of access in a variety of ways, e.g., physical, visual, visuo-kinetic, social, cultural, access to information, resources, and/or safety. Yet rather than a property solely of built environments, it is understood in terms of affordance (i.e., possibilities for actions), and thereby thought of in relational terms. In *Urban Chandelier*, for instance, access is closely linked to safety; the aim is to make people notice the chandelier, arouse a sense of domesticity, and contribute to people feeling safe enough to venture in the alleyway. In the SLCC access takes a different role: it refers to possibilities for (inter-)action in the space inscribed within its material boundaries. The design of that "void" focuses on facilitating spatial communication pathways within visual distances and considers architecture's symbolic meaning. While ramps and elevators remain important and are powerful enablers for many people, they are but a few of the options to consider when thinking about access.

Moreover, our analysis suggests that while access may be an important step in dealing with human diversity, it is not the *only* step. The designers' vision of architecture reconciles use and expression; a lacking link between both is identified as disabling and/or poor design (Siebers 2008; Swain et al. 2013). There ought to be expressive components to access, and vice versa, functional components to expressive architecture. In fact, identity is entangled with sociocultural aspects embedded in the material world. Built environments pre-supposing a normative body may not only contribute to bodily discomfort for some people, but give the impression of being unfamiliar and strange within one's own community and culture (Tauke and Smith 2020). Contrarily, paying attention to expressive features in architectural design may prevent collisions between the individual and the social, and furthermore enhance connectedness to someone and/or someplace. It is not the case that architects in general do not consider usability and expressive components important, yet literature suggests that they are rarely touched upon in unison whenever disability intersects with design (Hamraie 2016; Pullin 2009).

Doing Something for More Than One Reason

In our research we explored the often rigid and troublesome contact points between design and disability experience. Studied from a particular angle, namely, the design practices and outcomes of architects who were born, or have become impaired, we have noted how the experiences of being disabled may influence these practitioners. In doing so, we have re-learned the design principle of "doing something for more than one reason." Certainly, this approach is applicable to *any* design and in multiple contexts, but it remains especially relevant in relation to disability to achieve design coherence, social impact, and enjoyment. These designers' practices and materialized outcomes confirm Franck and Lepori's perspective on the potential of considering, besides functionality, aesthetic/poetic components, and how the material relates to, and expresses, the self without separating them. Echoing H. Bauman's words, an interplay of all three gives rise to creating places to dwell, rather than spaces solely to be used (2014: 375, 394).

Society's tendency to understand disability experience as essentially negative remains prevalent; it is often associated with tragedy, an unsatisfactory life, and/or a fundamental loss. Disabled people being or counting as different and/or worse-off is often reinforced by the spaces and objects assigned to them (e.g., a "special" entrance through a secondary door). In our research, we noted design's power to increase or decrease people's experiences of feeling disabled, not only by permitting or denying access but also—or especially—through the manifold associations made and meanings attributed by society imprinted in architectural objects. The designs presented here are meant to be not *a formula* on how to integrate attention for "the disabled" within the overall design but rather illustrations of the manifold possibilities arising from the multiple and diverse experiences of feeling disabled interpreted in design.

While we could detect significant differences across all four designers' experiences and design outcomes, their approaches offer more than technical solutions to problems created by impairment. Our analysis suggests that the design outcomes presented here take into account functional needs, aesthetic/poetic aspects, and propose ways to sensitively connect human beings to the places they inhabit. Future research would benefit from exploring additional possibilities of intersecting disability and (architectural) design, and it may be up to designers with disability experience to do so.

Acknowledgments

We would like to thank all participants that contributed to this research for sharing their time and insights. We also appreciate Elizabeth Guffey's and Alison Kurdock Adams's interest in and enthusiasm for our work, and their help in preparing this manuscript. This research received funding from the Research Fund KU Leuven in the form of a C1-project [Grant No. C14/16/047].

Notes

1. Besides the four architects whose perspectives we studied, we also interviewed at least one person from their immediate surroundings, e.g., Hansel Bauman, whom we also refer to in this manuscript.
2. Stéphane Beel, interview by N. Pérez Liebergesell and P. W. Vermeersch, Machelen-aan-de-Leie, Belgium, February 27, 2019.
3. Stéphane Beel, interview by N. Pérez Liebergesell and P. W. Vermeersch, Tervuren, Belgium, August 23, 2018.
4. George Balsley, interview by N. Pérez Liebergesell and A. Heylighen, Washington DC, USA, June 19–21, 2017.

5. Hansel Bauman is an architect, partner at hbhm architecture, and was the executive director at Gallaudet Campus Design Program Development at the time we interviewed him. He is referenced in the capacity of participant and published author. He is the brother of Dirksen Bauman, a deaf studies academic and faculty member at Gallaudet University. To avoid confusion, Dirksen is referenced using his initial "D. Bauman," whereas "Hansel" is used when mentioned as interviewee, and "H. Bauman" when mentioned as published author.

6. Hansel Bauman, interview by N. Pérez Liebergesell and A. Heylighen, Washington DC, USA, June 20, 2017.

7. William Feuerman, seminar at KU Leuven, Leuven, Belgium, May 22, 2018.

References

Bauman, D., and J. Murray (2014), *DeafGain*, Minneapolis: University of Minnesota Press.

Bauman, H. (2014), "DeafSpace," in D. Bauman, and J. Murray (eds), *DeafGain*, 375–401, Minneapolis: University of Minnesota Press.

Bordas Eddy, M. (2013), *Let's Open Cities for Us—LOCUS*, Universitat Politècnica de Catalunya: Iniciativa Digital Politècnica.

Bordas Eddy, M. (2017), "Universal Accessibility: On the Need of an Empathy-Based Architecture," PhD Thesis, Tampere: Tampere University of Technology. School of Architecture. Housing Design. Vol. 26.

Boys, J. (2014), *Doing Disability Differently*, Abingdon and New York: Routledge.

Boys, J. (2017), "Architecture, Place and the 'Care-Full' Design of Everyday Life," in C. Bates, R. Imrie, and K. Kullman (eds), *Care and Design: Bodies, Buildings, Cities*, 155–77, Chichester: Wiley Blackwell.

Butler, R., and S. Bowlby (1997), "Bodies and Spaces," *Environment and Planning D: Society and Space*, 15 (4): 411–33.

Cassim, J. (2007), "'It's Not What You Do, It's the Way That You Do It:' The ChallengeWorkshop—A Designer-Centred Inclusive Design Knowledge Transfer Mechanism for Different Contexts," in C. Stephanidis (ed.), *Universal Access in Human Computer Interaction. Coping with Diversity*, Heidelberg: Springer, 4554: 36–45.

De Standaard (2011), "'t Groot lot De toevalstreffers, grote en kleine lotgevallen in het leven van Stéphane Beel / Architect," September 24. Available online: https://www.standaard.be/cnt/vl3g2vqh (accessed July 26, 2019).

Dokumaci, A. (2018), "Disability as Method: Interventions in the Habitus of Ableism through Media-Creation," *Disability Studies Quarterly* 38 (3).

Edwards, C., and G. Harold (2014), "DeafSpace and the Principles of Universal Design," *Disability and Rehabilitation* 36 (16): 1350–9.

Fitzsimons, J. K. (2012), "Seeing Motion Otherwise: Architectural Design and the Differently Sensing and Mobile," *Space and Culture* 15 (3): 239–57.

Fitzsimons, J. (2017), "More than Access: Overcoming Limits in Architectural and Disability Discourse," in J. Boys (ed.), *Disability, Space, Architecture*, 88–101, Oxon and New York: Routledge.

Franck, K. A., and R. B. Lepori (2000), *Architecture Inside Out*, New York: Wiley.

Gray, D. B., M. Gould, and J. E. Bickenbach (2003), "Environmental Barriers and Disability," *Journal of Architectural and Planning Research*, 20 (1): 29–37.

Guffey, E. (2018), *Designing Disability: Symbols, Space, and Society*, London and New York: Bloomsbury Publishing.

Hall, P., and R. Imrie (1999), "Architectural Practices and Disabling Design in the Built Environment," *Environment and Planning B: Planning and Design* 26 (3): 409–25.

Hamraie, A. (2016), "Universal Design and the Problem of 'Post-Disability' Ideology," *Design and Culture* 8 (3): 285–309.

Heylighen, A. (2015), "Enacting the Socio-Material: Matter and Meaning Reconfigured through Disability Experience," in G. Lindsay, and L. Morhayim (eds), *Revisiting "Social Factors." Advancing Research into People and Place*, 72–90, Newcastle upon Tyne: Cambridge Scholars Publishing.

Heylighen, A., P. Devlieger, and M. Strickfaden (2009), "Design Expertise as Disability," in J. Verbeke, and A. Jakimowicz (eds), *Communicating (by) Design*, 227–35, Göteborg, Sweden: Chalmers University of Technology/Hogeschool voor Wetenschap & Kunst-School of Architecture Sint-Lucas.

Holl, S., J. Pallasmaa, and A. Pérez-Gómez (2006), *Questions of Perception: Phenomenology of Architecture*, San Francisco: William Stout.

Hughes, B., and K. Paterson (1997), "The Social Model of Disability and the Disappearing Body: Towards a Sociology of Impairment," *Disability & Society* 12 (3): 325–40.

Imrie, R. (1998), "Oppression, Disability and Access in the Built Environment," in T. Shakespeare (ed.), *The Disability Reader: Social Science Perspectives*, 129–46, London: Cassell.

Imrie, R. (2015), "Doing Disability Differently: An Alternative Handbook on Architecture, Dis/Ability and Designing for Everyday Life," *Disability & Society* 30 (3): 486–8.

Ingstad, B., and S. R. Whyte (1995), *Disability and Culture*, Berkeley: University of California Press.

Kolson Hurley, A. (2016) "How Gallaudet University's Architects Are Redefining Deaf Space," *Curbed*', January 13. Washington DC, USA. Available online: www.curbed.com/2016/3/2/11140210/gallaudet-deafspace-washington-dc (accessed May 2, 2020).

Leder, D. (1990), *The Absent Body*, Chicago, London: University of Chicago Press.

Liebermann, W. K. (2019), "Teaching Embodiment: Disability, Subjectivity, and Architectural Education," *The Journal of Architecture*, 24 (6): 803–28.

Lifchez, R. (1986), *Rethinking Architecture: Design Students and Physically Disabled People*, Berkeley, Los Angeles, London: University of California Press.

Manley, S., A. de Graft-johnson, and K. Lucking (2011), *Disabled Architects: Unlocking the Potential for Practice*, Bristol: University of the West of England. Available online: uwe-repository.worktribe.com/output/958093.

Morris, J. (1998), "Feminism, Gender and Disability," Text presented at a seminar, Sydney, February. Available online: http://citeseerx.ist.psu.edu/viewdoc/download?doi=10.1.1.563.4580&rep=rep1&type=pdf.

Morrow, R. (2000), "Architectural Assumptions and Environmental Discrimination: The Case for More Inclusive Design in Schools of Architecture," in D. Nicol, and S. Pilling (eds), *Changing Architectural Education: Towards a New Professionalism*, 36–41, London and New York: Spon Press.

Morrow, R., and K. Moore (2004), "An Inclusive Design Dialogue on Ethics and Aesthetics," paper presented at the Open Space International Conference on Inclusive Environments, Edinburgh. Available online: https://pureadmin.qub.ac.uk/ws/portalfiles/portal/14447526/An_Inclusive_Design_Dialgoue_on_Ethics_and_Aesthetics.pdf.

Oliver, M. (1983), *Social Work with Disabled People*, Basingstroke: MacMillan.

Oliver, M. (2013), "The Social Model of Disability: Thirty Years On," *Disability & Society* 28 (7): 1024–6.

Owens, J. (2015), "Exploring the Critiques of the Social Model of Disability: The Transformative Possibility of Arendt's Notion of Power," *Sociology of Health & Illness* 37 (3): 385–403.

Pallasmaa, J. (2000), "Stairways of the Mind," *International Forum of Psychoanalysis* 9 (1–2): 7–18.

Pereira, C. M., T. Heitor, and A. Heylighen (2018), "Improving Pool Design: Interviewing Physically Impaired Architects," in P. Langdon, J. Lazar, A. Heylighen, and H. Dong (eds), *Breaking Down Barriers: Usability, Accessibility and Inclusive Design*, 77–87, Cambridge: Springer.

Pérez Liebergesell, N. (2020), "The Difference Disability Makes: Learning about Interactions with Architectural Design from Four Architects Experiencing Disability," PhD diss., KU Leuven: Leuven, Belgium.

Pérez Liebergesell, N., P. W. Vermeersch, and A. Heylighen (2018), "Designing from a Disabled Body: The Case of Architect Marta Bordas Eddy," *Multimodal Technologies and Interaction* 2 (1): 4.

Pérez Liebergesell, N., P. W. Vermeersch, and A. Heylighen (2019), "Through the Eyes of a Deaf Architect: Reconsidering Conventional Critiques of Vision-Centered Architecture," *The Senses and Society* 14 (1): 46–62.

Pérez Liebergesell, N., P. W. Vermeersch, and A. Heylighen (2021a), "Designing for a Future Self: How the Architect Stéphane Beel Empathises with Wheelchair Users," *The Journal of Architecture* 26 (6): 912–37.

Pérez Liebergesell, N., P. W. Vermeersch, and A. Heylighen (2021b), "Urban Chandelier: How Experiences of Being Vision Impaired Inform Designing for Attentiveness," *Journal of Interior Design* 46 (1): 73–92.

Plets, G. (2011), "Waterlanders / Stéphane Beel," *De Standaard*, March 19, 2011. Available online: https://www.standaard.be/cnt/gcs37ohpr?articlehash=2FD720EDDECC96E9653886BCE3F998CDF86245A6A5A40A923B024152691B71820B470793A1D1C6F6676059A8C46213E0ABB89EAD368FBC08CB3E9AB0A3BE9BE6 (accessed August 5, 2019).

Pullin, G. (2009), *Design Meets Disability*, Cambridge: MIT Press.

Reid-Cunningham, A. R. (2009), "Anthropological Theories of Disability," *Journal of Human Behavior in the Social Environment* 19 (1): 99–111.

Rieger, J., and M. Strickfaden (2016), "Taken for Granted: Material Relations between Disability and Codes/Guidelines," *Societies* 6 (1): 6–17.

Siebers, T. (2008), *Disability Theory*, Ann Arbor: University of Michigan Press.

Stilgoe, J. R. (1998), "Lions and Tigers and Stairs, Oh My!" *Boston Society of Architects*, *Practice and Technology* 2 (1): 18–20.

Swain, J., S. French, C. Barnes, and C. Thomas (2013), *Disabling Barriers—Enabling Environments*, London: SAGE.

Tauke, B., and K. Smith (2020), "Marginalized by Design," *Journal of Interior Design* 45 (1): 5–12.

Titchkosky, T. (2011), *The Question of Access: Disability, Space, Meaning*, Toronto, Buffalo, London: University of Toronto Press.

Toro, J., J. Kiverstein, and E. Rietveld (2020), "The Ecological-Enactive Model of Disability: Why Disability Does Not Entail Pathological Embodiment," *Frontiers in Psychology* 11 (June): 1162.

Verhulst, L., C. Elsen, and A. Heylighen (2016), "Whom Do Architects Have in Mind during Design When Users Are Absent? Observations from a Design Competition," *Journal of Design Research* 14 (4): 368–87.

Vermeersch, P. W., and A. Heylighen (2010), "Blindness and Multi-Sensoriality in Architecture. The Case of Carlos Mourão Pereira," in R. L. Hayes and V. Ebbert (eds), *The Place of Research, the Research of Place*, 393–400, Washington, DC: Architectural Research Centers Consortium (ARCC).

Vermeersch, P. W., and A. Heylighen (2013), "Rendering the Tacit Observable in the Learning Process of a Changing Body," in N. Nimkulrat, K. Niedderer, and M. Evans (eds), *Proceedings of EKSIG 2013: Knowing Inside Out—Experiential Knowledge, Expertise and Connoisseurship*, 259–70, Loughborough: Loughborough University.

Winance, M. (2014), "Universal Design and the Challenge of Diversity: Reflections on the Principles of UD, Based on Empirical Research of People's Mobility," *Disability and Rehabilitation* 36 (16): 1334–43.

Zumthor, P. (2006), *Atmospheres*, Basel: Birkhäuser.

Zumthor, P. (2010), *Thinking Architecture*, Basel: Birkhäuser.

Case Study

3 Brett's Leather Case

JAIPREET VIRDI

Figure 3 Eleonora M. Kissel, *Portrait of Miss Dorothy Brett*, 1946. Gift of the artist. Courtesy of The Harwood Museum of Art.

It seems like an ordinary object. A dark-brown leather case approximately 4 × 4 × 7 inches, with a long and thick leather shoulder strap. It could easily be mistaken as a camera bag, were it not for the slight gap between the cover flap and the case edges—exactly wide enough for wires to trail outward. This was an object of immense value, handmade with bartered leather and adorned with pieces of silver and turquoise sourced from the Pueblo market, crafted by Taos-based painter Dorothy Eugénie Brett (1883–1977) for a single purpose: to house her hearing aid.

Supposedly deafened at nineteen following complications from appendicitis, Brett made use of various acoustic aids throughout her adulthood: auricles, trumpets, carbon devices, and vacuum tube hearing aids—devices that she collectively referred to as her "ear machines." They became indispensable for her navigation through multiple soundscapes, and in so doing, became intertwined with her body. They are never mere objects but rather "my ears" or "my aids," intimate extensions of Brett's ear, though they often fizzled, hummed, and clanked, exposing themselves—and thus, Brett—even when no attempt was made to conceal them. Of all the ear machines, none were as precious as "Toby," Brett's 14-inch ear trumpet that speakers had to awkwardly "bark down" on (Luhan 1932: 122). It joined her auditory journey around 1918 and remained her most faithful device until the emergence of subminiature vacuum tube hearing aids in the late 1930s. They were powerful instruments, but finicky and fragile at times, requiring regular maintenance, repair, and battery replacements; as useful as they were, they could also be costly.

With vacuum tube hearing aids, the movement *of* the body, as much as the placement of the aid *on* the body, determined the effectiveness of the machine. For the instrument to work properly, it was imperative that the microphone and receiver not be obstructed, and that wires were loose enough not to restrict movement. This could be challenging for users who strapped the receiver and external battery packs in harnesses underneath their clothing, for the fabric rustling against the microphone distorted sound quality. Some found it easier to carry the device in shirt pockets and strap the batteries on waist belts—options that could be constrained by gendered conventions for dress. Though hearing aid companies offered their own brand of carriers and harnesses, their standardized design did not meet the needs of all users. Thus, some users designed their own carriers: a woman frustrated by how the earpiece wire restricted her body movement made a pocket attached to her brassiere to wear her aid without adding bulge; a soldier remade his flannel jacket to house extra pockets to protect his device from the weather.[1]

A user design of hearing aid carriers provides us with material insight into the everyday experience of wearing technologies and how disability is tied to performance: improving technological limitations, aligning the machine to the body, and adjusting, tinkering, maintaining the body/machine interface to increase efficiency, if not assimilation, into the able-bodied world. This suggests that disability objects convey specific representations that move beyond their assistive features. As Abigail Mann and Katherine Béres Rogers argue, assistive technologies incorporate aspects of the Harawayian cyborg to minimize feminized self-negation, such that objects can become crucial for how disabled people mediate their world. Harriet Martineau's (1802–76) ear trumpet, for instance, is not just a tool she uses but an object "integral to her views and her selfhood, allowing her to practice her methodology and further her objective stance" as a deaf writer experiencing the world (Mann and Rogers 2011: 249). Similarly, Brett's ear machines embody her claiming of space, an insistence to be recognized as a deaf woman, and when they were housed inside the case, the case both protected the device and emboldened her assertiveness.

Brett carried her leather case everywhere, it seemed. Novelist William Goyen wrote of this, somewhat cruelly: "She carried her hearing-aid amplifier in a container the size of a cereal box in the crook of her arm and against the huge breast the way a woman carries a lap-dog" (Goyen 1999). Friends became accustomed to Brett positioning the case in the center of a table to ensure that they spoke clearly into her instrument; sometimes the flap of the case was opened to better receive sounds through the hearing aid microphone (Manchester [1933] 2006: v). The case is prominently captured in numerous photographs of Brett out and about in New Mexico, nestled underneath her arm or held in front of her body. When Henri Cartier-Bresson travelled through Taos for his 1947 cross-country road trip, he photographed artists in their homes or workplaces as a commission for *Harper's Bazaar*—including the wild-haired, smiling Brett wearing an embroidered jacket and standing inside her home against a wall adorned with Pueblo artifacts and her paintings. A wire trails from her ear into the leather case, which she holds in her right hand against her hip, slightly angling it toward the camera. Brett's relaxed pose and the open case flap come across as confident and comfortable—within the portrait the case becomes, in a sense, an extension of her, a part of her essence.

The same assertion is present in Eleonora M. Kissel's 1946 portrait of Brett, seen above. It is reminiscent of other portraiture of deaf subjects, including a 1786 mezzotint of geologist James Hutton holding an ear trumpet to his ear, Joshua Reynolds' *Self Portrait as a Deaf Man* (c.1775) showing him cupping his ear with his hand, and an 1832 illustration of Harriet Martineau in the same cupping gesture. As with these figures, we come to believe Brett's deafness, but we are also made aware of her independence—if not dominance—and the transformative power that comes from connecting a disability object to its person. The deliberate positioning of the case on Brett's lap, as well as the earpiece wire, signifies a performative relation between Brett, the object, and the (hearing) audience.[2] The case draws our attention to its hidden components, while the leather and jewels on its exterior are as reflective of Taos aesthetic as the embroidered jacket and the antique Mexican tan-colored felt hat embroidered with gold flowers that was a gift from Mabel Dodge Luhan. "You may not find it resembles your heart's desire and will therefore hate me for bringing it," Luhan wrote to Brett, "but one must take these risks. It is not too exaggerated or conspicuous to *wear*" (quoted in Hignett 1984: 229). Together, the case, jacket, and hat perfectly encapsulate an artist whose "feminist spirituality and offbeat counter-cultural values" were as renowned in Taos as her eccentric flair and bold paintings of Pueblo ceremonials (Rudnick 1996: 112–13).

The leather case of Dorothy Brett was made solely for her, a comfortable companion for carrying her hearing aid. It is part of a legacy of user design and adaptation that conceptualizes disability experience "through function in the material" rather than cure or rehabilitation (Guffey and Williamson 2020: 5). Body-worn hearing aids, such as the one Brett favored, eventually phased out by the 1980s and were replaced with models designed to be worn in or behind the ears. User preferences for aesthetic customization, nevertheless, remained throughout the decades: instead of carriers, deaf people have modified their instruments directly, offering insights, supplies, and advice in deaf newspapers or virtual community groups for decorating their hearing aids—and later, cochlear implants—to make them more visible (Profita et al. 2018). Collectively, these DIY adaptations demonstrate the scope of personal aesthetics and design for assistive technologies, but more importantly, they showcase the creative possibilities that arise when pushed back against the medical gaze of disability. With the alternative—the *disabled gaze*—we receive a powerful affirmation, one that celebrates disability and encourages difference.

Notes

1. *The Silent World* (March 1947), 280; Steven M. Spencer to Norton Canfield, September 25, 1946, Norton Canfield Collection Ms 1293, Box 7. Manuscripts and Archives, Sterling Memorial Library, Yale University.
2. On "performing power," see Böhme 2014: 201.

References

Böhme, B. (2014), *Fetishism and Culture: A Different Theory of Modernity*, trans. Anna Galt, Berlin: de Gruyter: 201.

Goyen, W. (1999), *Three Women: A Memoir by William Goyen*, Austin: Harry Ransom Humanities Research Center.

Guffey, E., and B. Williamson (2020), "Introduction: Rethinking Design History through Disability, Rethinking Disability through Design," in E. Guffey, and B. Williamson (eds), *Making Disability Modern: Design Histories*, 1–13, New York, NY: Bloomsbury Press.

Hignett, S. (1984), *Brett: From Bloomsbury to New Mexico, a Biography*, London: Hodder and Stoughton.

Luhan, M. D. (1932), *Lorenzo in Taos*, New York: Alfred Knopf.

Manchester, J. (2006), "Introduction," in Dorothy Brett, *Lawrence and Brett* (eds), *A Friendship*, Reprint, Santa Fe: Sunstone Press.

Mann, A., and K. B. Rogers (2011), "Objects and Objectivity: Harriet Martineau as Nineteenth-Century Cyborg," *Prose Studies* 33 (3): 241–56; 249.

Profita, H., A. Stangl, L. Matuszewska, S. Sky, R. Kushalnagar, and S. Kane (2018), "'Wear It Loud:' How and Why Hearing Aid and Cochlear Implant Users Customize Their Devices," *ACM Transactions on Accessible Computing* 11 (3): Article 13.

Rudnick, L. P. (1996), *Utopian Vistas: The Mable Dodge Luhan House and the American Counterculture*, Santa Fe: University of Mexico Pres.

Case Study

4   Zebreda Makes It Work! and the "Key" to Innovation

ELIZABETH GUFFEY

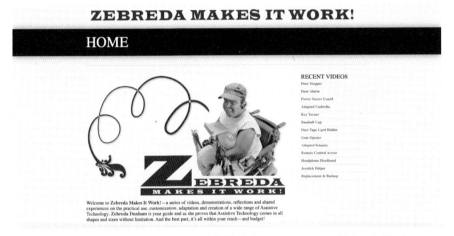

Figure 4 Website "Zebreda Makes It Work!" 2016. Image courtesy of Zebreda Dunham.

The t-shaped piece of metal appears unprepossessing. Attached to an electric wheelchair, it is easy to miss. But looks can be deceiving. It's a key turner with a horizontal plate that allows people who cannot easily grasp and turn a key in a lock to easily use it. This "zKey Turner" won a 2015 RESNA (Rehabilitation Engineering and Assistive Technology Society of North America) prize, an award that recognizes the "development of innovative, low-cost technologies that could be easily replicated in under-resourced countries" (RESNA 2015). Designed by Zebreda Dunham, a Black wheelchair user born with arthrogryposis multiplex congenita, RESNA publicity suggested that the key turner was a device that can "open doors" anywhere (RESNA 2015). But the case for Dunham's resourcefulness is not this simple and RESNA's hype implicitly passes over the dimensional ingenuity of Dunham's key turner. This chapter probes the fuller implications of this and other example of Dunham's innovations, examining how they often solve immediate access problems while also subverting ordinary protocols for caregiving, the typical supply chains for assistive technologies, and the very domains of life where those technologies are most thought to "assist."

The case for Dunham's resourceful designs for assistive devices can be registered on many levels. To be sure, they have been lauded as an example of the inventiveness of disabled innovation (Meissner et al. 2017). They have also attracted attention from makers looking for alternatives to the professionalized world of assistive technology (Bassi et al. 2019; Hendren et al. 2016) to academics researching Human-Computer Interactions (HCI) (Robinson 2018). That Dunham's ingenuity first gained attention through her website also highlights a twenty-first century blossoming on the internet. Indeed, social media has allowed people with disabilities to widely spread stories of their own modification, repurposing, and invention of designs; often these are shared among the disability community, as examples of what people with disabilities have done in their daily life to make something work better for them (Robinson 2019). At the same time, none of these accounts still adequately address Dunham's full resourcefulness.

To fully understand the import of this making practice, I want to suggest the subversive elements that are also present here, in addition to Dunham's ingenuity. In fact, there has been little investigation of the subversive elements that can guide such making; similarly, there is almost no discussion of how race, class, and gender plays into such making cultures (Woods 2019). In this case study, my investigation of the Key Turner and Dunham's website Zebreda Makes It Work! argues for us to recognize her design process as not only opening doors but also representing a form of agency represented by non-compliance and disability resistance.

Trying to Control It: Design and Subversion

Dunham uses design to fill a gap between her needs and available manufactured goods; at the same time, however, the "problems" she solves are often not typically the first needs addressed by conventional Assistive Technology (AT). For instance, Dunham wears a stiff-brimmed cap not only for sun protection but to use the visor for pushing buttons on key pads. This adaptation arose from necessity; when her storage unit stopped using an automatic door opener late at night, she recognized that she could find herself locked in. As an expert in her own life experiences, Dunham is very clear about her own immediate needs. When Dunham was confronted with the inaccessible keypad in her storage unit, she decided to "use my head," hoping to find a way to "Let me just try to control it …" (Dunham 2020). But the desire to find inexpensive and immediate solutions motivates much of her design practice as well.

If Dunham's design practice suggests a consistent interest in security, self-management and control, these themes are often deemed secondary by AT professionals. The latter usually design rehabilitation devices with a focus on cure. When questions of security are addressed, they often focus on bodily health and safety. The literature is filled with references to anti-slip mechanisms, fire safety, and many other well-meaning designs, but they rarely address the desire for personal privacy, autonomy, and security. However, Dunham's designs often revolve around security concerns in the real world and her grasp of safety is quite different. When Dunham designed a Joystick Helper in order to "allow me to keep a hold of the joystick when running over … rough terrain," for example, she describes it as "a real safety feature" (In the Space 2021).

Dunham designed the key turner and used the brimmed baseball hat as part of a larger plan to rent a storage facility for her possessions. Dunham's apartment is filled with neat compartments of duct tape, metal parts, and other materials saved as potential supplies. Dunham also supplements her income by collecting and recycling bottles and cans; ultimately as Dunham's activities fell under the scrutiny of the authorities at her living facility, she felt it necessary to move much of her possessions to a storage facility away from her home; in so doing, she had to hack a number of security features at the storage place, which was not fitted for someone who doesn't use their hands. The key turner was needed to lock the facility door. Similarly, using the hat to type in a code into a security pad was necessary to enter. To leave after hours meant using a pedestrian door and this had a handle that she could not use; to operate doors like this, Dunham developed a special door hook opener.

While these devices were deemed important for establishing a secure location for her possessions, Dunham also felt compelled to control security in her living quarters. Sometimes her inventions are intended to give more access, as with the door stopper she developed; the latter uses a product designed to keep a space closed was actually used to do the opposite—to innovate a simple pulley that, when attached to her wheelchair, allows Dunham to easily open her door. But others were designed specifically to allow for more privacy. For example, her low-tech door alarm effectively allows her to monitor who enters and leaves her living space; essentially it is composed of small stainless steel cotter pins hanging on a string, and they clatter when the door is opened and closed.

Many of these designed objects form a pattern of making and subversion in a deeper sense. At one point, for example, the previous authorities at the assistive living facility where Dunham lives began insisting that Dunham could not be assisted with eating and must be moved out. In the end, Dunham developed a number of inexpensive systems for feeding herself.[1] These include a potato masher in a metal pipe attached to her chair; propped to her elbow, she can eat finger foods. Alternately, she has also designed her pulley spoon, a device which raises a spoon from a bowl to her mouth. To a similar end, she developed the "eating assistant," a kind of foam tray that allows food to be placed at different levels for eating, allowing her to judge and adjust how she can more easily access various food types at different heights. Even as Dunham is involved in micro-resistances, these actions do not occur in a void; her practice falls within the processes of design and should be acknowledged as such.

"It Usually Starts with a Problem"

Praised as "a frame of mind about assistive technology" (Punzalan 2012), the website Zebreda Makes It Work! began as a series of videos posted online by AT professional Martin Sweeney. The pair had already been presenting Dunham's DIY AT practice at training sessions and conferences for AT professionals in the field. With titles like "Zen & The Art of No-Tech Assistive Technology," these presentations emphasized Dunham's range of activities. In her website videos, Dunham explains her process of designing an umbrella holder, a pair of scissors, or a joystick helper, and she repeatedly emphasizes their motivation: "it usually starts with a problem" ("Zebreda Makes It Work!" 2013).

As a problem-solving practice, Dunham's work combines design with fabrication or "making." Crucially, however, Dunham does not use her hands; her process is a tight collaboration with various individuals who assist her in realizing and refining her concepts. This approach, Dunham recalls, can be traced back to a third-grade teacher who carried out her directions for class art projects. In her current, lived practice, Dunham employs internet search engines to find and assemble collections of images that resemble or otherwise share components of her conceived object. She then conveys these images, as well as her own verbal descriptions, to collaborators who gradually follow her directions, ultimately executing her ideas. Dunham's collaborators reflect her large social network, from personal friends to service providers to unhoused individuals living on the streets of her community. For simple and fast jobs, she will often ask for help from the maintenance workers at her facility for living. More complex tasks have led her to a clerk at her local bank who helps during lunch hours. In some ways Dunham's living quarters in an assisted living space are packed with stuff neatly ordered in boxes on shelves, making it into a kind of warehouse stocked with materials that are largely found on the street or cheaply bought from hardware and home improvement stores. Calling the space "my lab," Dunham notes how much of what is in there can be put together to make different devices (In the Space 2021). Because Dunham has no shop or workspace, she often works with sales associates at hardware and home improvement stores (the latter being trained in mechanical processes like cutting or drilling and having access to store tools). As Dunham describes this making process she is quite explicit in directing these associates. Dunham waits for them to have free time, then clearly describes to her collaborators how "I need to put that [there or] lay that beside something else and then tape it together or weld it together … whatever needs to be done … that's how I make things work" (In the Space 2021).

Ultimately, Dunham is eluding more than the rules and guidelines of the nursing home where she lives; she also evades the typical profile we often associate with innovative makers. A Black disabled woman with no college degree, Dunham herself diverges from the white men usually associated with technical creativity. Recent scholarship has questioned theoretical foundations of the maker movement, echoing Britton's assertion that power, access, and status are deeply enmeshed in questions of race, gender, and class. For Britton, such narratives reinforce "an engrained culture of white masculinity in the design and deployment of technology" (Britton 2015). Whatever the methods, the space, or the things in it, the "key" to Dunham's agency is perhaps also different from the entirely autonomous design processes we take for granted in conventional narratives of innovation.

A master of finding collaborative means of making access, Dunham's expertise is evident in the assistive devices she designs as well as the web blog she authored with yet another collaborator, AT advisor Marty Sweeney. In all these activities, she is comfortable in the role of "creative director" and clear about what she wants done. Collaborative allyship is the real key to understanding her processes. If anything, this is more subversive than the entirely autonomous cases of designing that we normally celebrate. This very agency is conjoined with a practice of subverting our expectations of traditional design. Dunham destabilizes the ways we usually understand caregiving, how assistive technologies are made, and even what aspects of living actually need assistance.

Which needs in life are thought to be genuinely urgent, which are more superfluous, and who decides? In this case, Dunham has made access where little exists, carving out a livable niche, often in the face of power structures that may be invisible to professionals creating assistive technologies. Moreover, Dunham's suite of objects can be tied to a substantial heritage of DIY making, tinkering, and hacking that happen outside the public eye (Williamson 2012), and outside the rarified realms of professionalized expertise in the AT laboratories that fill university buildings, as well as corporate research and development operations. Above all, it suggests a form of design agency that can all too often pass unobserved.

Note

1. Dunham notes that the facility was sold and is now under new management.

References

Bassi, E., M. Salvodelli, and R. Hulskes(2019), "Process for Creating Made 4 You Careables.Org Platform." Available online: https://www.careables.org/wp-content/uploads/2019/09/made4you-_-deliverable-3.1.pdf (accessed September 25, 2021).

Britton, L. (2015), "Power, Access, Status: The Discourse of Race, Gender, and Class in the Maker Movement," Technology and Social Change Group. *Making and the Maker Movement: A Democratizing Force or an Example of Cultural Reproduction?* (blog), March 18. Available online: https://tascha.uw.edu/2015/03/power-access-status-the-discourse-of-race-gender-and-class-in-the-maker-movement/ (accessed September 25, 2021).

Dunham, Z. (2020), interview with author, Pasadena, CA.

Forlano, L. (2016), "Hacking the Feminist Disabled Body," *The Journal of Peer Production* 8. Available online: http://peerproduction.net/issues/issue-8-feminism-and-unhacking-2/peer-reviewed-papers/issue-8-feminism-and-unhackingpeer-reviewed-papers-2hacking-the-feminist-disabled-body/ (accessed September 19, 2021).

Hendren, S., and C. Lynch (2016), "This Counts Too: Engineering at Home," *Engineering at Home*. Available online: http://engineeringathome.org/manifesto (accessed October 2, 2021).

In The Space (2021), "In the Space with Zebreda Dunham [EPISODE 4]," *YouTube video*, 28:12, posted May 21. Available online: https://www.youtube.com/watch?v=JPamY-GYITA.

Meissner, J., J. Vines, T. McLaughlin, J. Nappey, J. Maksimova, and P. Wright (2017), "Do-It-Yourself Empowerment as Experienced by Novice Makers with Disabilities," in *Proceedings of the 2017 Conference on Designing Interactive Systems*, 1053–65, New York: Association for Computing Machinery.

Punzalan, R. (2012), "Zebreda Makes It Work!" *Where It's AT. The Ability Tools Blog. A Program of the California Foundation for Independent Living Centers* (blog), December 11. Available online: https://abilitytools.org/blog/zebreda-makes-it-work/.

RESNA (2015), "Unique Key Turner Wins RESNA 'DIY' Assistive Technology Design Contest," *Rehabilitation Engineering and Assistive Society of North America* (blog), July 2. Available online: https://resna.itswebs.com/About/RESNA-News/RESNA-Blog/unique-key-turner-wins-resna-diy-assistive-technology-design-contest-1 (accessed October 2, 2021).

Robinson, J. (2018), "A Phenomenological Look at the Life Hacking Enabled Practices of Individuals with Mobility and Dexterity Impairments," Syracuse University. PhD dissertation.

Robinson, J. (2019), "Individuals with Physical Impairments as Life Hackers?: Analyzing Online Content to Interrogate Dis/Ability and Design," in *The Routledge Companion to Disability and Media*, 306–15, New York: Routledge.

Williamson, B. (2012), "Electric Moms and Quad Drivers: People with Disabilities Buying, Making, and Using Technology in Postwar America," *American Studies* 52 (1): 5–30.

Woods, P. (2020), "(Re)Making Whiteness: A Critical Discourse Analysis of Equity-Based Maker Literature," in *Proceedings of the 2019 Connected Learning Summit*, 189–97, Irvine, CA: University of California at Irvine.

"Zebreda Makes It Work!" (2013), *Wayback Machine*. Available online: web.archive.org/web/20130914203533/ http://www.zebredamakesitwork.com/ (accessed October 2, 2021).

Case Study

5   Privileging Agency: A Conversation with Designer and Disability Advocate Jessica Ryan-Ndegwa

ALISON KURDOCK ADAMS

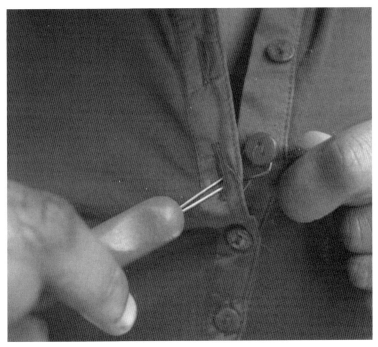

Figure 5 Hair-clip button hook designed by Jessica Ryan-Ndegwa. Image courtesy of Jessica Ryan-Ndegwa.

Recognizing the needs of the individual in the design process and pushing back against the hegemonic pressures of Universal Design, Ryan-Ndegwa argues, advances the notion that the personal nature of disability must be foregrounded in conversations around agency and inclusion. As the founder of the UK platform Design for Disability, Ryan-Ndegwa reworks traditional medical aids used by the disabled community to meet the unique needs and aesthetic preferences of her clients. Ryan-Ndegwa's lived experience as a disabled person informs her conviction that there are multiple ways of achieving a desired outcome and the Design for Disability client is an expert in their needs. Above all, their voice must be privileged in the design process.

One of Ryan-Ndegwa's goals is to ensure the disabled community is visible in conversations around art practices and cultural production. In addition to her design work, she serves as a consultant, speaker, and curator at a variety of cultural organizations including the Institute for Contemporary Arts in London and the Tate Exchange. Frustrated by the way disabled people are represented or, conversely, erased from conversations in the arts and, more broadly, in and around the topic of inclusion, Ryan-Ndegwa hopes to use her platform to educate and advocate for the disabled community through actions which center individual approaches to design, artistic, and cultural production by putting people first.

Tell me about your practice, Design for Disability. How did it develop?

I studied product and furniture design in university. For my dissertation, I examined whether people who identify as disabled are better at designing products for other disabled people. When I graduated I began to work on the concept of how to change the way medical product aids are perceived in public and that was the genesis of Design for Disability. I also started an entrepreneurial business boot camp. People were interested in what I was doing and I started working with different charities and companies doing some writing and speaking on these issues. This work expanded into blogging and writing for Tate's Exchange in partnership with A New Direction charity, which works with deaf, disabled, and neurodivergent young children and also working to co-curate exhibitions and galleries that had an inclusive design focus. Today, I am thinking about the ways individuals who identify as disabled can partici-pate in the conversation about disability inclusion in design—whether that be product or graphic design or any type of design practice.

How did you come to embrace the idea of user-initiated design in your own work, and why do you think it is so important to privilege the personal experi-ences of your disabled clients in the creative process?

My belief in the bespoke is rooted in my own experiences with Universal Design products. I used to use a zipper pull aid to help me button up my clothes. Typically, it features a big white handle with a little hook on the end. I was given that product free of charge by the National Health Service, but it just sat on my wardrobe in my bedroom because I didn't like the stigma associated with it and I didn't want to take it out of my house. Of course, nobody wants to be carrying around this long, unsightly product everywhere with them in public. You are given this tool, but there is no consultation about your personal needs or style preferences or how you may use this product aside from maybe what color you'd like the tool to be. Having used these hideous looking medical and orthopedic products growing up encouraged me to take a closer look at these tools and factor in the experiences of those who actually have to use them.

I believe it is really important for my clients to feel that products are accessible and inclusive. Yes, it is hard to design for every individual. Yes, it is hard to design bespoke products. When I started Design for Disability, I wanted to change the face of how items designed for disabled people are perceived in public. I tried to create a consultative relationship between the user and the designer. The ideal end result of this relationship is a product designed and made for one individual; that person can use it however they want and that is especially important.

Did your early and formative experiences as a disabled person inform your belief in bespoke design?

I used medical aids as a small child myself growing up with cerebral palsy (CP) and I did not like the idea of these hideous looking orthopedic products. It wasn't until I was enrolled in a mainstream school environment where I thought, "Hang on a minute, I'm doing things very differently than the others."

I think I've always tried to bridge the gap between mainstream and non-mainstream because I experienced those exchanges as a child. My parents were both in the medical field and I've been exposed to that because I went to occupational therapy or physiotherapy, and speech and language therapy when I was young. Furthermore, I was initially enrolled in a mainstream school and then I switched to a specialized school as I got older. And that in itself was a very big mental change because you go from thirty kids in your class to five. When you are in a class of thirty-plus students at a mainstream school, you are not getting one-on-one support and you feel like you are missing out on your education and lagging behind a bit on your learning and understanding. And of course having CP-related short-term memory and word finding difficulties adds to that disadvantage.

My parents made the important decision to enroll me in a school for dyslexic students which was unusual. I'm not dyslexic and I'm not dyspraxic, but I share similar attributes to dyslexic or dyspraxic students because of my short-term memory and my word comprehension difficulties. Switching to a class of six students at a specialized school where I was able to receive individualized atten-tion from educators helped expand my learning and was influential for me. I think that flexibility and willingness demonstrated by my family to seek out unconven-tional and beneficial experiences for me as part of my early education was why I wanted to try and fuse those medical and design disciplines in my adult life and in my design practice.

How does your design practice provide a sense of agency to your disabled clients?

Disabled people are not some otherworldly group. We are human beings. Sometimes, society doesn't accommodate different abilities. When you are sitting down with a person who is disabled, my advice would be to just talk to them and have a normal conversation, because once you are in a relaxed state and frame of mind, you start learning about the other individual: what their joys are in life, what they like doing, what they want to be doing. An important aspect of design and designing for anyone is to try and imagine what situation they are living in, or working in, or whatever is not properly fulfilling or helping or benefiting them and changing that dynamic. At the end of the day, you are trying to change how society works and give agency to your clients through the design process.

For instance, one of my clients had use of only one of his hands. I had several conversations with him about his own experiences with the zipper pull aid. I asked him a series of questions: What do you think about the product? Do you like the way that it looks? If I was to change it for you, what would you want to be changed? It was an open, honest, friendly conversation. He revealed that he loves wearing dog tags and they held a personal significance for him and were part of his aesthetic. Based on those insights I incorporated a hook on the back of the dog tag that allowed him to open the hook on a pivot joint. Using this product, he could open things just by pulling it off of his neck, untwisting the hook, zipping up, and putting the hook back onto his neck. It is a product that shows personality, discretion, multi-functionality, and inclusivity, and is fashionable which was important to my client.

That product is designed and made for one individual and they can use that product however they want. If I were to show that same zipper pull to ten different people, I would probably generate ten different design outcomes. The dog tag product worked in this case because it symbolized who the client was aesthetically while also operating as a functional tool.

As you continue to advocate for inclusion and visibility of the disabled within the design world, what are your hopes and future goals for pushing this conversation forward?

When you talk about inclusion, disability is usually the last issue people think about. Design for Disability is trying to change this and broaden the topic of inclusion to encompass disabled people. It is still very, very difficult to design an inclusive product, but part of that work is creating products for people who identify as disabled which are not considered ugly, clinical or poorly made but factors in the voice of the client. I think striving for disability inclusion is going to take up my entire lifetime. I am twenty-seven now, but I will be talking about this issue for decades to come.

Case Study

6   Rehabilitation Technology at the Self-Help Shop Then and Now

BESS WILLIAMSON

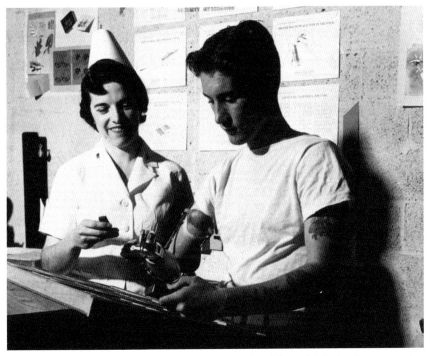

Figure 6 Lieutenant Geraldine Barthelemy, occupational therapist, instructs an amputee in the use of his prosthesis, 1952. Image courtesy of National Library of Medicine.

Since at least the 1960s, disabled people have critiqued the clinical gaze of medical professionals, trained to treat non-normative bodies in terms of pathology and seek the "fixes" of treatment and cure. The "social model" and its more recent permutations have done much to identify disability as a social and political concept, and to locate disabled people out in their own worlds and communities rather than within the institutional walls of hospitals.[1] Still, medical experiences do shape disabled life, including the devices and spaces that disabled people use to make their worlds accessible. In a design world that often ignores or actively excludes disabled people, medical or "assistive" technology is a form of design that is often fraught with its own power imbalances and social assumptions.

In thinking about agency, we might recover design practices that focus on individual bodies and personal needs: design for rehabilitation, or the hands-on, customized practices of occupational therapists, prosthetists, orthotists, and other specialists associated with medical care. These professions have long material histories that interweave with craft traditions of leatherwork, carpentry, metalsmithing, plastics, and 3D printing (Ott 2002). They also cross a variety of social lines. Prosthetics and orthotic makers have connections to saddle and other leather-making fields, earning them, in the First World War era, the moniker "buckle-and-strap men" and associations with manual labor (Gritzer and Arluke 1985). On the other hand, customized tools of everyday life such as adaptive typewriters and kitchens designed for wheelchair use have, since the mid-twentieth century, been the purview of occupational therapy and other female-dominated professions focused on the rationalization of the home (Penner 2018; Puaca 2016).

In the twentieth century, mostly women medical specialists as design workers developed customized, patient-focused products and spaces that still influence today's design world. These women, trained in occupational and physical therapy, rehabilitation science, home economics, and fashion design, framed their work not in terms of typical design concerns of form and function but in terms of outcomes for their patients' ability to perform typical activities of life such as work, family caregiving, and self-care. This work foreshadows recent design discourses about "designing with" rather than "designing for" disability. However, it also raises key issues around power and control in design.

Braces and Kitchens: The Self-Help Shop

One of the most prominent sites of mid-twentieth-century rehabilitation medicine—and its related design and technology work—was the New York Institute of Physical Medicine and Rehabilitation (IPMR). Founded in 1947, IPMR was a department of New York-Bellevue Hospital that deliberately stood apart from the "acute" stages of injury or illness, and instead focused on the transition, as founder Dr. Howard Rusk put it, "from bed to job" (1949). Moving disabled people from physical injury or ailments into active lives, Rusk argued, was a social and psychological project to enable patients "to live as full and completely self-sufficient a life as possible with [a] disability" (Rusk 1949: 84).

Within the IPMR, patients encountered a range of technologies that aimed to support and rehabilitate their bodies. This often meant strict and challenging exercises focused on navigating an inaccessible world, such as prodding patients with paralyzed lower bodies to walk using crutches. But it also meant a focus on aspects of that world that could be changed through a kind of tinkering that Rusk and his colleagues dubbed "self-help." The IPMR included a "Self-Help Shop" where patients could find both off-the-shelf and customized equipment, from crutches and wheelchairs to large-handled cutlery, electric shavers and irons, and Velcro-fitted clothing. The Self-Help Shop also kept tools and materials to make or adapt these items, including fabric, leather straps, and soldering equipment. In the 1940s, Rusk recruited the well-established designer and psychologist Lillian Gilbreth to design a kitchen for the "handicapped homemakers" who came into his care (Puaca 2016). Gilbreth incorporated design elements such as easy-to-reach stove buttons, open storage, and retractable work surfaces that were familiar from her decades of work on efficiency in home design (Mandel 1989: 317).

For the therapists in charge of the Self-Help and Housekeeping department of IPMR, technology was a part of a philosophy of rehabilitation that emphasized individual achievement and independence. The Self-Help Shop—as its name suggests—offered a design methodology that engaged individual patients in finding and learning to use these tools to support a vision of work and life on their own. The department director, occupational therapist Muriel Zimmerman, described former patients who worked as assistants in the shop as "disabled pioneers" who were "making use of mechanical devices to live a full and functional life" (1955). For them, she seemed to imply, technological work itself was a form of rehabilitation.

In the Self-Help Shop, therapists and their patients—including several patients who became paid workers—designed with a focus on function and adaptability. They embraced new materials such as plastic and synthetics with a focus on making familiar routines easy to do, such as combing hair, shaving, or pulling on pantyhose (offering a padded hook with an extended handle). These nonstandard approaches to these tools and their sheer variety set this design work apart from the standardized and sleek ideals of modernism in the same time period. These were, rather than singular solutions to the concerns of daily life, works of "maintenance": the unglamorous, long-term processes of fixing, updating, and regulating technologies, rather than moments of invention that tend to get more historical attention (The Maintainers 2019; Mattern 2018). These products also likely had a longer and more variable life cycle than is typically accounted for in standard designs. They required testing, adapting, and readjustment by their users over time, making them design ideas with multiple iterations and life histories.

Who Is a Designer?

The history of assistive design raises questions about agency and ownership. In photographs of rehabilitation practices, we see mostly white women in uniforms directing disabled patients in the use of adaptive tools or accessible kitchens. No doubt, their prescriptions were sometimes poor fits to the real lives of the patients, who are rarely named and often seem to avoid the gaze of the camera or look at it skeptically. The women therapists, too, worked within existing structures of power and knowledge that limited their ownership over their designs. Their work was carefully documented in research reports and internal journal publications at IPMR and other sites, but was often attributed to male supervisors in books and writings for a broader audience.

The adaptive and customized works of sites like the Self-Help Shop are at times difficult to distinguish from the homemade designs of amateur makers who were disabled themselves. While women rehabilitation experts published reports on "handicapped homemakers," disabled people showed off their own adaptations and product recommendations in community publication such as the newsletter *The Toomey J Gazette*, published in the 1950s and 1960s, which was started by a network of former patients and volunteers from the Toomeyville Junior Polio Hospital (Foertsch, 2007; Williamson, 2012). The *Gazette* showed DIY approaches to ramping houses, arranging kitchens, and selecting tools such as mouthsticks or dictation machines. Today, we can find similar reports of invention or technical expertise on blogs, Twitter, and YouTube. This work constitutes what scholars Kelly Fritsch and Aimi Hamraie call "crip technoscience," or others name #cripborg maintenance or lifehacking (Hamraie and Fritsch 2019; Jackson 2018).

In recent years, designers have shown an interest in both medically informed and DIY or community-driven design as sources of design knowledge. In the methodology known as Design Thinking, designers are encouraged to observe or consult users in the making of new products or services. They take various hands-on approaches such as acting out user routines or visiting the relevant spaces or sites associated with their imagined user group (IDEO, 2003). But what is rarely included in this work is recognizing the existing design relationships: that medical providers and therapists already perform in designing, as do disabled people themselves, alone or with family or other helpers. Little examined are the power dynamics, gain or loss of agency, and hidden messages in these relationships.

What would designers learn if they identified rehabilitation technology as design, and disabled people as user-designers for whom the process of design rarely ended at discharge from a clinic or hospital? First, they may identify the constant exchange between patient and care provider, and that these exchanges were often frustrating or disappointing. Further, they might observe that no one person can be credited for the making or success of a product, given that disabled people bring their own knowledge to this relationship and may alter the design over time. Who designs and who is credited for design are necessary questions in designing with disability.

Note

1. For an extended discussion and critique of the medical or "individual" model of disability, see Kafer 2013.

References

Foertsch, J. (2007), "'Heads, You Win': Newsletters and Magazines of the Polio Nation," *Disability Studies Quarterly*, 27(3). Available online: http://www.dsq-sds.org/article/view/30/30.

Gritzer, G., and A. Arluke (1985), *The Making of Rehabilitation Medicine: A Political Economy of Medical Specialization, 1890–1980*, Berkeley and Los Angeles, CA: University of California Press.

Hamraie, A., and K. Fritsch (2019), "Crip Technoscience Manifesto," *Catalyst: Feminism, Theory, Technoscience* 5 (1): 1–34.

Jackson, L. (2018), "We Are the Original Lifehackers," *The New York Times*, 30 May. Available online: https://www.nytimes.com/2018/05/30/opinion/disability-design-lifehacks.html (accessed June 1, 2021).

Kafer, A. (2013), *Feminist, Queer, Crip,* 4–10, Bloomington, IN: Indiana University Press.

The Maintainers (2019), "About Us," The Maintainers. Available online: http://themaintainers.org/about-us (accessed October 17, 2019).

Mandel, M. (1989), *Making Good Time: Scientific Management, the Gilbreths Photography and Motion Futurism*, Santa Cruz, CA: M. Mandel, 317.

Mattern, S. (2018), "Maintenance and Care," *Places Journal*, November. Available online: https://placesjournal.org/article/maintenance-and-care/.

Ott, K. (2002), "The Sum of Its Parts: An Introduction to Modern Histories of Prosthetics," in K. Ott, D. Serlin, and S. Mihm (eds), *Artificial Parts, Practical Lives: Modern Histories of Prosthetics*, 1–43, New York: New York University Press.

Penner, B. (2018), "The Flexible Heart of the Home," *Places Journal*, May 29. Available online: https://doi.org/10.22269/180529.

Puaca, L.M. (2016), "The Largest Occupational Group of All the Disabled: Homemakers with Disabilities and Vocational Rehabilitation in Postwar America," in M. Rembis (ed.), *Disabling Domesticity*, 73–102, New York: Palgrave Macmillan.

Rusk, H. A. (1949), *New Hope for the Handicapped: The Rehabilitation of the Disabled from Bed to Job*, 1st edn, New York: Harper.

Williamson, B. (2012), "Electric Moms and Quad Drivers: People with Disabilities Buying, Making, and Using Technology in Postwar America," *American Studies*, 52(1): 5–30.

Zimmerman, M. (1955), "Accent on Progress," *IPMR: A Chronicle of Independence*, Fall 1955: 19–21.

Case Study

7 Beyond the Bespoke: Agency and Hands of X

ANDREW COOK AND GRAHAM PULLIN

Figure 7 Hands of X installation in Cubitts eyewear, London, 2017. Photo by Andrew Cook/Studio Ordinary.

Our practice is disability focused, yet embraces culture and fashion as a challenge to narrower definitions of "function." Frances Corner writes, "Faster than anything else, what we wear tells the story of who we are—or who we want to be. It is the most immediate form of self-expression" (2014). We believe that wearers or users of disability objects should have agency, allowing the opportunity to take control of the stories that these objects tell about who they are.

We can also borrow a useful framework from fashion to help explore different approaches to design for one. Although the terms "bespoke" and "made-to-measure" are often used interchangeably, they are two fundamentally different models of service. A bespoke garment is entirely designed and made from scratch in consultation with the customer. Made-to-measure involves a standardized pattern and manufacturing process which is adapted in structured and constrained ways to the customer's measurements, and manufactured using their specification of materials. Ready-to-wear or off-the-peg garments do not offer any level of customization.

Each of these models has implications for cost to the wearer. Designing and making for one can be expensive in a commercial context. The economies of scale that most design and manufacturing industries rely on to operate can fail to apply in all kinds of ways, from designers' time to bulk-sourcing identical components. Bespoke items are expensive, often prohibitively so. Made-to-measure, while invariably higher cost than ready-to-wear, can offer a real sense of control and ownership at a much more reasonable cost.

We believe that there are opportunities for economically viable—and economically accessible—disability-related design for one, through coherent, structured, and constrained services that are not fully "bespoke," but still allow wearers/users to make choices that fundamentally define their product. Our research has shown that a sense of ownership is fostered through the act of making choices, even when these choices are highly constrained.

Hands of X

Hands of X is a research project that prototyped a service for wearers to make nuanced choices about the materials that their prosthetic hand would be manufactured from.

Hand prostheses, like many other disability objects, are prescribed to the wearer based on consultation with a prosthetist that tends to focus almost exclusively on functional requirements. While the wearer can make some aesthetic choices, these tend to be limited to a choice of skin tone in an anatomically "realistic" glove. For some robotic hands, the wearer can choose to wear these gloveless, where the material palette tends to be distinctly high-tech: carbon fiber shells, alloy chassis, and black silicone gaiters. This is a "ready-to-wear" model, albeit one where there are very few choices.

"Prescription" is at odds with a sense of ownership. As the late Eddie Small, one of our mentors and a prosthetic hand wearer since childhood, said while discussing his prosthesis, "when have I ever thought that this arm was mine? Not at all. Never, ever, ever have I ever thought that it's part of me" (Schiller 2019). Eddie spoke of his childhood fear of damaging his prosthesis because of his feeling that it belonged to someone else, coming with a sense of responsibility to look after it on behalf of its prescribers, the limb fitting service (Small 2017).

At the other end of the spectrum are services that offer fully bespoke prostheses. Functional artist and trained prosthetist Sophie de Oliviera Barata makes incredibly realistic prosthetic gloves for individuals, matching clients' skin color and texture, hair patterning, and even tattoos. Through her Alternative Limb Project, she also produces remarkable pieces of prosthetics-as-art, exploring form, material, and function with clients in extraordinary, and often quite extreme, ways (de Oliveira Barata n.d.).

In Hands of X, wearers could prototype hands in combinations of materials from a limited palette of woods, acetates, leathers, felts, and metals to specify a hand that told a story about who they are. This is a made-to-measure model of service, with defined product forms and constrained choice of materials. Yet after trying out combinations, recombining and refining, trying on and comparing, almost all of our testers and mentors arrived at a point where the whole "clicked," and many said something like "that's it!", or even "that's my hand."

Hands of X was installed as an "experience prototype" within Cubitts eyewear in London. At the time, Cubitts were striking in offering a relatively constrained choice of frame shapes, yet each in a nuanced choice of materials. This (also found in furniture manufacturers such as Maruni, for example) both inspired our approach to Hands of X and provided the perfect backdrop for the experience, working very hard to set our visitors' expectations and expectation of the choice available to them.

How Much Choice Is Enough Choice?

Ownership was a theme that surfaced repeatedly during our conversations with wearers around Hands of X. Even though the choices were fundamentally constrained, the act of making these choices gave wearers a sense of agency that they hadn't experienced in prosthetics services before. No testers complained that there wasn't enough choice, and all were able to specify a hand that they felt was fitting for them (Schiller 2019).

Choice in Eyewear

Eyewear is the most obvious example of an object that was once considered primarily an assistive device, but which is now considered—for many people—at least as much a fashion accessory (Pullin 2009).

In a long and complex history, one fundamental element of the destigmatization of eyewear is the increase in choice of shape and material seen in the mid-twentieth century as fashion-conscious brands entered the marketplace.

In 1948, the UK's National Health Service (NHS) offered thirty-three adult frame styles, a range which remained the same for thirty-five years, when one new frame shape was added. The overseeing Ministry of Health continuously railed against offering "too stylish" frames, strictly limiting the number of acetate frame shapes (more fashionable than metal frames at the time) and colors offered. Manufacturers who sought to offer slightly adapted, more fashionable variations on NHS frame patterns were refused licenses (Gooding 2021). In hindsight, eminent eyewear designer

Laurence Jenkin considers that the NHS frames were actually well-resolved, yet the lack of perceived choice and the denial of any connection to fashion rendered them stigmatizing nonetheless: an illustration of how impossible it is to disentangle wearable disability objects from the culture around anything wearable (Jenkin, Pullin, and Ingham 2019).

The market was ripe for competitors willing to challenge the status quo, from experimental enfants terribles like Cutler and Gross to Jenkin's Anglo-American Shuron and others who offered reasonably priced, nuanced takes on classic tortoiseshell frame shapes (Handley 2011).

In 1985, a voucher system was introduced that allowed patients to choose their own "private" frames, effectively ending the NHS frame range. Still, those thirty-three shapes, some in six colors, is probably far more aesthetic choice than you still are offered as a wearer of a prosthesis, hearing aid, or wheelchair cape.

If you have visited a dispensing optician in the past thirty years, you will be familiar with the overwhelming amount of choice offered. In among shelves of frames, there is a high chance that you can find a pair of glasses that tells the world a story about who you are—or who you want to be—that you are happy to tell.

Made-to-Measure Eyewear

This ready-to-wear model of eyewear is not the only possibility, though. With control of the mainstream eyewear market in the hands of three or four multinational conglomerates, the choice is fairly homogeneous. Many independent eyewear brands offer bespoke services (with the expense that implies). Cook has been experimenting with Laughing Stock, an eyewear provider more akin to made-to-measure service.

At Laughing Stock, Cook is a designer and maker of eyewear, but his service model is inspired deeply by his experience on Hands of X, based on fundamentally limited choice, but aiming to foster a deeper sense of ownership than a typical high-street optician. Cook offers a range of less than ten shapes at any one time, occasionally retiring one shape in favor of a new one. All frames are made from ox horn, a natural material and by-product of farming which offers infinite, nuanced variation in color and figuring, from pale blond to coal black.

The client can try on test frames in the basic library of shapes and sizes to decide a shape. They then choose two pieces of horn from an extensive stock (for frame front and sides), using a shape mask to get a sense of how the figuring will work in glasses form. The frames are then made from these pieces of horn, in the shape and size chosen by the client.

In the role of Laughing Stock client, Pullin found that the choice of specific material pieces felt somehow deeper than a choice between materials. In ways hard to articulate, some pieces "spoke" to him while others did not. As a result, the object seemed to feel like something stumbled upon—discovered—and perhaps a different sense of ownership results. Since wearing the glasses for several years their irreplaceability means that he never considered changing them, as he might have with previous pairs. They took on more of the relationship that he has with a piece of furniture or a loved item of clothing.

We have taken this experience—the nuance of our relationships with everyday objects—into Studio Ordinary, our interdisciplinary research studio at the meeting point of design research and critical disability studies, co-founded with Fiona Kumari Campbell and other colleagues. In Studio Ordinary we are looking again at disability objects as we might any other object, where design choices speak of complex and nuanced identities beyond disability.

In some respects, this means designing these objects as *unremarkable*, and thus challenging the narratives of triumph and/or tragedy so often associated with them. We are designing disability objects that neither aim to "disappear" nor loudly demonstrate their remarkable technological advancement, but rather aim to work as elements of everyday life. Ironically, unremarkableness is still a radical stance here, but we hope to play a part in its deradicalization.

References

Corner, F. M. (2014), *Why Fashion Matters*, London: Thames & Hudson.

de Oliveira Barata, S. (N.D.), [*Limbs Gallery*]. Available online: https://thealternativelimbproject.com/limbs/ (accessed November 8, 2021.)

Gooding, J. (2021), "Rather Unspectacular: Design Choices in National Health Service Glasses," *Science Museum Group Journal* 7: 7.

Handley, N. (2011), *Cult Eyewear: The World's Enduring Classics*, London: Merrell.

Jenkin, L., G. Pullin, and C. Ingham (2019), *Prosthetics Meets Eyewear*, Dundee: V&A Museum.

Pullin, G. (2009), *Design Meets Disability*, Cambridge, Mass.: MIT Press.

Schiller, J. (2019), Hands of X.

Small, E. (2017), *RE: Interview for Hands of X*, type to Pullin, G.

Case Study

8 Re-imagining Access and Its Pedagogies

MAGGIE HENDRIE, JOSHUA HALSTEAD, ROBERT DIRIG, ELISE
CO, AND TODD MASILKO

Figure 8 Library display incorporating digital technologies, Mohammed Bin Rashid library
(MBRL), Dubai. Photo by Giuseppe CACACE / AFP via Getty Images.

Increased awareness and the fundamental right to access educational materials are
identified in section 508 of Americans Disabilities Act (ADA). However, the implications and consequences in the digital world of archives are less developed. The
accelerating pace of technology requires an equal focus on co-design with communities (see White House 2016 Disability and Inclusive Tech Summit). Universal Design,
focusing on the end product rather than the process, aims to make products and
environments usable to all without specialized modifications, which risks effacing
the particularities of embodied experience. Still, as Jonathan Hsy pointed out in
2016, it serves as a "motivating fiction" (Godden and Hsy 2018: 105). In more recent
years, technology companies and designers have become aware of "inclusive"

design developing checklists, preferences, and some integrations. But this does not ensure that people actually want to use the technology or that it matches their search, use, and workflow practices. This requires participatory and, more recently, pluriversal design.

In 1993, Ronald Gilardi published "The Archival Setting and People with Disabilities: A Legal Analysis" (Gilardi 1993: 704–13). More recent guidelines move beyond ADA compliance (Society of American Archivists 2019), (Snider 2014: 137–54), (White 2013: 12, 28), and make a case for improved websites and finding aids and emphasize the benefits of universal accessibility, usability, and meeting the Society of American Archivists (SAA) ethical codes. With this in mind, ArtCenter College of Design's Interaction Design Department, DesignMatters Department, and Library conducted a series of classes, symposium, and development studios beginning in the spring of 2021, which challenged ArtCenter students to incorporate human-centered design processes into innovative experiences that improved accessibility of digital archive collections.[1] Building on existing guidelines, and research frameworks, the opportunity to craft accessible archives foregrounded the principle that access is knowledge production: a dynamic, generative activity that goes beyond the checklists and the constraints of universal design to include the unique dimension of nuanced human variations. "Reimagining Access: Inclusive Technology Design for Archives and Special Collections" aimed to leverage emerging technologies and participatory design methodologies for inclusive, useful, and compelling access to these archives and others, for people with a broad spectrum of bodymind experiences, i.e., visual, hearing, mobility, and cognitive.[2] Our case study aims to demonstrate that galvanizing disparate pedagogies, facilitating participatory design, and ideation and prototyping results in a deliberate and reflexive process, proposing not only new modes of access but an innovative approach to teaching design.

Toward a Pedagogy of Access

Above all, the project developed a situated pedagogy of access, rooted in student and participant knowledge production from lived interactions with digital ecosystems. Taken together, these perspectives informed—and sometimes de—and reconstructed—how conventional design guidelines were communicated and mobilized to accent not only the tools of digital access, but the politics of access making. This pedagogical approach challenges design to go beyond the limited realm of solutionism. The socio-technical politics of access underpinned the program class, opening conventionally closed spaces in many art and design institutions.

Our approach centers digital design on diverse scenarios, not only types of content or technology platforms, employing participatory prototyping to identify guidelines, inverting the guidelines-to-application process. ArtCenter's Interaction Design department partnered with DesignMatters, the College's long-standing social innovation program, to bring together a teaching team—Elise Co, Joshua Halstead,

Todd Masilko, and Robert Dirig—combining expertise in creative technology, critical disability studies, archives, industrial, and interaction design.[3]

We began with a two-day symposium in January 2021, and then the following two terms a series of studio classes started with the history, techniques, and mission of archives. In further online sessions with participants, students shared and developed an overall goal (e.g., modularity, multi-sensory, adaptability), based on people's research styles and workflow strategies. Each team focused on a different aspect of accessibility in technology from customizable interfaces to alternative forms of navigation. A unique component of the studio was the creation of Best Practices for Accessibility Design. Compiled as a student reference, it includes categories such as Navigation and Information Architecture, Document Structure, Content and Functionality, Keyboard Support, and a list of web checker tools.

To prepare for participatory sessions, students crafted prompts and accessible prototypes in relevant technologies (e.g., applications, website tools and mobile services, and adaptive tools) based on insights from participants. Students utilized real data and examples from the ArtCenter Archives web pages into their prototypes, showing how their concepts are not only speculative but plausible. Given the restrictions of Covid-19, in-person sessions moved online, which, while unexpected, gave students a firsthand experience of limitations and affordances of participants' digital environments. During virtual co-creation sessions, people demonstrated methods they intuitively would use when online searching, sharing the steps they would take to use databases and aggregators, and access digital archival records in a variety of media such as a handwritten note, an oral history, or a photograph.

Initial prototypes investigated use of categorization systems, hierarchy structures, rich alt-text, metadata, captions, and audio design but also subjective experiences such as distraction, browsing, relatable content, and personal workflows. A key part of pedagogy in these activities are the questions, which prototypes (or part of prototypes) do we work with, and what fidelity are we creating? At key milestones—midterms, reviews, and planning sessions—the advisory group came together to discuss insights and alternative points of view based on lived experience with varied disabilities and archives, highlighting points of tension and intrigue.

Pivotal Insights

Initial prototypes focused on specific thematic approaches; an accessibility checker for archivists used upon ingest of digital records; audio-first experience design; Pinpoint, a tool to support find, retrieve, and export workflow based on the entire user journey; and reflowing categories into blocks and coded tagging to support Bring Your Own Device. But during this process, certain pivotal insights informed each iteration of prototype development, including the following:

- Leveraging existing assistive technologies and users' own workflows in an ethos of "Bring your own devices." Many designers know that a large number of people with disabilities use assistive technologies to access digital environments, but it's rare to see a website that mobilizes this knowledge and integrates it into its form and structure.

- People who are blind or have low vision use spatial orientation. Students' original assumptions were to not focus on the visual but discovered, for example, that the mouse is used in navigation functions as a spatial affordance. Archivists often depend on conventional functions of the body to interpret media within digital collections, for example, relying on hearing to watch videos. Unique, personal, and diverse modalities of learning apply to everyone; a visual learner may be blind and benefit from the spatial orientation that comes with using a mouse.

- Audio instructions have much potential to be a structured audio language. This prompts the question, "What would an audio-first archives experience be like?"

- The archivist experience is core to the user's experience. Many accessible solutions rely on core archival and interaction patterns which are often very text driven, relying on a conscious arborescence and reader tools.

- Searching and retrieving. Accessible tech does not always take into account context searching, such as finding aids. Many current browse structures could be more than reiterations of archival structures and collections; they could rely on other adjacencies and common threads.

Unique workflows. It is important to move from a content and UI-centered approach to consider users' workflows, integrating how people use the outcomes of their searches through save, composition, posting, sharing, and integration with other tools.

Conclusion

Participatory design, rich communications with a diverse advisory team with direct experiences with disability, and project-driven learning required sustained, years-long programs, and consistent funding. These are rare circumstances in present-day education. But specific pedagogies in design education also need to be further developed. "Participatory design" is a term that covers multiple methods, practices, and domains. In fact, specific pedagogies in design education need to be further developed. Design schools are grounded in a culture of making as much as theory; they include craft, experimentation, prototyping, assessment, and real-world experience. Transformational learning theory and new omnichannel pedagogies create new paths to this learning for more design students and creative tech practitioners. As many technology companies and institutions shift from engineering-driven to design-led, we have an opportunity to advocate that the design in question is fully participatory. Educating students in these methods calls for a community of practice and rich relational design.

Acknowledgments

This project was made possible in part by the Institute of Museum and Library Services (IMLS grant number LG-246431-OLS-20).

Notes

1. ArtCenter College of Design's Archives and Special Collections collects, preserves, and makes available the records of the College and other rare and unique materials that helps tell the stories of people and communities that shape the history of art and design. With grant support from the Institute of Museum and Library Services (IMLS), the Archives in partnership with SAA, will eventually recommend project insights to be added to existing national guidelines.
2. For further documentation see https://designmattersatartcenter.org/proj/reimagining-access-inclusive-technology-design-for-archives-and-special-collections/.
3. To frame the project, we formed an advisory group; participants from SAA's Accessibility and Disability Section, The Braille Institute, Michigan State University's IRB oversight and commissioned Usability/Accessibility Research and Consulting (UARC) Group at Michigan State University, Director Sarah Swierenga and Senior User Experience Researcher Jennifer Ismerle, to develop a User Experience Research Guide. It is important to note that as a small Art and Design College currently without its own IRB, this oversight and training in Human Subject Research, constitutes a fundamental component of student preparation and continuing practice in ethical engagement.

References

Gilardi, R. L. (1993), "The Archival Setting and People with Disabilities: A Legal Analysis," *American Archivis*t 56 (4) Fall: 704–13.

Godden, R., and J. Hsy (2018), "Universal Design and Its Discontents," in D. Kim, and J.Stommel (eds), *Disrupting the Digital Humanities*, 91–116, Goleta, CA: Punctum Books. Available online: https://doi.org/10.2307/j.ctv19cwdqv.9.

Snider, L. (2014), "Access for All: Making Your Archives' Website Accessible for People with Disabilities," in K. Theimer (ed.), *Reference and Access: Innovative Practices for Archives and Special Collections*, 137–54, Lanham: Rowman & Littlefield.

Society of American Archivists (2019), *Guidelines for Accessible Archives for People with Disabilities*. Available online: https://www2.archivists.org/sites/all/files/SAA%20 Guidelines%20for%20Accessible%20Archives%20for%20People%20with%20 Disabilities_2019_0.pdf.

White, S. (2013), "Disability: Uncovering Our Hidden History," *Archival Outlook* (November/ December): 12, 28.

Section 2 Equity

Introduction

What is equal is not always fair, and what is fair is not always equal.

While the word "equity" often blurs into the term "equality," the two words have very different meanings. Equality treats all people the same, in terms of rights, opportunities, and status (Policy & Projects Officer Community Services Division, 2013, p. 13). The vast variety of human difference, however, suggests that equality may not always be possible or even desirable. Equity recognizes that individuals have different background, circumstances, and abilities; support and resources are offered so that all people can attain the same outcome. It is multiple means for the same end.

Recognizing that it is impossible to eliminate all forms of inequity without taking larger systems into account, in "Equations for Reducing Disability Stigma through Design Equity" Joshua Halstead examines disability design's complex relationship with the status quo. Paradoxically, treating differentness in identical ways risks creating overt forms of design discrimination. Design equity, he notes, can mean recognizing—rather than suppressing—difference by designing to meet specific needs. Halstead outlines seven emerging frames that can be considered in disability design, addressing questions around stigmatized interactions and work being done to increase exponentially disabled people's participation in the world around them.

If equality has often translated into a one-size-fits-all approach to disability design, ideas of equity in some ways seem to echo changes in designing and making. Where the pressures of mass production once meant that the same design must be made used by everyone, the early 2000s brought new potentialities. Technological changes made possible a range of new activities, including rapid prototyping tools and 3D printing, as well as access to online communities. The maker movement suggested that equity might be achieved by allowing anyone to custom design, create designs for one, or bespoke assistive products. Emeline Brule's "Making Equity: How the Disability Community Met the Maker Movement" examines this initial promise, raises the increasingly significant challenges it has presented in reality, and proposes several solutions to these issues.

Disability design that is more inclusive of designers who identify as disabled can change the scope of hackerspaces and crafting. Nevertheless, inaccessible maker tools and limited direct support for individuals with physical impairments can challenge the idea of makerspaces as liberatory. Specifically looking to provide equity in the spaces where this occurs itself, Katherine Steele describes her own quest to make a fully accessible maker space in "Shaping Inclusive and Equitable Makerspaces." Steele outlines the goals of the project to increase bespoke making, as well as persistent challenges faced in its implementation. In the end, Steele suggests, such barriers may in fact represent opportunities for accelerating innovation.

Even as the processes of designing and making shift, so too do definitions of disability and their implications for achieving equity in other ways. The significance of sensory experience is highlighted by Maitraye Das, Katya Borgos-Rodrigues, and Anne Marie Piper. In "A Case Study of Skilled Craftwork among Blind Fiber Artists," they study vision-impaired people's weaving, noting how embodied interactions, often based in tactile and acoustic sensations, can help us understand and learn from under-valued narratives of making and engineering.

The expansiveness of ideas around equitable outcomes has also provoked an investigation of design's role in shaping sensory experience. Of course, variations in ability related to sight, hearing, smell, touch, or taste are highly individual; providing equity here is always tricky for designers. Accommodating for mobility impairments as well can seem especially daunting. Peter-Willem Vermeersch and Ann Heylighen describe how co-design helped address these challenges at the Multisensory Museum. By drawing the museum visitor into the space through all the senses (sound, touch, smell, vision, motion), they aimed to create a museum accessible to all, shaped by lived disability experience.

Recognizing the particularities involved in designing for the senses and robustness of our lives includes, David Serlin argues, our sexualities. Serlin purposes a different form of sensory equity by analyzing the designing of the Enby sex toy. In "The Politics of Friction: Designing a Sex Toy for Every Body," Serlin notes how the Enby was conceived as an assistive device: less as a "toy," and more as a prosthetic or a wheelchair. In this way it functions much like others intended to be extensions of the body helping the user accomplish a sensory goal. But Serlin also pushes us to consider disability not only in terms of sexual pleasure or as a site contestation or difference but as an opportunity for innovation.

While challenging, designing sensory experiences equitably can still be easier than shaping fair and accurate ways to depict and describe them. In "The Face-Based Pain Scale: A Tool for Whom?," Gabi Schaffzin examines the design and development of the ubiquitous Wong Baker FACES pain scale as a form of visual communication, as well as its ability to equitably describe sensation. By relating pain back to the body, he notes how we overlook the possibility that pain affect can be present anywhere and everywhere. Rather than treating pain equitably,

Shaffzin argues that the scale is the product of health systems that have prioritized speed, efficiency, and proof over caring.

In addressing questions of equity, some designers argue that we must change internal dynamics within the profession. The disability justice movement has prioritized work of multiply-marginalized disabled activists of color like TL Lewis, Leah Lakshmi Piepzna-Samarasinha, and Alice Wong. These voices extend discussions of disability and difference to include questions of race and intersectionality. Natasha Trotman's "Next Practice: Toward Equalities Design" addresses the intersection of disability and visibility of marginalized populations and argues for a post-normal equity that could be called equalities design. As Trotman suggests, this would recognize a range of social and structural challenges faced by people with disabilities, especially when they embrace multiple identities. Trotman argues that different forms of lived experience—including race and gender as well as neurodivergence—should be taken into account and better represented within the profession of design itself.

Key Points

- Care and allyship in design carry various forms of responsibility.
- Recognizing multiple needs and values means accepting that universality cannot be achieved.
- Community endeavors inevitably mean identifying tensions between access needs; use these to highlight opportunities for flexibility, adaptability and innovation.
- Accessible spaces and designs are never "done" and rather should and will adapt and change with the community.
- View all aspects of making equity not as "accommodations" for specific users but as part of larger processes.
- Expanding our understanding of varieties of embodied experience means changing our understanding of what constitutes an "assistive device."
- Disability activism can be perpetuated through design, speaking to both individuals who are disabled and those otherwise marginalized because of race or class.
- A range of disability experience is left out of design discourse, including that of disabled Black, Indigenous, people of color (BIPOC) and those who identify as neurodiverse, mad, and sick.
- The intersectional nature of disability both broadly and specifically within design contexts is often unnoticed or disregarded.

9 Equations for Reducing Disability Stigma through Design Equity

JOSHUA HALSTEAD

Design's dialogue with disability equity may now be traced over several decades but its result can be generalized into a trichotomic equation: Equity (E) = the status quo (SQ) − stigmatized interactions (SI) × exponential access to participation (P2); rewritten: (SQ SI) P2 = E. As simple as this equation may seem, it is important to define its terms. By status quo, I mean the sociocultural construct of "normality" in a specific time and place. Stigmatized interactions result in this context when individuals or groups embody attributes, behaviors, or legible features that are socially marked as undesirable, thus prompting a perceptual separation from "normality." Participation is synonymous with access. And yet, is any equation that involves stigmatized interactions really all that simple?

Values-led design approaches (e.g., barrier-free design, universal design, participatory design, design thinking, inclusive design) focus on increased participation rates instead of confronting stigma. Based on these approaches, design interventions such as curb cuts, assistive technologies, and the guidelines based on the Americans with Disabilities Act legislation all build (or retrofit) material arrangements with multiple access points to serve a heterogeneous audience. Nevertheless, disabled people continue to experience multivalent oppression. Material (re)arrangements simplify the phenomenon of disability while disregarding "conceptual entanglements" (Barad 2007) and key intersectional power structures introduced through academic practices like critical law, race, and gender studies.

The equation above illustrates how refocusing on stigma reduction along with access and participation can lead to holistically equitable design outcomes. However, the question remains: What is stigma and how can we reduce it? How might design fit into this framework? For the believers and optimists, design is a promise of hope. How can we achieve greater equity by supporting and encouraging design that doesn't just focus on transforming lives but that fundamentally enriches them? How can we expand its purview from providing answers to foregrounding questions? Once better understood, reducing disability stigma can be challenged. This chapter studies stigma, the design status quo, and access to participation, and then outlines how emerging frameworks for increasing disability equity in design are aiming to do this work.

Changing Design Stigma

Even if we neatly translate design's dialogue with disability into mathematical terms, stigma (SI) remains a looming constant. In ancient Athens, a "stigma" was a literal brand mark on the neck or shoulder that distinguished soldiers of Sparta from former slaves. It was, as psychologist Dr. Stephen Hinshaw writes, "a mark of shame" (2010) that signifies membership in an out-group. Once expressed physically, stigma today has become transformed. Although it can be expressed as SI in a mathematical equation, it is dominantly psychological but it also continues to be deeply expressed in design.

The concept of stigma has broadened considerably since antiquity. Published in 1963, sociologist Erving Goffman's *Stigma: Notes on the Management of Spoiled Identity* suggested that stigma is an "attribute that is deeply discrediting" (1963: 2). Whether the color of one's skin, one's body, religion, or a range of other attributes, stigma makes over individuals, taking them into a "discredited" social status (Goffman 1963: 41). Because stigma conveys devalued stereotypes about personal attributes, it becomes part of constructed identity. Although this definition remains influential today, Goffman's model overemphasized behavioral drivers and precluded stigma's effect on interconnected relationships. A later definition proposed by sociologist Bruce Link and Jo Phelan (2001) includes structural discrimination. By looking at how larger systems can encompass stigma, this work "opens the door for us to begin to elucidate the ways that power shapes the distribution of stigma within a social milieu" (Kleinman et al. 2009: 418). Further, anthropologists have positioned stigma as embedded in "moral experience" (Yang et al. 2007; Yang et al. 2008). Sustaining moral status, *therefore*, becomes dependent on meeting social norms, and stigmatization occurs when individuals do not meet in-group requirements.

Applied to racial and sexual minorities, women, left-handers, adoptees, delinquent youth, disabled people, and others, stigma comes in many categories: self-stigma, public stigma, stigma by association, and structural stigma (Bos et al. 2013). The project of reducing stigma, thus, very much hinges on which form is meant to be changed. Self-stigma and public stigma are of immediate interest because of their relationship to design and hold a knotted reflexivity. Defined by prejudice and discrimination, public stigma is most often observed and studied; when individuals assume and take in these public attitudes—and often experience negative consequences—self-stigma occurs.

While definitions of stigma have existed for some time, strategies for challenging or even erasing stigma are increasingly under discussion. On the surface, it might seem that open acceptance of a stigmatized identity might be a key here. In dealing with these issues, designers have also underestimated complex social factors users experience but also the ways in which design practice can heighten—not lessen—stigma. Against this backdrop, several design frameworks that address disability stigma are emerging:

- **Representation:** *positioning projects to combat disability stigma and exclusion.*

  How disabled people are represented pictorially influences how they are perceived in society and draws connections with stigma. In recent years, a number of design projects have been instigated to combat all-too-common images depicting disability as tragic and infantile. Representing disability in a positive light both graphically and pictorially is an observable trend in graphic design. From building out an inclusive emoji collection to curating a collection of authentic images and architecting symbols that visualize the invisible, designers are noticing how pictures influence societal stigma.

  Several threads bring these projects together, and one of them is introducing a more capacious pallet of embodiments. In 2019, Apple created an expanded emoji collection featuring people using a variety of assistive technologies like wheelchairs, canes, and hearing aids, as well as pictographs symbolizing invisible disabilities (Apple Newsroom 2016). The emojis are also interracial and gender-inclusive. Notably, Apple collaborated with disability organizations like the National Association of the Deaf, the Cerebral Palsy Foundation, and the American Council of the Blind. Beyond honoring the disability rights epithet "nothing about us without us," collaborating with disability organizations is a step toward emancipatory methods (e.g., participatory action research) recommended by disability studies scholars.

  > Even further, because the current International Symbol of Access omits people with invisible disabilities, designers are experimenting with newer icons; these efforts can build awareness of the ever-present disability community who do not make use of wheelchairs. Arguing that these designs will provoke questions and dialogue, at least one group has created icons depicting invisible disabilities such as schizophrenia, depression and anxiety, and learning difficulties like dyspraxia.
  >
  > (Dawood 2018)

  Other projects involve broadening the imagery available to designers and the public alike. Collections of stock imagery are beginning to highlight and bring together representations "that break stereotypes and more authentically portray[s] individuals with disabilities" (Getty Images 2018). Increasingly, such curation includes participatory collaboration with disability communities, picturing disabled people mothering, playing sports, painting, in family, and—importantly—in community. Such work goes to great lengths in order to humanize subjects and avoid falling into rhetorical tropes such as the supercrip (i.e., depictions of individuals "overcoming" their disabilities).

- **Shifting the landscape:** *engaging and broadening the spectrum of understanding about difference as people with disabilities are expressing their experiences and are more open about their disabilities.*

Although disability culture and identity have been fundamental building blocks for disability rights movements since the late 1960s, many designers are becoming acquainted with political definitions of disability—such as the social model—for the first time. Disability has become a trending topic in design fields outside of rehabilitation engineering, with great potential for cross-disciplinary collaboration. More and more people are, as activist Simi Linton called it "claiming disability" (Linton 1998). In design terms, this can be seen variously. In some cases, for example, wearers proudly reveal bionic arms or legs, in contrast with those who prefer to "pass" as able-bodied. These positions can sometimes leave those in the middle with a false dichotomy and wishing for a more nuanced conversation about the elastic qualities of identity. Finding balance between claiming disability and passing as nondisabled is a reality of disability phenomena that designers should be aware of, as it will impact not only those who use their designs but how funds will be allocated for research.

Addressing the Design Status Quo

Design has long been considered to have a practical purpose—namely to answer real-world problems. Above all, functional design is meant to work easily, performing an assigned task with a minimum of strain, stress, breakdowns, or errors. Clear and easily achieved functionality has been associated with "normality" and can be seen as design's status quo. On the other hand, in and outside the disability community there has been greater acceptance of disabilities as part of a broader spectrum of human differences, or what some nondisabled design stakeholders may characterize as "normal." In recent years, this has shaped a fundamental desire in the disability community to shift the narrative from "disability as a problem." Moving along this spectrum—from a traditional medical model that says disabled people must either be "fixed" or adapt to a more inclusive social model that views society and inaccessible environments as the problem—is evident across the disability movement. There still exists a significant gap between assertions of design's status quo and shifting narratives of problems, solutions, and normalcy within the disability community.

At times, this disparity can challenge—and sometimes be in direct conflict with—design's often proud identity as a problem-solving art. Designers often start their processes by identifying problems and then work deductively in order to remedy them through a refinement process known as iteration. In recent years there has been considerable interest in putting people at the center of design solutions. Too often, however, the disability "problem" can use stigmatizing terms. Positioning design as solving problems related to struggling or tragic disabled people is an example of ableistic prejudice that inadvertently further marginalizes disabled people.

Even designers' initial directive or project description, the design brief, often adheres to stigmatizing conventions. Design briefs are often shaped by the assumption that disabled people are excluded from society by their bodily impairments; therefore, we (i.e., medical professionals and engineers) must restore "normal functioning" through design interventions. Seeking restoration tacitly implies that Assistive Technologies (AT) are designed for a "separate species," that is users with diagnostic "impairments" that might be considered grossly abnormal (Hendren 2017). Designing from this paradigm propagates false narratives and affirms cognitive divides between designers and "the disabled." It can also lead to disability designs that perpetuate stigma. As historian Ashley Shew writes, "The awfulness it is to go out as a young person with a walker, for instance, is why I might not use my walker more often" (2017). Researchers Kristin Shinohara and Jacob Wobbrock found that AT was being abandoned at high rates if the device brought "unwanted attention" and made the individual "feel self-conscious in social contexts" (2011). For example, text-to-speech applications activated in a lecture hall, library, or office cubicle could be problematic. Technology use, then, is determined by social factors. As Shinohara and Wobbrock note, we must understand that "functionality and usability do not live in a social vacuum" (2011).

Rather than treating the design status quo as an activity that attempts to simplify problems, some designers have begun to embrace design's potential to engage the deep contradictions and complexities here. Several important notions are shaping this discourse:

- **Disability as design problem:** *challenging positions that present the disabled body/mind as a "problem" to be solved by designers.*
  Design differentiates itself from other art forms in its commission to solve problems. This sentiment can be observed from the Bauhaus to Stanford's Hasso Plattner Institute of Design, aka "the d.school." But disability is often problematized in order to validate design intervention. The problematization of the disabled body/mind has especially become notable in answer-driven approaches that erase or exclude disabled expertise and designers. (See Bennett and Rosner 2019; Jackson 2018.)

    Chief among these methods is Design Thinking, an approach that has influenced the field far beyond design education programs. As a mode of working, its raison d'être is teaching people how to approach complex problems through empathy. This method, however, has been criticized for the ways in which it marginalizes disabled people in the design process. Above all, as disability studies scholar Cynthia Bennett suggests, "acts of empathy building may further distance people with disabilities from the processes designers intend to draw them into" (Bennett and Rosner 2019). Instead of working directly with disabled people—or even turning to the insights of disabled designers—this process can effectively shut them out.

    If Design Thinking distances designers from genuinely engaging disabled people and their lived experience, this lack of exposure may also cut designers off from nonmedical theories of the body. Disability activists like Liz Jackson and Alex Haagaard of the Disabled List posit that Design Thinking places the "problem" of disability within the body instead of society (May 2018). In so doing, they draw from the social model of disability, which offers alternatives to the problematizing of disabled bodies. Returning to the design-disability relationship, then, it is much less likely for designers to ask questions about the disability category itself than to default to the assumption that disabled bodies need "fixing." In this context, design's relationship to disabled bodies works through older and more questionable paradigms, including the fix-it approach that focuses on the individual and not society.

- *Corporate engagement: making disability issues more legible to designers and the general public means building on existing disability-driven design work.* The economic value of designing accessible products and spaces is not new—it was the foundation from which Universal Design emerged following the Second World War. This has formed the status quo for disability design to this day. But this work has, at times, been deeply exclusive, marginalizing women, Black families, immigrants, and even disabled designers. By developing frameworks that consult with the disabled people who are most impacted by the products and services, there is potential for better products and more equitable access to those products. People with disabilities are often driving the innovation, whether as independent entrepreneurs or as workers within a larger corporate entity. The investment in disability design is not always motivated by profit, with many large companies taking up disability inclusion and accessible design in ways that seem genuine and are often not advertised or publicly visible.

   In the 2010s, companies like Microsoft, Google, and Apple all invested in projects at the intersection of graphic design, computer science, and disability inclusion, each with their own approach. Microsoft has steadily increased their focus on accessible technology since the launch of their Inclusive Design Toolkit in 2016, and is helping fund entrepreneurial projects as well as providing start-ups with technological resources and guidance. Similarly, Google is focused on inclusive technology, but with an aim to enable creators, marketers, and designers to build more inclusive products and designs through a resource center that offers access to step-by-step lessons that are easy to digest across platforms. Apple decided to broach disability representation itself through a gender-and-race inclusive emoji collection, featuring people using assistive technologies like wheelchairs, canes, and hearing aids as well as pictographs symbolizing invisible disabilities. With hardware and the technology industries as a whole, integration of voice technology, controllers with large buttons that can be used with any appendage, eye-tracking remote controls, and numerous other adaptable assistive devices that work with standard products are increasingly available. This might indicate that accessible technology is in itself considered increasingly "innovative" by mainstream standards. However, very few organizations are attributing value to existing disability-driven design work or partnering with disability organizations and individuals.

Exponential Access to Participation

Some designers are approaching the question of disability equity through activist frameworks based on rights and social justice. Three reasons shape this shift: (1) increasing involvement in disability advocacy/activism, (2) a desire to challenge older stigmatizing approaches by bringing disability perspectives into shared design futures, and (3) a general interest in larger systemic change. Among those designers who have disabilities themselves, advocacy/activism concerning disability rights can be integral to their design practice. For example, Victor Pineda and Aimi Hamraie both identify as disabled and designed their professional and academic careers around promoting access and asking critical questions around how material world-building intersects with prejudicial, able-bodied worldviews. Though not disabled themselves, others such as Sara Hendren and Jos Boys center disability rights and justice frameworks by challenging ableist notions that design's purpose is to neutralize the affect disability engenders. Increasingly, there has been a deep desire not only to integrate disability perspectives into design work but to use this work as a platform highlighting the importance of disability rights and justice in the world.

The emerging activist-designer paradigm marks a turning point. Many philosophical or methodological frameworks, including methodologies like Universal Design, are known to promote power asymmetries. Increasingly, designers are putting marginalized people who are overlooked or otherwise forgotten at the center of their processes and work (Design Justice Network, n.d.). Disabled or not, those designers who take this approach have a commitment to working with disability communities as co-designers. Political frameworks such as disability justice call attention to the social model of disability. The latter continues to be the primary framework in use for designers focused on rehabilitation and assistive devices. But this assumes that equity can be achieved through structural independence alone. As Aimi Hamraie argues in *Building Access*, creating accessible spaces and products is good, but if Black and brown bodyminds are overpoliced when they use them, our notion of "accessible" design is too narrow yet (Hamraie 2017). As activist-designers engage with disability communities through a more nuanced understanding of design's role in promoting equity, frameworks drawn from disability justice and critical disability studies will likely proliferate. Several key points include:

- *Justice-centered frameworks: integrating disability as part of justice frameworks that address race, gender, class, and more has the potential to advance disability issues both broadly and specifically within design contexts.*
  In invoking "justice-centered" approaches, designers are critiquing the historical tendency to provide access only for those for whom it is politically and economically intended. In the years after the Second World War, for instance, housing developments offered accessible accommodations, first to white veterans who were recipients of the GI Bill and were often redlined from Black communities (Hamraie 2017). In the first wave of Universal Design as well,

track homes were similarly built with white wheelchair users in mind. Though such discrimination may be more subtle today, foregrounding questions of justice or to critically engaging with the equity-value means thinking about participation. Notable is the influence disability activists are having in popular media. This includes projects such as the San Francisco-based media project Disability Visibility (Wong 2020) and #SayTheWord campaign. Devised by disability community activist Lawrence Carter-Long, the latter urges people to use the word *disabled* and draw attention to terminology (Forber-Pratt 2020). Such efforts reveal the more varied nature of disability, making room for (D) isability pride and identity to spread within public discourse on topics such as diversity, women's rights, and LGBTQIA+ liberation.

Designing through a disability justice framework means questioning who typically occupies the center of design philosophies touting "accessibility." Often white, male, heterosexual privilege is assumed; fundamental considerations, for example, looking at how identity can shape accessibility across different contexts, can be omitted.

- *Exclusions and underrepresentation: recognizing that a number of disability communities are being left out of design discourse. Among them are disabled BIPOC and those who identify as neurodiverse, mad, and sick.*

A so-called disability caste system can exist within institutions and even disability culture itself. As disability studies scholar M. Deal notes, "a hierarchy of impairment exists from the perspectives of both disabled and non-disabled people" (Deal 2003). Some reasons for this circumstance are related to funding allocation, ethnicity, and other stigma-led affects. Disability communities often mention the existence of "disability culture," and though such a culture certainly exists, scholars admit it is immensely diverse. Further, Deaf culture(s) has historically distanced itself from identifying with disability cultures, and the umbrella "disability" political identification has recently broadened its landscape to include people who identify as mad, sick, and chronically ill. Lastly, the lack of BIPOC representation that plagues design disciplines as a whole is amplified in the disability community; the same structural inequities leading to Black, indigenous, people of color (BIPOC) discrimination in the US educational, healthcare, and criminal justice systems are also prevalent in design spaces.

Similarly, in contrast to popular UD-based philosophy, designers are beginning to acknowledge a multiplicity of identities at work composing disabling experiences. Some thirty years ago, Kimberlé Crenshaw first coined the neologism "intersectionality" but it has particular relevance to disability design (1989). Although Universal Design still has relevance in the industry, the totalizing methodology risks to invisiblize intersectional marginalization. As a response, several actors and companies are foregrounding intersectionality to protest institutionalized supremacy in the industry.

With this in mind, neurodiverse and disabled BIPOC have been breaking conventional binaries. Social consciousness around gender-fluidity has contributed to the (de)medicalization of the disability category in favor of a more intersectional and cultural approach. This blurring of boundaries, however, has not contributed to a substantial shift and whose perspectives influence design projects and resources. The relationship between design and neurodiversity, for example, remains dominantly therapeutic within rehabilitation or transition programs, and disabled BIPOC continue to be underrepresented in academic and professional spaces.

One model of intersectional design might be found in adaptive fashion specifically, because garments need to have aesthetic value as well as functional value. In other words, clothing needs to be tailored to how individual bodyminds move through myriad environments—all specific to individual clients. Much of why this has not taken shape already in fashion design is because designers have been basing their clothes on a supremacist template (i.e., white, fit, nimble bodyminds). But gender- and race-neutral forms can be folded and widened to fit many different embodiments. Sky Cubacub's "A Queercrip Dress Reform Movement Manifesto" (Wong 2020), for example, urges a custom-made gender nonconforming approach that "celebrates each wearer's complex intersections of identities, giving light to each one and providing an option for all of them simultaneously." As the designer notes, "Feeling confident in one's appearance can revolutionize one's emotional and political reality" (Wong 2020: 92).

This emphasis on tangible and intangible realities is helping reshape a wide-ranging and expansive discourse on exclusion, stigma, and participation in design. As we move away from more institutionalized approaches, and their very clear and even prescriptive ways of shaping access, we are faced with something different. More amorphous, speculative, and critical work is shifting the nature of equity in disability design. Newer understandings of disability are expanding this discourse still further. Neurodiverse, mad, and people who identify as sick have long been stigmatized and are only now beginning to gain attention in design circles. The goal in this and in years to come is to change this part of the equity equation, reshaping future work. Only in so doing can we confront stigma and truly create disability design equity.

References

Apple Newsroom. (2016), "Apple Offers a Look at New Emoji Coming to IPhone This Fall," Available online: https://www.apple.com/newsroom/2019/07/apple-offers-a-look-at-new-emoji-coming-to-iphone-this-fall/ (accessed December 23, 2021).

Barad, K. (2007), *Meeting the Universe Halfway: Quantum Physics and the Entanglement of Matter and Meaning*, Durham, NC: Duke University Press.

10 Making Equity: How the Disability Community Met the Maker Movement

ÉMELINE BRULÉ

I first read about the Open Hand Project and e-NABLE initiatives in 2013. Both were filling the mainstream news with heart-warming accounts, all centered on the exciting potential of anyone planning to 3D-print customizable upper-limb prosthesis. A father made a "special" prosthetic hand for his own son. A teen produced mechanical fingers for a neighborhood kid born without any. Both groups were sharing their designs, inspiring a movement that seemingly revolutionized what could be made and by whom. Over time, these initiatives have taken separate paths. The Open Hand Project has become the Open Bionics company. It still produces myoelectric prosthesis, but no longer uses hobbyist printers and has not shared the blueprints of their latest product, the Hero Arm.[1] The Hero Arm, however, has been clinically tested, approved, and is offered through clinics, whereas e-NABLE has refined a small number of designs, to be used at one's own risks and printed by volunteers.

But in 2013, these two projects were still a promise: that computer-controlled production tools such as 3D printers could enable anyone, including disabled people, to become "makers" and design and produce assistive products at a low cost and locally. What if any person might design and produce their own technologies? Might this new form of production remake systems of inequality, oppression, and injustice? Rooted in ideas of open-source software and electronics hacking, the global "maker movement" began to take shape in the 1990s. The movement increased its influence after the financial crisis of 2007–8. Its central promise—the ability to manufacture anything at any time at will—was claimed as a democratization of production (Gershenfeld 2005). Furthermore, if anyone could "make" anything, passive consumers might be transformed into active makers and creative citizens. But as illustrated above, 3D-printing underpins very different approaches to the design of assistive products, and interactions between makers and the disabled community take many shapes.

In this chapter I introduce central discourses and hopes for encounters between the making and disability community, but also discuss why they are a limited help in facing the challenge of bringing assistive products to all who need them. I draw on seven years of involvement, meeting stakeholders in this space, collecting projects documentation and exhibition catalogs, reviewing research, or attending events: a patchwork ethnography. I do not aim at mapping this field,[2] instead teasing tensions at its core.

My first task then is to circumscribe the topic. While I consider many do-it-your-self (DIY) practices and crafts as belonging under this umbrella, I focus on initiatives using automated production tools and electronics, instead of, for instance, hobby-ist making of adapted clothes. Similarly, while I cursorily refer to digital fabrication in medicine, medical implants or models are beyond the scope of this chapter, as they present its specific set of safety and organizational issues. In discussing the promise of digital fabrication and making, I look at the topic through three perspec-tives: the types of objects that digital making is framed as uniquely positioned to produce, the actors involved in sustaining making these initiatives, and the technical benefits of digital fabrication beyond hobbyists. I conclude with a discussion of the persistent—and inevitable—challenges to making for access to assistive products. Prototyping is easy; developing as well as maintaining a product is hard.

A History of Making

There is a long history of disabled people designing and sharing ideas for custom-as-sistive technologies. For instance, polio survivors documented and shared their experimentations and home alterations through a magazine initially called the *Toomeyville Gazette* from 1955 to 1998 (Williamson 2019). But this type of commu-nity sharing can be traced even further, for instance to the *Bulletin mensuel de l'Union des Aveugles de Guerre* (Monthly Bulletin of the Union of Blind Veterans) published from 1919, which included an open rubric used by members to communicate about adaptations they had developed.[3] As Liz Jackson put it, people with disabilities *"are the original lifehackers"* (2018).

By the 2000s, however, the possibilities surrounding custom-assistive technolo-gies appeared to shift radically. In their article spearheading research into making for accessibility in the field of human-computer interaction (HCI), Hurst and Tobias (2011) highlight the work of a volunteer creating assistive or adapted objects in a home workshop; they asked how the computer-controlled fabrication tools and hobby-ist electronics platforms that were increasingly available in the 2000s could expand these practices, for both disabled people and their able-bodied family and friends. Among those tools, the 3D-printer stood out. Essentially, it seemed to promise that any user could download the file of an object, push a button, and obtain a high-fi-delity copy. The actual construction process occurs by adding material in strata, following a digital model. There are a variety of approaches to doing so, but fused deposition modeling, which consists in melting plastic (for instance, *Ultimakers* or *Makerbots*), is historically the most common.

The seeming simplicity of this process was key to the emergence of the maker movement, which often promised a more equitable approach toward design and production. Emerging in the early 2000s, the maker movement built on traditions of DIY, craft, and open-source hardware and software (Turner 2018). Unlike these earlier movements, which required the patient development of skills, this newer kind of automation promised the easy production of material goods, putting the means of production back in the hands of the people, at least according to public coverage (Hepp 2020). In practice, their use required developing an infrastructure (Davies 2017) of websites for sharing and documentation such as Thingiverse and Instructables; physical makerspaces to meet and provide access to more complex or large machines like laser cutters, further visibility-making practices, and recruiting and supporting new members; events and demonstrations framing making as a new path to innovation, economic development, and for education; and user-friendly 3D modelling tools supporting beginners with creating their first objects, possibly leading to the development of more advanced engineering skills, and transforming users into makers (Roedl et al. 2015).

In reflecting on this history and these realities, I should note that this movement has never been homogeneous. I myself have been involved with projects for social and digital inclusion and the empowerment of young people and people with disabilities for many years. In late 2014, sometime after I first learned about the Open Hand Project and e-NABLE initiatives, I started studying an organization providing services to visually impaired children and adults undergoing sight loss in southern France. A small group of workers who were interested in making for accessibility had recently become interested in the local makerspace, and they had a partnership with HCI researchers at the local university. I stayed for eighteen months for field work and continued doing interviews and collecting their documentation of their making practices for four more years. Throughout, I was involved in making myself, focusing especially on more complex three-dimensional representations, for instance tactile globes and insects (Brulé and Bailly 2021).

In parallel, I became personally more involved in a local makerspace, which had several initiatives in that area: supporting the printing of hand prosthesis, often for educational purposes as an introduction to 3D-printing; helping individuals seeking to repair assistive or adapted products to organizing events for designing new accessible objects, such as physical games; or more complex assistive technologies requiring electronics and software design. I was encouraged in 2016 to join one of these initiatives, E-Fabrik, because makerspace employees knew of my research. E-Fabrik sought to strengthen social solidarity through the co-design of assistive products, inspired by the Fixperts project.[4] E-Fabrik first focused in 2015 on involving secondary school students in designing and building custom objects with people with disabilities receiving services from, or institutionalized in, partner organizations. In 2016, it attempted to match more experienced makers and disabled individuals. From 2018, it trained young adults from Seine Saint-Denis, an underprivileged urban area, to use digital fabrication tools and develop design skills, as part of a national scheme to develop workers' digital skills.[5] Rather than an accredited diploma opening employment as makers for accessibility, trainees receive support to develop professional and social skills and usually go on to further training or toward socio-educational work.[6]

I draw on these experiences to write about the multiple configurations of collaborations between the making and disability communities. And clearly, from the

Toomeyville Gazette to E-Fabrik, the ultimate goal of these initiatives is to make design and fabrication more equitable and responsive to individual needs. Nevertheless, the variety of E-Fabrik's projects and goals reflects the wide range of objects and people under the umbrella of making and disability.

The Objects of Making

Although this is not an exhaustive mapping of the field, the promise behind digital fabrication and making rests in part on the types of objects that proponents claim it is uniquely positioned to produce. This discussion focuses on these objects, and also some of the tensions surrounding them. One key argument for digital fabrication in the design of assistive products is that it enables the production of objects that could not be produced otherwise. Customizable prostheses are the best example of how making captured the popular imagination. I focus on objects that are *customizable* automatically or semi-automatically and *empowering* objects that go beyond assistive functions, aiming to convey identity or empowerment through participation in the design process.

The ability to customize or make something tailored to an individual is an important aspect of the promise of digital design and fabrication of assistive products. To design a prosthesis, there are a number of parameters (e.g., length, width, design of a cover) and constraints (e.g., weight, mechanical properties such as stiffness) that may vary from one person to the other. Parametric modeling is an approach to design enabling automatic changes to an object based on the input of different parameters value, or to explore solutions optimizing different constraints. For more complex shapes, a model could include a part based on a 3D scan. This is the approach used in GripFab, a design tool for occupational therapists to create custom grips for everyday objects (Buehler et al. 2014). In contrast, previous methods of automation have relied on a range of standardized sizes, necessary to create the molds for plastic, or other industrial fabrication processes. The conjunction of wider availability of parametric modelling tools (for instance, the Makerbot Customizer available on Thingiverse or the LimbForge project for prostheses specifically) and of reliable 3D-printers for production makes customization by the actual user of an assistive device feel possible.

Part of the promise of customization is the ability to cut out intermediaries, or accelerate their work, improving the availability of assistive products. For instance, obtaining a custom-fit prosthesis involves a lengthy process. First, the user must secure funds for these highly specialized objects. Next, he or she must meet a prosthetist, itself a fairly rare type of expertise. The latter may then outsource production or request the assistance of colleagues in order to make the prosthetic device itself. Each step in this process lengthens the time between the appearance of the need and receiving a prosthesis. The initial appeal of using parametric customizable models is considerable. Yet, achieving that promise is often difficult. e-NABLE, for instance, is limited to below-elbow prosthetics despite efforts to expand, for instance, to leg prosthetics. Moreover, the promises of automation may hide the complex manual work required to finish, assemble, and fit these devices. I spent ninety minutes of an e-NABLE workshop held at the 2018 edition of the Mozilla Festival, an event dedicated to open technologies, polishing just two knuckles. The parametric, customizable, Knick's prosthetics finger similarly requires significant manual work, as described in its documentation. In other words, digital fabrication does require labor, but it shifts who can undertake it and where it takes place.

But customization remains only one argument for this sort of making; the design of assistive products can also foster making for empowerment and the participation of disabled people in the making process. It follows that disabled people could become designers and create products for needs otherwise overlooked or ignored, or products that are too costly otherwise because they are manufactured in small numbers. The activist Raul Krauthasen, for example, designed and printed a wheelchair ramp (Rose 2014). Empowerment is also a core value of the research about making for accessibility. Hurst and Tobias's (2011) influential article on making for accessibility frames both participation in the making process and the type of objects produced as empowering. Similarly, De Couvreur and Gossens argue that involvement in making is key to living an independent life, because it allows designing for highly personal goals, situations, and skills, and a focus on personal aesthetics. Calling their approach "design for (every)one," they argue that making is a new approach to personal rehabilitation engineering, lifting the stigma of using assistive products and positively impacting self-perception (2011). They give examples of co-created designs, including a guitar slider, an adapted badminton shuttle, and a device for eating ice-cream bars. With examples like these in mind, I define objects for empowerment as objects crafted for or with individuals, that cannot be automatically customized through parametric models, and that may diverge from needs that are considered essential by rehabilitation specialists, for instance enabling a focus on conveying identity.

Again, outside academic circles, prosthetics have been some of the best known of these empowering objects. Prosthetics or prosthesis attachments made to fit the activities of the wearer are nothing new, but it is unlikely professional prosthetists could develop many of these for playful or imaginative purposes. One widely publicized object is the 2016 Project Unicorn, a 3D-printed arm prosthesis designed with a ten-year-old girl. A digitally fabricated arm, the prosthesis shoots glitter from one end.[7] Here, 3D-printing and electronics prototyping kits enable rapid iterations at lesser costs, while the use of plastics offers flexibility for the design of the shape. Free hobbyist modelling software does open avenues for the autonomous fabrication of simpler designs. Tinkercad, for instance, is based on the assembly of basic geometric shapes by addition and subtraction and is used in educational contexts (Hansen et al. 2017). Hand drawings, commonly used in other DIY traditions such as fanzines, can be scanned for a laser cutter, or shapes can be prototyped with paper or cardboard and applied to other materials. It enabled the Quietude project, for instance, in which Deaf participants drew hearing aids as jewelry. But these types of objects and design processes are close to DIY traditions and often remain prototypes. Indeed, the fully realized design of Project Unicorn's model arm required the expertise of an industrial designer.

The need for more specialized knowledge brings out another characteristic of the maker movement: online documentation and communication systems allowing free access to models and tutorials for inspiration, sharing knowledge and guidelines for new volunteers, collaborating worldwide, or asking for help from other experts.[8] National and international DIY competitions often supported by more generalist disability organizations, like Papas bricoleurs (DIY-Dads), which started in 1998, now named Fablife, have aimed to encourage these collaborations. De Couvreur and co-authors (Ostuzzi et al. 2017), who have run a program matching designers, rehabilitation specialists, and disabled users to produce these empowering *designs for one* for close to a decade, propose to build typologies of design features, for situations where parametric design is not possible. For instance, they attempted to systematically explore how two surfaces can be joined or handles that can be added on objects. This modular approach to design, aiming at scaffolding what amateurs can do through simple guidelines, goes beyond assistive products for people with physical disabilities. Nevertheless, projects like these suggest another singular aspect behind digital making, namely the sheer variety of people involved in—and often necessary for—such undertakings.

The People in Making

Figure 9 A series of objects made using digital fabrication for visually impaired children. Objects were made at or with the Centre d'Education Spécialisée pour Déficients Visuels, Institut des Jeunes Aveugles of Toulouse, France. This work is licensed under a Creative Commons License.

The initial promise of initiatives like Open Hand Project and e-NABLE was that their designs could be made by anyone. As I have outlined in the previous section, making and disability initiatives are built not only around certain types of objects but also around collaborations, with making in itself sometimes framed as an empowering process. In practice, however, just who is actually making and using these devices? First, I consider the various roles of *disabled makers*, and the immediate community of family and friends. I then discuss partnerships with *educational institutions* or *disability professionals*. I conclude with the networked approach aiming at independently matching *amateur makers* with users.

The promise of the maker movement is that users could become designers (Roedl et al. 2015). Rose's coverage on making for accessibility emphasizes the ability to design for oneself and the ability to share and improve designs with other disabled people (2014). Disabled makers argued it could lower the price of pieces of specialized equipment such as wheelchair cup holders or allow them to resolve everyday problems they encounter such as using a straw. But such making practices could also provide new employment opportunities or a path into the design and engineering industry (Meissner et al. 2017). This is, for instance, one of the stated aims of the BOOST program bringing together disabled youth and makers. To support disabled makers, HCI scholars have proposed adapted design and prototyping tools (Siu et al. 2019), and investigated how to make makerspaces more accessible (Brady et al. 2014).

This DIY approach to design can be complemented with what some (e.g. Tehel 2019) call "Do-It-Together design." Calling for disabled people to work with designers or others, this approach allows for the sharing of expertise (Tehel 2019). It follows that makers and researchers have strived to identify stakeholders and partners for all stages of the process. Disabled people's immediate community members, often including family and friends, are commonly identified as partners for making. Making initiatives often concentrate their focus on younger disabled people, framing their principal users as children; parents' involvement is seen as supplementing the work of disability professionals, and the involvement of peers as a means to develop mutual respect and opportunities for social interaction. Parents are already involved in identifying accessibility needs and possible solutions, from identifying and buying mainstream products that are or can be adapted to their child's needs[9] or making small tweaks such as adding sticky pads to common household objects like plates so they stay in place while eating (Hook et al. 2014). But in this context, digital making has encountered significant obstacles. When invited to expand these low-tech practices using digital fabrication, parents face significant issues. In reality, many lack the time or confidence to do so, while others worry about the safety of the objects they would design from scratch or print out. They do, however, feel confident about making repairs, if parts were available: another area in which digital fabrication could be useful (Hook et al. 2014). Peers' involvement concerns different types of objects, more oriented toward playing or media, as they would between nondisabled children: Kim et al., for instance, proposed a tool for children to make accessible tactile pictures out of building blocks like Legos, much like one would make a scrapbook or card for a friend (2014).

While family and friends can work on these projects, the need for cheap or free labor and technical skills means that educational institutions, especially universities, can also be partners of choice. Students may be asked to collaborate with occupational therapists to design one-off assistive devices (De Couvreur and Gossens 2011), develop interactive prototypes as part of class projects (Brulé and Bailly 2021), or explore how to make makerspaces accessible (Worsley and Bar-El 2020) as a means to teach technical or creative skills and accessibility through an authentic task. Some making initiatives, like E-Fabrik, also establish themselves as vocational training programs, thereby ensuring the involvement of students until completion of the project. Others like Fixperts offer educational content that teachers can use, then publicize the results. In their messaging, they evoke problem-solving skills and making as a form of citizenship. This should be understood within a broader history of involving students in initiatives for development. Engineering without Borders, for example, organizes competitions between undergraduate programs, aimed at solving a problem far removed from students' experience.

And yet such approaches carry their own risks with disability activists highlighting the limitations, or even damages of these approaches. Ashley Shew has described these impulses as techno-ableism (2020) while Elizabeth Guffey and Bess Williamson suggest that the desire to "cure" disability through newer technologies might constitute a newer *design model of disability* (Williamson and Guffey 2020). Liz Jackson coined the term "disability dongle" for design concepts that purport to address a problem in style, but fail to understand and answer accessibility issues.[10] The dongle embodies the aspirations of many young designers and is a particular concern with student projects. In my relatively short teaching career, I met no less than seventeen students proposing "technologies to guide the blind." Depending on the fashion of the moment, these may involve drones, robots, or smart textiles. While earnest young designers want to produce impactful products, students may lack the time and guidance to fully research needs, or avoid simpler products and focus on aesthetics to gain advantage in course evaluation or even look for potential for public coverage. Emphasizing the value of small and collaborative DIY projects may avoid this pitfall.

Disability professionals also play a role in digital fabrication projects. I discuss earlier in this chapter research and projects aiming at changing disability professionals' practices, especially occupational therapists', by introducing digital fabrication tools and the design and engineering skills for making. Maker Nurse,[11] for instance, provide tools, space, and an online sharing infrastructure for nurses. For disability professionals, this is a way to see their often overlooked (Hofmann et al. 2019; Royer 2015) creativity recognized. Here, making is presented as a driver for innovative care practices, with the goal of improving services at no or low cost.

However, the extent to which digital fabrication and making is changing existing professional practice is unclear. For example, Slegers et al. suggest that occupational therapists are less likely to believe hobbyist 3D-printing would change their profession after using it, in part because they believe that collaborating with professional design-ers would be necessary (2020). In my own research on special education for visually impaired children, I have observed this problem often with disability professionals working as tactile document makers. Digital fabrication tools can complement their existing toolset; nevertheless, they cannot replace fundamental equipment such as tactile image makers. In fact, 3D printers are more likely to fail, and prints often require hand finishes. They also found that while 3D models are sometimes helpful, tactile or bas-relief representations are often better indicated. Moreover, while many models are shared online, educational materials need to be adapted for local contexts and then to individual children. These issues often meant that digital fabrication added to the costs and to the workload of document makers; maintaining the skills need to make such changes was difficult, often necessitating that extra staff with design and engineering skills had to be hired. Such users continued to support digital fabri-cation, and especially using laser cutters. At the same time, however, after six years of collaboration with makers, only one member of staff remained highly involved in making (Brulé and Bailly 2021).

Encouraging amateur makers has proven an alternative route taken by initiatives such as Makers Making Change, E-Fabrik, or Match My Maker. These groups aim to find makers with engineering or computer programming skills to help out with design-ing or building solutions to a problem they identify. Their involvement may be limited to a short period of in time, in contrast with disability professionals investing and being supported in developing making skills. Because these volunteer makers often get involved of their own volition, they also lack the incentives typical of others, for example, students working on a project for school. In the end, volunteer participation from the beginning to end of each project can vary greatly.

In these issues, digital fabrication and making echoes the difficulties of the open-source movement in using a decentralized and unpaid community to maintain software projects (Eghbal 2020). In my experience as both a maker and a researcher, it is difficult to recruit volunteer makers in the local making community for an acces-sibility project; this is often why many projects turn to students for help (Brulé and Bailly 2021). Researchers have attempted to identify the motivations for makers to get involved in accessibility work and how it occurred (e.g., Hoffman et al. 2016). Some volunteers have developed this work as a hobby (Hurst and Tobias 2011) and receive moral rewards or public exposure for their involvement. At the same time, not unlike earlier participation in the open-source software movement, volunteers' involvement is usually limited to a one-off project or event and remains their only form of participation (Eghbal 2020). Projects of limited complexity and clear guid-ance, for instance printing an e-NABLE hand or the production of visors during the 2020 Covid pandemic, can easily re-produce simple, single designs. More complex work requires more complex and ongoing collaborations. The Unicorn Project, for example, was developed by a ten-year-old child who collaborated closely with a professional industrial designer. To not only develop but maintain and improve projects like, this can require vast resources to pay designers and engineers instead of only involving volunteers. For instance, Makers Making Change, a nonprofit that connects makers, disability professionals, and disabled people, received a large grant to develop a mouth-controlled computer input meant to enable people with limited motor skills to operate a computer. Conversely, the Open Hand Project, which was originally funded through crowdsourcing, raised venture capital from investors to become Open Bionics. The latter initiative allowed them to hire engineers, establish a lab, and produce low-cost customizable prosthetics. Ultimately, approaches to making for disability that casually connect demands and makers are likely to result in widely different outcomes, with more complex or less easy to show off projects receiving far less attention.

Maintenance, Repair, and Innovation: A Different Economy of Scale

So far, I have outlined how these tools have been understood as a way to dramatically change who can get involved in making, as well as the ways they have—and have not—met those expectations. But another way to look at digital fabrication is as an industrial advantage, spurring new businesses and enabling not only customizable objects but also a different approach to distribution. Moreover, while digital fabrication was reserved for prototyping historically, computer-controlled fabrication at scale may improve mechanical performance. Although these practices may seem distant from the initial promise of casual and creative forms of digital making, it still offers a complementary approach to understanding or building new initiatives that leverage digital fabrication tools. I will focus on two aspects potential advantages, specifically digital fabrication for *small series* and hopes that making models already openly available could foster innovation. In these ways, the making movement still offers an invitation to rethink how we produce products more broadly, using different scales of manufacturing and taking advantage of each one.

Repairing assistive products remains one of the areas of digital making which disabled people as well as their immediate community might find highly effective and also practical (Hook et al. 2014). When a disability organization asked me in 2015 to make a copy of a screw for a needed repair, I thought I had found a great example of what digital fabrication could achieve. This screw was not standard and unavailable (a wider issue that recent "Right to Repair" legislation aims to address); replacing the bed transfer device it was part of would be expensive. Repairing accessible and assistive products can present hefty price tags, as replacement parts are often difficult to source and sometimes have to be made individually or in very small production volume. Industrial grade 3D-printers or computer-controlled drills, for instance, can use materials such as metal rather than the less permanent plastic used by hobbyists (Chekurov et al. 2018). At the same time, when I was first approached about this problem in 2015, I rapidly realized that the 3D scanners I had access to were not precise enough, but also our drilling machines could not produce this screw safely.

But indeed, a local company owning industrial computer numerical *control* (CNC) milling machines agreed to produce a copy at no cost.

More generally, improving the production of small product series could make them more affordable. For instance, I found that tactile document makers often laser-cut and then hand-paint accessible rulers every year (Brulé and Bailly 2021: 10). This is less expensive to make than buy, even though making them using digital fabrication tools at hand is likely less efficient in terms of energy and labor and hardly require creative thinking. Similarly, bottle openers for people with arthritis are needed in large enough numbers and can be produced with traditional manufacturing techniques and are sold at a low cost. There are models that can be downloaded and 3D printed locally, but it is unclear if using digital fabrication results in a product as robust or as efficiently manufactured. But improvements to production can be found beyond digital fabrication. The Adaptive Design organization builds custom cardboard seats for disabled children, largely by hand. The making movement could be an invitation to rethink how we produce products more broadly, using different scales of manufacturing and taking advantage of each one.

Finally, another argument for providing open access and encouraging digital making is that they could speed innovation, inviting more people to iterate and improve designs. There are good reasons to believe this type of decentralized innovation can work, from scientific innovation contests to open-source software.[12] Regardless of the short-term design outcomes, creating assistive products in maker spaces can have profound implications for civic participation, the consolidation of accessibility as a shared value, the development of skills, and the creation of formal and informal communities well-placed to rethink approaches to manufacturing. From this perspective, open-source plans for assistive products would enable designers and engineers to learn more easily from the work of others. But the path to a global community involved in accessibility innovation is not so clear. Sophisticated myoelectric prostheses can be especially difficult in this regard; Hackaday listed four open-source myoelectric hands projects in 2016, but only the Open Hand Project appears to have gone beyond prototyping, and it is unclear whether makers built upon each other's work. In their study of models for protective equipment, Mack et al. found that innovation mostly originated in existing professional teams. Amateur makers would innovate at the periphery, for example proposing tweaks for using a different printer (2022).

Making as a Powerful Horizon for Equality

As I was writing this chapter and discussing it with other makers, we struggled to understand a paradox: it feels like we have achieved so much yet so little through making. There are many hopes and promises, but just as many feelings of failure. Competing explanations and recommendations follow from this paradox. I have been peripherally participating in these initiatives for years; while digital fabrication is sometimes linked to arguments for customization or empowerment, I am still struck by the frequent emphasis on digital making as *decreasing costs of assistive products*. This has been the case in with e-NABLE and OpenBionics, as well as many of the digital making in education initiatives I have joined. Disability professionals have turned to digital fabrication tools and maker approaches to cut costs, and educational institutions, especially universities, often provide cheap or free labor and technical skills for digital making. We certainly should incentivize manufacturers to keep prices low, but by emphasizing how making drives down the costs of qualified workers, we also avow an acceptance that states will not take responsibility toward disabled citizens. Often I have expressed concerns that positioning digital making as an alternative to state-supported services would only contribute to more responsibilities being transferred over to unpaid volunteers. In most cases these workers must be trained, but may not be able to contribute to the community for long, or who might propose ideas whose maintenance cannot be ensured.

A counterargument is often expressed as a variation of this quote: making *"is better than nothing."*[13] These technologies are no longer new, and it is still clear that the ways they allow customization and empowerment have the potential to move design with disability in a new direction. As we begin to assess over a decade of digital making, however, I want to emphasize *equality in accessing assistive products*. This presents the need for a state-operated approach[14] to develop and maintain new assistive products taking advantage of innovations in manufacturing, based on employing professionals to provide products for all. This does not preclude regularly trying to expand the group of professionals to work on certain problems through competitions or calls to makerspaces, or supporting disabled individuals in developing and sharing their everyday hacks. Others are concerned acting toward institutional change would have no results, at least for the foreseeable future. They instead advocate for emphasizing *the innovation potential* that can funnel funding to the people who can develop assistive products at lower costs with responsible entrepreneurial practices, and that we just need more time for prototypes to come to fruition. They rightly point that this is more attractive for public institutions in a context of austerity measures. What concerns me is that funding innovative practices may draw resources away from disability organizations, especially as they are already asked to provide more services than their original mandate; this scenario comes at the risk to see it used for day-to-day functioning and have organizations compete for sources of funding that are ever less sufficient.[15] I summarize these discussions because they show that the same technologies, while accompanied by a certain set of values (Davies 2017; Turner 2018), can be recontextualized in different ways in the service of accessibility.

When we examine the design implications for these new technologies, we make assumptions about what they allow: the transfer of labor, a decrease in skills needed to accomplish the same goals. This view oversimplifies the complex organizational work that was necessary to bring about the open-source software movement, which additionally draws on a much larger and well-resourced group of software professionals. Moreover, when discourses on making and disability have focused on empowerment, projects held as successes that expanded beyond individual proto-types and have spread to countries with low access to assistive products, such as e-NABLE, are still to be evaluated.[16]

To summarize and conclude, media, civic, and disability organizations have framed the maker movement and its tools as a significant opportunity for decentralized and rapid innovation in accessibility. In these ways, the making movement still offers an invitation to rethink how we produce products, moving us beyond the mass-pro-duced solutions of earlier decades. But the groups involved in digital making vary in terms of motivations, organization, and focus. They often emphasize the moral value of volunteering and center empowerment and artifacts as a means to effect change. This can translate into a materialization of hopes for an inclusive future. But while initiatives like Open Hand Project and e-NABLE often provide compelling stories and can bring communities together, they downplay the difficulties to bring about the advantages of digital fabrication for manufacturing. In that regard, they reflect concerning trends that focus on innovation rather than maintenance, or that emphasize autonomous access to technologies rather than concerted training as a path to progress and justice.

Notes

1. The company announced through social media in 2018 the files would be available, but they currently are not. See https://twitter.com/openbionics/status/991691284162195457.
2. I will mostly refer to projects, but there are atlases of maker spaces interested in accessi-bility, such as https://www.careables.org/community-map/ or http://wiki.fablab.fr/index.php?title=Groupe_Travail_Accessibilit%C3%A9_Handicap.
3. An example can be found in Volume 1, May 1919 edition, p.20.
4. Fixperts is an initiative encouraging students to design for a disabled person in their community.
5. La Grande École du Numérique (*The Great School of the Digital*).
6. According to their website, see list of Project References at conclusion of this chapter.
7. See https://jordanreeves.com/project-unicorn.
8. There's a long tradition of studies into documentation, in particular different types of tutorials, and their importance in the informal and decentralized learning advocated by many makers. I would recommend Torrey et al. (2007).
9. For an example, see the crucial role in iPad cases in the use of alternative communica-tion devices in Alper (2017).
10. Liz Jackson, a disability activist, designer, and curator, coined the term *disability dongle* in 2019 as "A well intended elegant, yet useless solution to a problem we never knew we had. Disability Dongles are most often conceived of and created in design schools and at IDEO." The implications of this type of products are outlined in a later Vox article: https://www.vox.com/first-person/2019/4/30/18523006/disabled-wheelchair-access-ramps-stair-climbing (accessed December 14, 2021).

11. Maker Nurse initially was supported by MIT, simultaneously highlighting the role of educational institutions in making for accessibility and the role of a technological imaginary in which MIT retains a place of choice.
12. Lakhani and coauthors have long investigated the conditions under which these processes are possible. See, for instance, Lakhani et al. (2013).
13. It is worth noting that there are astoundingly few initiatives to structure international collaborations around assistive products. This is changing; in 2021, the World Health Organization published guidelines on minimum requirements for assistive technology and products.
14. The latest example in my notes is from an online accessibility hackathon on April 29, 2021, while discussing priorities for makers aiming to improve accessibility. Over the years, I have heard this from researchers, designers, makers, and disability activists. This discourse illustrates that many, despite their involvement in making and believing in its potential, recognize the limitations of current practices while arguing that the current state of access to assistive tools justify any alternatives.
15. This goes beyond the scope of this chapter, but as an example, the disability organization studied during my thesis provided educational services to more children than stated in the regional agreement for funding. For years, they received additional annual funding, until they did not. Disability organizations are incentivized to develop their own resources to compensate for state public austerity measures, including through research and the provision of services beyond their core missions. A 2018 report, "Scenarios for the Evolution of National Institutes of Deaf and Blind Youth," makes visible this evolution of funding. Long funded at state level as the first schools for disabled children, it argues that this separate status prevents them from competing for additional sources of funding for research or innovative practices. I do not doubt the appropriateness of public funding needs to be regularly examined. However, expanding responsibilities of public educational organizations to make them more responsible financially has often resulted in decreasing public funding rather than increasing educational equality, as has previously been the case for French universities.
16. Fiedler et al. (2018) proposed a study, but to my knowledge results have not been published.

References

Bennett, C. L., E. Brady, and S. M. Branham (2018), "Interdependence as a Frame for Assistive Technology Research and Design," in *Proceedings of the 20th International ACM Sigaccess Conference on Computers and Accessibility*, 161–73, New York, NY, USA: Association for Computing Machinery.

Brady, T., C. Salas, A. Nuriddin, W. Rodgers, and M. Subramaniam (2014), "MakeAbility: Creating Accessible Makerspace Events in a Public Library," *Public Library Quarterly* 33 (4): 330–47.

Brulé, E., and G. Bailly (2021), "'Beyond 3D printers': Understanding Long-Term Digital Fabrication Practices for the Education of Visually Impaired or Blind Youth," in

Proceedings of the 2021 CHI Conference on Human Factors in Computing Systems, 1–15, New York, NY, USA: Association for Computing Machinery.

Buehler, E., A. Hurst, and M. Hofmann (2014), "Coming to Grips: 3D Printing for Accessibility," in *Proceedings of the 16th International ACM SIGACCESS Conference on Computers & Accessibility*, 291–2, New York, NY, USA: Association for Computing Machinery. *Bulletin mensuel de l'Union des Aveugles de Guerre* (Monthly Bulletin of the Union of Blind Veterans). Available online: https://argonnaute.parisnanterre.fr/ark:/14707/a011447430312YuCgOW/af4e3d2895 (accessed 2 December 2021).

Chekurov, S., S. Metsä-Kortelainen, M. Salmi, I. Roda, and A. Jussila (2018), "The Perceived Value of Additively Manufactured Digital Spare Parts in Industry: An Empirical Investigation," *International Journal of Production Economics* 205: 87–97.

Davies, S. R. (2017), *Hackerspaces: Making the Maker Movement*, Cambridge and Malden, MA: Polity Press.

De Couvreur, L., and R. Goossens (2011), "Design for (Every) one: Co-creation as a Bridge between Universal Design and Rehabilitation Engineering," *CoDesign* 7 (2): 107–21.

de Oliveira, F., R. G. Pétreault, F. Carayon, T. Leconte, and P. R. Ambrogi (2018), "Scénarios d'évolution des instituts nationaux des jeunes sourds et des jeunes aveugles (Scenarios for the evolution of national institutes of Deaf and Blind Youth)," Available online: https://www.igas.gouv.fr/IMG/pdf/2017-069R.pdf (accessed December 2, 2021).

Eghbal, N. (2020), *Working in Public: The Making and Maintenance of Open Source software*, San Francisco: Stripe Press.

Fiedler, G., S. Savage, J. Schull, and J. Mankoff (2018), "The Case For Broad-Range Outcome Assessment across Upper Limb Device Classes," *Canadian Prosthetics & Orthotics Journal* 1 (1): 1–4.

Gershenfeld, N. A. (2005), *Fab: The Coming Revolution on Your Desktop–from Personal Computers to Personal Fabrication*, New York: Basic Books (AZ).

Hansen, A. K., E. R. Hansen, T. Hall, M. Fixler, and D. Harlow (2017), "Fidgeting with Fabrication: Students with ADHD Making Tools to Focus," in *Proceedings of the 7th Annual Conference on Creativity and Fabrication in Education*, 1–4, New York, NY, USA: Association for Computing Machinery.

Hepp, A. (2020), "The Fragility of Curating a Pioneer Community: Deep Mediatization and the Spread of the Quantified Self and Maker Movements'," *International Journal of Cultural Studies* 23 (6): 932–50.

Hofmann, M., J. Burke, J. Pearlman, G. Fiedler, A. Hess, J. Schull, and J. Mankoff (2016), "Clinical and Maker Perspectives on the Design of Assistive Technology with Rapid Prototyping Technologies," in *Proceedings of the 18th International ACM SIGACCESS Conference on Computers and Accessibility*, 251–6, New York, NY, USA: Association for Computing Machinery.

Hofmann, M., K. Williams, T. Kaplan, S. Valencia, G. Hann, S. E. Hudson, and P. Carrington (2019), "'Occupational Therapy Is Making' Clinical Rapid Prototyping and Digital Fabrication," in *Proceedings of the 2019 CHI Conference on Human Factors in Computing Systems*, 1–13, New York, NY, USA: Association for Computing Machinery.

Hofmann, M., U. Lakshmi, K. Mack, R. I. Arriaga, S. E. Hudson, and J. Mankoff (2022), "Making a Medical Maker's Playbook: An Ethnographic Study of Safety-Critical Collective Design by Makers in Response to COVID-19," *Proceedings of the ACM on Human-Computer Interaction* 6 (CSCW1): 1–26.

Hook, J., S. Verbaan, A. Durrant, P. Olivier, and P. Wright (2014), "A Study of the Challenges Related to DIY Assistive Technology in the Context of Children with Disabilities," in *Proceedings of the 2014 Conference on Designing Interactive Systems*, 597–606, New York, NY, USA: Association for Computing Machinery.

Hurst, A., and J. Tobias (2011), "Empowering Individuals with Do-it-yourself Assistive Technology," in *The Proceedings of the 13th International ACM SIGACCESS Conference on Computers and Accessibility*, 11–18, New York, NY, USA: Association for Computing Machinery.

Jackson, L. (2018), "We Are the Original Lifehackers," *The New York Times*, 30 May. Available online: https://www.nytimes.com/2018/05/30/opinion/disability-design-lifehacks.html (accessed December 2, 2021).

Kim, J., A. Stangl, and T. Yeh (2014), "Using LEGO to Model 3D Tactile Picture Books by Sighted Children for Blind Children," in *Proceedings of the 2nd ACM Symposium on Spatial User Interaction*, 146–6, New York, NY, USA: Association for Computing Machinery.

Lakhani, K. R., H. Lifshitz-Assaf, and M. L. Tushman (2013), "Open Innovation and Organizational Boundaries: Task Decomposition, Knowledge Distribution and the Locus of Innovation," in Anna Grandori (ed.), *Handbook of Economic Organization*, 355–82, Northampton, MA: Edward Elgar Publishing.

Meissner, J. L., J. Vines, J. McLaughlin, T. Nappey, J. Maksimova, and P. Wright (2017), "Do-it-yourself Empowerment as Experienced by Novice Makers with Disabilities," in *Proceedings of the 2017 Conference on Designing Interactive Systems*, 1053–65, New York, NY, USA: Association for Computing Machinery.

Oehlberg, L., W. Willett, and W. E. Mackay (2015), "Patterns of Physical Design Remixing in Online Maker Communities," in *Proceedings of the 33rd Annual ACM Conference on Human Factors in Computing* Systems - *CHI '15*, 639–48, New York, NY, USA: Association for Computing Machinery. Available online: https://doi.org/10.1145/2702123.2702175.

Ostuzzi, F., L. De Couvreur, J. Detand, and J. Saldien (2017), "From Design for One to Open-Ended Design. Experiments on Understanding How to open-up Contextual Design Solutions," *The Design Journal 20* (sup1): S3873–83.

Roedl, D., S. Bardzell, and J. Bardzell (2015), "Sustainable Making? Balancing Optimism and Criticism in HCI Discourse," *ACM Transactions on Computer-Human Interaction (TOCHI)* 22 (3): 1–27.

Rose, D. (2014), "Could 3D Printing Provide New Solutions for Disabled People?" *BBC News*, January 31. Available online: https://www.bbc.com/news/blogs-ouch-25947021 (accessed December 2, 2021).

Royer, M. (2015), "De l'instrument à la prothèse: ethnographie de trajectoires d'objets biotechnologiques en cancérologie (From Instrument to Prosthesis: Ethnography of the Trajectories of Biotechnological Objects in Cancerology)," PhD diss., EHESS, Paris.

Shew, A. (2020), "Ableism, Technoableism, and Future AI," *IEEE Technology and Society Magazine* 39 (1): 40–85.

Siu, A., S. Kim, J. Miele, and S. Follmer (2019), "ShapeCAD: An Accessible 3D Modelling Workflow for the Blind and Visually-Impaired Via 2.5D Shape Displays," in *The 21st International ACM SIGACCESS Conference on Computers and Accessibility (ASSETS*

'19), 342–54, New York, NY, USA: Association for Computing Machinery. DOI:https://doi.org/10.1145/3308561.3353782.

Slegers, K., K. Kouwenberg, T. Loučova, and R. Daniels (2020), "Makers in Healthcare: The Role of Occupational Therapists in the Design of DIY Assistive Technology," in *Proceedings of the 2020 CHI Conference on Human Factors in Computing Systems*, 1–11, New York, NY, USA: Association for Computing Machinery.

Tehel, A. (2019), "Do It Yourself: la fabrication numérique comme empowerment des corps handicapés?" *Terminal. Technologie de l'information, culture & société*, 125–6. Available online: http://journals.openedition.org/terminal/4967.

Torrey, C., D. W. McDonald, B.N. Schilit, and S. Bly (2007), "How-To Pages: Informal Systems of Expertise Sharing," in *ECSCW 2007*, 391–410, London: Springer.

Turner, F. (2018), "Millenarian Tinkering: The Puritan Roots of the Maker Movement," *Technology and Culture* 59 (4): S160–82.

Walter, M. (2016), "Hackaday Prize Entry: Open-Source Myoelectric Hand Prosthesis," *Hackaday*, May 26. Available online: https://hackaday.com/2016/05/26/hackaday-prize-entry-open-source-myoelectric-hand-prosthesis/ (accessed December 2, 2021).

Williamson, B. (2019), *Accessible America: A History of Disability and Design*, New York, NY, USA: NYU Press.

Williamson, B., and E. Guffey, eds (2020), *Making Disability Modern: Design Histories*, London: Bloomsbury Publishing.

World Health Organization. (2021), "First Ever Global Guide for Assistive Technology to Improve the Life of Millions," March 2. Available online: https://www.who.int/news-room/feature-stories/detail/first-ever-global-guide-for-assistive-technology-to-improve-the-life-of-millions.

Worsley, M., and D. Bar-El (2020), "Inclusive Making: Designing Tools and Experiences to Promote Accessibility and Redefine Making," *Computer Science Education*, 1–33. Available online: https://www.tandfonline.com/doi/full/10.1080/08993408.2020.1863705.

Project References

Adaptive Design: adaptivedesign.org
BOOST, a program of Born Just Right: boostxbjr.org/about
Careables: careables.org
E-Fabrik: efabrik.fr/parcours
e-NABLE: enablingthefuture.org/about
Fablife/Papas bricoleurs et mamans astucieuses: fondationleroymerlin.fr/realisations/32-actualites
Fixperts: fixing.education/fixperts
Ikea This Ables: thisables.com/en/new-developments
Limbforge has merged with Victoria Hand Project: victoriahandproject.com/history-timeline
Makers Making Change: makersmakingchange.com
Match My Maker: matchmymaker.de

My Human Kit/Human Lab: myhumankit.org/le-humanlab

New York Public Library program: https://www.nypl.org/about/locations/heiskell/ dimensions

Open Hand Project, which became Open Bionics: openhandproject.org, openbionics.com

Project Unicorn: jordanreeves.com/project-unicorn

Case Study

11 Shaping Inclusive and Equitable Makerspaces

KATHERINE M. STEELE

Examining Makerspaces

Figure 10 Students offer input on making makerspaces more accessible to people with disabilities. Courtesy Dennis Wise / University of Washington.

bespoke: made for a particular customer or user

Makerspaces are often used to help build new assistive technology and increase accessibility; however, many of these spaces and tools remain inaccessible. We need to make sure disabled people can access these spaces and create the products and designs that they actually want.

—DO-IT Scholar

To enable user-initiated design or design for one, we must consider creating equity through our design spaces—the physical spaces, digital tools, and communities within which we build and create. There is a deep history of examples to learn from, like New York University's shop that provided a place to build and make for the Second World War Veterans (see Chapter 7) to today's online communities like e-NABLE that are challenging the status quo of prosthetic design and provision (see Chapter 10). This kind of equitable making requires flexible, inclusive spaces with supportive communities.

These communities have been dedicated to the iterative process of learning, adapting, and re-creating. Making their culture as they make within their spaces. Part of the power of these spaces is this iterative process. Having the grace and humility as a community to know that the space can never be "done" and rather should and will adapt and change with the community. A bespoke, iterative process.

It is a process I have also witnessed and participated in numerous times during my career. From navigating access to old machine shops to imagining the design of new makerspaces. Entering the door of each new space and considering, what does this space say about who can build? Who can create?

As one example, makerspaces have been created in many communities over the past two decades—in schools, libraries, and garages. These spaces have accelerated the access to fabrication tools and created communities of DIY innovators (Morocz et al. 2015; Taylor et al. 2016). In 2015, I partnered with our community at the University of Washington makerspaces to evaluate and improve the accessibility of a makerspace for people with disabilities. Working with campus community members and a team of DO-IT Scholars (Disability, Opportunity, Internetworking, and Technology—a program that prepares high school students with disabilities for success in college and careers), we examined the space, participated in design activities, and reimagined inclusive options for making (Steele et al. 2018). Through these activities we identified many exciting possibilities and tensions which shape how we improve access and support equity through bespoke design.

The Equitable Makerspace

Entering a makerspace often makes you feel like a kid in a candy shop—so many new tools, things to learn, and opportunities to create. Ideas for engaging and making bespoke creations flowed as the students explored the space. However, we quickly realized that many of the tools and equipment were not accessible or inclusive to many people in our group. Many tools, from computer-aided design software to electronics to 3D-printing, present persistent barriers. These barriers represent opportunities for bespoke making to accelerate innovation.

As happens in any community endeavor, we also identified tensions between individuals. When brainstorming solutions, we often faced apparently opposing opinions. For example, the students who use power wheelchairs loved how many of the tools and tables were on wheels. This allowed them to easily push items and reconfigure the space. However, the students in our group who are blind found this frustrating. As they created mental maps of the space, knowing that tools and tables could be in different spaces each time they entered the space made them wary of engaging.

While tensions often feel like insurmountable or frustrating barriers—arguments often made in opposition to the utility of universal or inclusive designs—they highlight opportunities for adaptability and innovation that can benefit all users of a maker-space. Being in a space, trying new things, grappling with the tensions, as well as building community through these experiences is part of bespoke making. In this case, it led to some simple changes and rules: textured tape on the floor could be used to identify walkways to the home location of key tools and equipment, improving the overall flow and usability of the space.

The equipment, training materials, and space itself all offer opportunities for bespoke making and innovation to increase inclusion and access. If viewed as just "accommodations" for specific users, we can miss the chance for identifying opportunities for innovation and reconsidering our design processes. We have found similar observations in every space we have investigated from machine shops to engineering labs to electronic workbenches. We have developed basic guidelines, checklists, and ideas to support access and inclusion in these spaces (DO-IT 2021). I view these resources as working documents, representing opportunities for innovation and needs for bespoke making.

Makerspaces are about community. We need to ensure everyone from the community can participate.

—DO-IT Scholar

Examining Making

There is enormous potential in creating equity through bespoke design. The potential for the objects that we interact with every day to be custom-fit to ones' body. To adapt, learn, and change with us over the course of each day, and across our life span. If done with intention, this potential represents an intriguing frontier (Campbell 2003). Why must our clothes, our smartphones, our chairs be based on some artificial "population-based" measure that ends up fitting no one and compromising each body?

In addition to designing the methods for bespoke design, we must also examine who is creating, or allowed to create (Eason 1995). If bespoke designs arise solely from traditional design teams, there is a risk that simplifying assumptions and norms about the "average" user will remain, built into the infrastructure and market research (Colusso et al. 2019; Frontiers 2021). Without examining bespoke making—customizing the processes and methods for creating bespoke designs—we risk fumbling the enormous potential, or even building exclusionary barriers.

As a mechanical engineer, I often think about—and honestly, am intimidated by—the daunting challenges of bespoke making. Especially when considering the current practices for fabrication and design. The tools and machines we often use to shape and form our creations require significant training and can pose safety concerns to every body.

I often quip to computer scientists that software is easy but *hard*ware is hard. In the digital realm, I see clear pathways and affordances that can enable ability-based making (Wobbrock et al. 2011). Digital assistance—from 3D printers to computer numerical control milling machines—provide a link between adaptable digital interfaces and physical making (Bennett et al. 2019; Bosse et al. 2020; Buehler et al. 2014), but there are still many tools that currently do not offer such affordances. While physical tools and machinery may offer challenges for innovation, these challenges do not give us the excuse to create one-size-fits-all technology, devices, or environments. Beyond the need for education, training, and practice, I do not want different classes of tools or machines to exist based strictly upon one's body. Bespoke making is asking how can we ensure that our making ecosystem—from our homes to our makerspaces to our machine shops—can enable each user?

Examining Makers

While we have focused thus far on the physical spaces and tools that enable bespoke design, there is still the question of who is making? People with disabilities are underrepresented in the workforce. In engineering, less than 10 percent of undergraduate students identify as having a disability, with even fewer in the workforce (National Center for Education Statistics 2015; National Science Foundation 2017). To leverage the innovation of bespoke and user-initiated design, we must ensure our makerspaces, labs, educational programs, and tools are open and inclusive, and be more discerning as we evaluate the hardware that comes out of them (Bennett and Rosner 2019; Hurst and Tobias 2011; Ladner 2014).

We need to build the pipelines to support and encourage people with disabilities to pursue careers in engineering, design, and related fields. In our work with the University of Washington makerspace, while we were examining the space and offering recommendations, we were designing activities to also hopefully spark an interest in engineering and design among the high school students. Not that we can claim that these small activities influenced their career choices but we have seen multiple of the DO-IT Scholars who participated go on to complete STEM degrees.

We hope that they will continue to identify as makers and creators—building the processes, tools, and products to support their own goals through bespoke design. Bespoke design can spur innovation and create new frameworks for *who* can design and *how* we evaluate impact, creating ripple effects with each creation.

References

Bennett, C. L., A. Stangl, A. F. Siu, and J. A. Miele (2019), "Making Nonvisually: Lessons from the Field," in *21st Int ACM SIGACCESS Conf Comput Access*, 279–85, New York, NY, USA: Association for Computing Machinery. Available online: http://doi.org/10.1145/3308561.3355619.

Bennett, C. L., and D. K. Rosner (2019), "The Promise of Empathy: Design, Disability, and Knowing the 'Other.'," in *Proc 2019 CHI Conf Hum Factors Comput Syst*, 1–13, Glasgow, Scotland, UK: ACM. Available online: https://dl.acm.org/doi/10.1145/3290605.3300528.

Bosse, I. K., and B. Pelka (2020), "Peer Production by Persons with Disabilities—Opening 3D-Printing Aids to Everybody in an Inclusive MakerSpace," *J Enabling Technol*. Emerald Publishing Limited; 2020 Jan 1; 14 (1): 41–53.

Buehler, E., A. Hurst, and M. Hofmann (2014), "Coming to Grips: 3D Printing for Accessibility," in *Proceedings for the 16th International ACM SIGACCESS Conf Comput Access*, 291–2, New York, NY, USA: Association for Computing Machinery. Available online: http://doi.org/10.1145/2661334.2661345.

Campbell, R. I., R. J. Hague, B. Ener, and P. W. Wormald (2003), "The Potential for the Bespoke Industrial Designer," *Des J* Routledge; Nov 1, 2003 6 (3): 24–34.

Colusso, L., C. L. Bennett, P. Gabriel, and D. K. Rosner (2019) "Design and Diversity? Speculations on What Could Go Wrong," in *Proceedings 2019 Design Interactive System Conference*, 1405–13, New York, NY, USA: Association for Computing Machinery. Available online: http://doi.org/10.1145/3322276.3323690.

DO-IT. (2021), "Resources," Available online: https://www.washington.edu/doit/programs/accessengineering/resources (accessed 05/2021).

Eason, K. D. (1995), "User-Centred Design: For Users or by Users?" *Ergonomics* 38 (8): 1667–73.

"Frontiers | DIY Health and Wellbeing: The Hackers and Makers Outpacing Manufacturers and Researchers [Internet]," [cited May 27, 2021]. Available online: https://www-frontiersin-org.offcampus.lib.washington.edu/10.3389/conf.FPUBH.2016.01.00080/event_abstract.

Hurst, A., and J. Tobias (2011), "Empowering Individuals with Do-It-Yourself Assistive Technology," in *Proc 13th Int ACM SIGACCESS Conf Comput Access*, 11–18, New York, NY, USA: Association for Computing Machinery. Available online: http://doi.org/10.1145/2049536.2049541.

Ladner, R. (2014), "Design for User Empowerment," in *CHI 14 Ext Abstr Hum Factors Comput Syst*, 5–6, New York, NY, USA: Association for Computing Machinery. Available online: http://doi.org/10.1145/2559206.2580090.

Morocz, R., B. D. Levy, C. R. Forest, R. L. Nagel, W. C. Newstetter, K. G. Talley, and J. S. Linsey (2015), "University Maker Spaces: Discovery, Optimization and Measurement of Impacts," Georgia Institute of Technology; 2015 June [cited May 27, 2021]; Available online: https://smartech.gatech.edu/handle/1853/53812.

National Center for Education Statistics. (2015), "Digest of Education Statistics," Available online: https://nces.ed.gov/programs/digest/d15/tables/dt15_311.10.asp.

National Science Foundation. (2017), "Women, Minorities, and Persons with Disabilities in Science and Engineering," Last modified January 2017. Available online: https://www.nsf.gov/statistics/2017/nsf17310/.

Steele, K., B. Blaser, and M. Cakmak (2018), "Accessible Making: Designing Makerspaces for Accessibility," *Int J Des Learn. Association for Educational Communications & Technology* 9 (1): 114–21.

Taylor, N., U. Hurley, and P. Connolly (2016), "Making Community: The Wider Role of Makerspaces in Public Life," in *Proceedings 2016 CHI Conf Hum Factors Comput Syst*, 1415–25, New York, NY, USA: Association for Computing Machinery. Available online: http://doi.org/10.1145/2858036.2858073.

Wobbrock, J. O., S. K. Kane, K. Z. Gajos, S. Harada, and J. Froehlich (2011), "Ability-Based Design: Concept, Principles and Examples," *ACM Trans Access Comput* 3 (3): 9: 1–9:27.

Case Study

12 A Study of Skilled Craftwork among Blind Fiber Artists

MAITRAYE DAS, KATYA BORGOS-RODRIGUEZ, ANNE MARIE PIPER

Figure 11 Helen, a blind fiber artist, working on a tote bag with blue and black yarns, c. 2019. Photo courtesy of Maitraye Das.

Helen is a blind fiber artist who works at a communal weaving studio in Chicago. The studio—which is located within a residential community for people who are blind or visually impaired—is filled with looms of varying sizes, neatly organized shelves packed with colorful yarns, and bins containing an assortment of other weaving materials. Throughout her ten years weaving, Helen has created a wide range of products including table runners, dishcloths, white cane holders, purses, and more. In the weaving studio, she joins other blind weavers who come together every week to work on personal and communal projects. One afternoon, we observed Helen working on a full-sized floor loom to create a tote bag with black and blue yarns. Her choreographed hand movements sent the shuttle (i.e., a carrier device for yarns) from one hand on one side of the loom to the other hand poised waiting on the opposite side. Helen skillfully sensed the sound of the wooden beater as she pushed it against the woven fabric, forming a rhythmic pattern as she worked and signaling the end of a sequence. She periodically laid a hand on the array of yarns to check whether the fibers were under appropriate tension and thus composing a cloth of uniform density.

These embodied interactions, grounded in tactile and acoustic sensations, form an accessible language for making and design. Yet, weaving is a complex practice of making that can take years to master. In the most basic sense, weaving involves two sets of yarns or threads that are interlaced at right angles to form a cloth. The longitudinal threads are called the warp and the lateral threads are the weft. The warp threads are held stationary in tension on the loom, while the transverse weft thread is drawn through and inserted over and under the warp. The process of weaving involves deciding upon an arrangement of yarns and patterns for a project, tracking placement of yarns as they are woven together, detecting possible mistakes in the woven fabric, and maintaining awareness of the state of the entire loom system. Weavers also engage in a form of algorithmic thinking as they systematically interlace yarns and repeat and vary numerical sequences of patterns. Thus, studies of weaving help understand the foundations of early computing and expose nondominant narratives of making and engineering (Rosner et al. 2018).

This case study details a community-based weaving studio for blind artists as a rich site of learning, making, and skilled practice.[1] Our case study is grounded in long-term participant observations as volunteers in the community weaving studio coupled with contextual interviews with these weavers and their sighted instructors. Our ethnographic approach is an attempt to come alongside these individuals and be with this community (Bennett and Rosner 2019), although we bring with us inherent power differentials as researchers, engineers, designers, and sighted people. Over the course of our field work, we worked alongside nineteen weavers, all of whom were legally blind, ranging from partial vision loss to total blindness due to a variety of conditions (e.g., glaucoma, optic nerve atrophy, diabetic retinopathy, nystagmus, and retina detachment). These weavers had varying levels of experience in the studio, ranging from three months to fifteen years. We also worked alongside three sighted instructors who had been working with residents in the studio for seven months to twelve years. Our own analytic views align with the philosophy of our field site, which aims to foster individual potentials and autonomy, as well as feminist disability scholarship.

The weaving studio is located within an assisted living facility for people who are blind or visually impaired. While all community residents are visually impaired, the vast majority also have chronic health conditions (e.g., hearing, cognitive, or motor impairments, cancer, and diabetes) and are low income. The studio is open four or five days a week, typically with two, two-hour working sessions per day. Community residents work alongside volunteers in the studio. The residents work on various weaving projects such as rugs, coasters, dish towels, tote bags, bookmarks, baby blankets, belts, and cane holders. Residents also participate in communal projects in which they work together to create tapestries or artistic rugs, which have previously been exhibited in local art centers. Their work is displayed in the studio and common spaces within the community. In accordance with an agreement between the organization and residents, residents may keep half of the products they make. They can choose to sell their products or keep them for their personal use or other purposes. The remaining products go to the organization and are sold to the general public, which helps support studio maintenance and buying tools and supplies.

To explore additional ways in which blindness and fiber arts can be experienced, weavers at the studio have produced "braille weaving" through which they embedded custom messages and meanings into the woven fabric. As the name of this technique suggests, "braille weaving" involves six distinct pieces of yarn, each with unique shapes or textures, which represent the six dots in a braille[2] character. Paul described this technique saying, "it's like you are pumping braille in a braille writer, but you're not. You're pumping it in the yarn." Weavers also regularly participate in community-wide projects, where they collaboratively create pieces that revolve around a particular theme. For example, in a project that involved sound, weavers added materials such as bells, tissue paper, bottle caps, guitar strings, and beads into a large cloth. Another piece that resulted from this collaboration was a purse with a pair of earbuds integrated into it, which were playing a recording of the weaver interacting with the loom components as they worked on the bag. Resulting artifacts are displayed in public exhibitions within the community and broader Chicagoland area.

This case of making not only illustrates how artifacts imbue disabled experiences but also surfaces how the very nature of this work is intertwined with societal expectations of disability, productivity, and value. While some weavers explained that they derived pleasure from their work, calling it a "fun" and "relaxing" experience, others turn to their work as a way to "keep the mind occupied" and distracted from stressful events in their personal lives. Lisa said, "I've gotten addicted to weaving, actually. What I'm weaving, it's my relaxation." Opening up about how weaving has helped him through difficult situations, Roy explained, "Because when you come and you've got something on your mind that's really heavy, then you come to weaving, weaving has helped to release it and move forward." Another weaver said of the studio, "This is the only place where I feel I belong." Others described how weaving motivated them to step out of their homes and "heal." Emma said, "It's like a workshop. For me, it's something … just to do and not stay in the room all day … It's hard, getting back into things after loss. For me, it's a good way to get back to where I was, but at the same time, in a new direction."

The physical act of making is a source of satisfaction and has value. Jim shared, "I get a kick out of using my hands, so this is something new and I like it because I can do it." Jen indicated that she enjoys "seeing how the product comes into being. And then that I can make something that I can use or somebody else could use." In addition to seeing how products emerge from their own hand work, weavers describe value in being able to gift their work to others. Jim said that it "makes me feel good" to see family members using the products he makes. Residents described personalizing aspects of their products (e.g., choosing yarn in accordance with the recipients' favorite colors). Lisa explained, "When I give something, I want that person to not only appreciate what's in my hand, but I think a piece of my soul ..." By gifting their work to meaningful individuals or someone in need, residents show care toward others. Gifting their work allows participation in a reciprocal relationship with others and helps shift power dynamics from receiving to giving support. That is, the act of gifting their work pushes back against the common frame of disabled people as being in a continual state of needing care.

In addition to gifting, the commodification of their products is particularly meaningful. Many of the weavers who work in the studio live on limited income and have multiple chronic conditions that prevent them from participating in other forms of employment. Receiving profits from a sold product can be a significant and important source of income for these weavers. Adam explained that the best part of weaving is "making the money. We get like half of what we sell. And the other half, they get to pay for the loom and the fabric." Some residents advertise their products to other people within their networks (e.g., through social media). Bill described selling his work on Facebook. "I try to sell all my work ... I've made well over $200 selling my scarves and hats," he said.

Weavers also described how their work can lead to broader societal recognition of their abilities and existence as a community. Helen explained that their work shows that people with vision impairments "are still able to do things ... Old, young, or middle-aged, that we're still able to learn new things to do, and to sell." Emma stated that public recognition of their work "will help communicate to people that we're not throwaways, we're not just helpless, we have something to offer." Helen was particularly vocal about the importance of recognition of their work by those outside of their community: "I wish I could tell them on the radio, even talk to somebody on [a local radio station] to come and see the weavers here, and then other people would buy and know more about the weaving, also, from the blind ... People should know more about the visually impaired life."

Many weavers expressed enthusiasm toward community projects and wanted their work displayed to the general public. Emma said:

> For me, as a designer, it's a great way to collaborate and also to do something that is beyond just placemats ... I think it [public exhibition] definitely would bring a lot of publicity for this type of facility ... our names will be up there, and I've asked them if I could take a picture of the one section I've done ... I would like to create a website and show that off, like a visual portfolio.

In having their work recognized by a broader audience, these weavers aim to show their worth as disabled people and encourage others. Lisa said:

> My weaving is my life, and legacy, and art. I want it to get out there so other people can know that they're free as well, despite their disabilities. They might not be able to talk, but they can talk through this ... Some people have blind children, kids with down syndrome. They can come here and learn [weaving] from us. I want to pass it on.

Lisa emphasized the expressive nature of weaving as well as a desire to pass on her skills, which is part of the community ethos.

Our case study joins that of many others who call attention to issues of power and the undervalued labor of certain communities, particularly those who do manual craft or handwork. Narrating undervalued stories of design and making, as we aim to do here, may be one way of broadening who is considered a maker and dismantling the elite status of design. Bennett, Peil, and Rosner caution, however, that "Celebrating design stories, then, may obscure the oppression underpinning their necessity" (2019). That is, framing weaving as meaningful and empowering may miss the fact that this labor emerges *because* of one's social position, limited options for employment, and financial constraints. Tellings of weaving as therapy, a job, giving focus for one's time, enabling gift giving, and a source of financial gain all speak to the necessity of this work. At the same time, weaving may be told as a practice of resistance that surfaces imposed expectations and competencies (Jungnickel 2015). The practice of selling one's work, which is meant to be empowering, may also disempower: selling one's work is rooted in capitalist ideals of what constitutes productivity and success, reaffirming a particular social ordering. As discussions of disability and design continue, collective reflection on how disabled labor and resulting products are valued—and which stories of design are told—is essential. Stories of disability and design more broadly must be told through, not apart from, the social, political, and structural forces that work to construct disability.

Notes

1. This case study is drawn from an earlier publication by the authors: Das et al. 2020: 1–15.
2. Braille is a tactile reading-writing system where each character is represented with six dots.

References

Bennett, C. L., and D. K. Rosner (2019), "The Promise of Empathy: Design, Disability, and Knowing the 'Other'," in *Proceedings of the 2019 CHI Conference on Human Factors in Computing Systems (CHI '19)*, New York, NY, USA: Association for Computing Machinery, Article 298, 13 pages.Available online: http://dx.doi.org/10.1145/3290605.3300528.

Bennett, C. L., B. Peil, and D. K. Rosner (2019), "Biographical Prototypes: Reimagining Recognition and Disability in Design," in *Proceedings of the 2019 on Designing Interactive Systems Conference (DIS '19)*, 35–47, New York, NY: Association for Computing Machinery. Available online: https://doi.org/10.1145/3322276.3322376.

Das, M., K. Borgos-Rodriguez, and A. M. Piper (2020), "Weaving by Touch: A Case Analysis of Accessible Making," in *Proceedings of the 2020 CHI Conference on*

Human Factors in Computing Systems (CHI '20), 1–15, New York, NY: Association for Computing Machinery. Available online: https://doi.org/10.1145/3313831.3376477.

Jungnickel, K. (2015), "Sewing as a Design Method," *Interactions* 22 (6): 72–5. Available online: DOI:http://dx.doi.org/10.1145/2834881.

Rosner, D. K., S. Shorey, B. R. Craft, and H. Remick (2018), "Making Core Memory: Design Inquiry into Gendered Legacies of Engineering and Craftwork," in *Proceedings of the 2018 CHI Conference on Human Factors in Computing Systems (CHI '18)*, 1–13, New York, NY: Association for Computing Machinery. Available online: https://doi. org/10.1145/3173574.3174105.

Case Study

13 Toward Sensory Equity: A More Inclusive Museum Space Designed from Disability Experience

PETER-WILLEM VERMEERSCH AND ANN HEYLIGHEN

Figure 12 Multisensory museum space (from left to right): *salon* with seating alcoves, *route* from the salon side with tactile guideline and dimmed lighting, tactile guideline detail, *route* from the bridge side. © Peter-Willem Vermeersch.

The Multisensory Museum presents a redesign for an art exhibition space at the Van Abbemuseum in Eindhoven, the Netherlands. Situated at the interface of research and practice in architecture, the project seeks to socially innovate the latter by developing a co-design method that engages people with disability experience and architects together (Heylighen et al. 2016). The result was meant to be an enticing space that draws the museum visitor in through all the senses (sound, touch, smell, vision, motion), giving architectural expression to inclusion and dialogue, and thus providing a new way of experiencing a museum visit. While the installation had multiple aims, one significant goal was to suggest how inclusive design might de-emphasize ideas of universality; instead it demonstrated how recognizing multiple needs and values through co-design can make for more equitable and just ambitions (Bianchin and Heylighen 2018).

In order to achieve this kind of equity, we posit that setting up co-design as a dialogue between designers and people with disability experience can inspire inclusive architecture with atmospheric aesthetics. Establishing co-design as a dialogue means gaining a mutual understanding of each other's experiences, which can be personal (from daily activities), theoretical (from academic research), or professional (from developed skill). Based in the context of architecture, the dialogue includes talk, gesture, and spatial representation. Throughout, the goal is to reach a creative exchange (Sanders and Stappers 2008) that results in a joint architectural concept that can be further developed in subsequent design activities. The dialogue provides insight into the how and why behind the concept, beyond knowledge in codes and guidelines. Such insight is crucial for designers to refine a concept into built space (Gray et al. 2003), moving through multiple dimensions of form, shape, material selection, construction detailing.

The theoretical basis for the project starts from a cultural model of disability, acknowledging the critiquing power of disability experience (Devlieger et al. 2003). This power has been investigated in relation to a visual bias in architecture (Dischinger 2006) and its design processes (Vermeersch and Heylighen 2013, 2021), which can potentially be overcome through involving people with a vision impairment as user/experts (Ostroff 1997). Involving people with different impairments and diverse experiences in building analysis has further consolidated this framework (Vermeersch and Heylighen 2015). In co-designing the museum space at Van Abbe, we eventually involved people with expertise and personal experiences with mobility, vision, and hearing impairment.

The co-design process at the Van Abbemuseum was organized around multiple sessions that were specifically structured to gain an understanding of each other's knowledge and experiences, and to go through some creative aspects of the design process, such as brainstorming and concept formulation. The ambition was to value user/experts' knowledge more or less equally as the architect's, with a focus on spatial experience. The architect provided skills in representation of form and spatial qualities to guide user/experts in expressing spatial experiences and interventions. All sessions aimed at dialogue, but were organized so that the lead was sometimes taken by the user/experts (e.g., during brainstorming) and sometimes by the designer (e.g., during concept formulation).[1]

The location for the design was a corridor on the museum's top floor that connects the elevator and a bridge through the atrium toward one of the main exhibition spaces. One side of the corridor was a dead end that looks out over the same atrium.

With the resulting concept, the user/experts and architect proposed a museum space with a clear identity and impact on art experience. The proposal divided the existing corridor into two distinct zones: the salon was intended as a resting point within the museum trajectory, while the route was meant to support motion. This division supported several key points:

- The *salon* would be an acoustically soft space, unlike the otherwise reverberating museum space. A sculptural acoustic damper was mounted on the window onto the atrium. Sound penetration was reduced, and signaled to the rest of the museum that something special was going on up there. The art was intended to be experienced from a seated position. The walls guided visitors toward seating alcoves which were positioned to turn people slightly toward each other, and around the artwork in a circle. Visitors using a wheelchair could complete the circle from their position coming from the corridor.

- The *route* would guide visitors into a specific path. This space did not allow two people to pass each other comfortably, thus encouraging people to keep moving and discouraging them to linger.

- On the *bridge* a second railing was mounted on top of the existing (closed) railing. At the underside a mirror was mounted, so that people in a seated position, or shorter persons could view the atrium through the mirror and over the railing. From the topside the mirror was concealed from view.

Based on the gained understanding of the user/experts' experiences, the concept from the co-design sessions, the deconstruction of its inclusive character, and the multisensory ambitions of the museum (in terms of art experience) and the architect (in terms of spatial experience), the concept was further developed into an architectural design. For this, a second architect joined the architect who organized the co-design workshops.

Investigations of a potential materiality and formalistic expression developed into an organic language based on a play between concave and convex shapes, loam plaster with multiple types of textures (both soft and rough), felt, and smell distributions. The place engaged with the different sensory systems to achieve corporeal awareness (Pallasmaa 2005). A dimmed lighting heightened the attention for the other senses. The bulbous walls in the *route* created shadow gradients and a softer acoustic aesthetic experience. The flowing guidelines made in smooth loam plaster were comfortable to the touch and accentuated the fluency of the body's motion through space. A smell designed for the *route* was distributed to engage with memories of past museum visits. In the *salon*, the walls moved from concave to convex to create a sheltering aesthetics and a restful place to start a dialogue with the artwork itself and its haptic representation. The felt alcoves focused the acoustics toward the seated visitor as a space of introspection. A second designed smell distributed here relates to the artwork and added an olfactory layer of aesthetics to its experience.

Following the co-design process, we discussed how multiple understandings of inclusion rose during the sessions and were present in the initial concept (Vermeersch et al. 2018). After the final implementation, we come back to our initial analysis:

- Inclusion as accessibility. Accessibility as a functional component of inclusion remains important (Heylighen et al. 2017). The final design tries to take up the issues raised in the workshops—which already surpassed accessibility norms—in a more integrated way. The chosen materiality and forms still allow for tactile guidance, turning circles, comfortable seating, and acoustic absorption.

- Inclusion as equality or exclusivity. Bianchin and Heylighen (2018) propose a way out of an apparent paradox in inclusive design by moving from a universal ambition toward a just ambition. The user/experts' intentions to nudge visitors to more equal experiences (all are invited to a seated vantage point to experience the artwork) or illustrate feelings of exclusion through equally exclusive solutions (the mirror in the atrium is only meaningful from a lower vantage point) explicitly accept that universality cannot be achieved and convey this message in an inviting way.

- Inclusion as identity. The ambition of the participants was to be explicit about the inclusive character of the design. By designing for multiple experiences, groups of people can identify with (parts of) the design. Implementing haptics in meaningful ways relates to vision-impaired people's experiences more closely, but can be appreciated by others as well. This translated in the final design as a design attitude to investigate how to integrate these meanings (Perez Liebergosell, Vermeersch and Heylighen, Ch 2) (e.g., selecting a haptically comfortable finish for the wheelchair inspired *route*), or tie them in with the main architectural language, when the 3D touch model is placed in a wheelchair accessible alcove.

- Inclusion as dialogue. It is the express hope of the user/experts that the design elements expressing identity form a basis for dialogue, operationalizing the cultural model of disability (Devlieger and Froyen 2006). For instance, the seating alcoves were carefully designed to provide good conditions for communication, both verbally (acoustic absorbing material, and acoustically focusing elliptic walls) and through sign language or lip reading (extra lighting); and supplemented with one alcove fit for standing persons and persons using a wheelchair.

- Inclusion as empathy. If empathy is understood as the sharing of an affect (Stueber 2018) with an important role for the body (Finlay 2005), this design potentially supports gaining empathy for each other. The built environment that the design provides does support dialogue not only linguistically but also materially by allowing visitors to be affected by the space (Latour 2004) and sharing that experience, specifically for those design elements that diverse people identify with.

To conclude, the project departed from an inclusive co-design process, and illustrates, through the inclusive qualities of the process as well as of the design, how the cultural model of disability can be applied to architectural design. The diverse experiential knowledge adds both to the architectural expression and the inclusive character of the design. By attempting to reach sensory equity through an inclusive/ exclusive dialectic in the design, the intention is to invite a dialogue to gain proper mutual understanding.

In video testimonials after the co-design sessions, the involved user/experts appreciated the genuine dialogue in that they felt heard, but even so that they gained a more profound understanding of professional design practice, and concerns of architects. Furthermore, being involved in a project with multiple groups raised their awareness of others' experiences and concerns. Ultimately, the design process and finished space were each important in different ways. Reflecting on the final built space, one of the user/experts with a mobility impairment noted how *"The design has undergone a substantial change after the [codesign] workshops, but I still recognize what we put forward."* Indeed, the final result was still quite familiar. In the end, she noted, it was not only familiar, it also *"feels like coming home."*[2]

Acknowledgments

We thank all the user/experts for their knowledge, time, and energy. Others involved: Jeandonné Schijlen (project initiation), Daniel Neugebauer (funding application), Marleen Hartjes (inclusive museum working), and Tomas Dirrix (architect final development). The project received funding from the European Research Council (grant nr. 335002), KU Leuven Industrial Research Fund (grant nr. HB/14/001), and Creative Industries Fund NL (grant nr. 16AC/031/02).

Notes

1. See Vermeersch et al. (2018) for a more detailed description of the process.
2. This observation was made by a participant at the symposium organized by the Van Abbemuseum in February 2019 which attracted an international public, people working at museums; academics in the field of museum studies, disability studies, and architecture; people with disability experience; and also workers for disability organizations. As part of the symposium, we visited the space for the first time with some of the user/experts that were involved in the co-design, and noted some of their observations. For more information on the presentations, see https://vanabbemuseum.nl/en/programme/programme/symposium-multisensory-museum/.

References

Devlieger, P., and H. Froyen (2006), "Blindness/City: A Disability Dialectic," in P. Devlieger, F. Renders, H. Froyen., and K. Wildiers (eds), *Blindness and the Multi-sensory City*, 17–38, Antwerpen: Garant.

Devlieger, P., F. Rusch, and D. Pfeiffer, eds (2003), *Rethinking Disability*, Antwerp: Garant.

Dischinger, M. (2006), "The Non-careful Sight," in P. Devlieger. et al. (eds), *Blindness and the Multi-sensory City*, 143–76, Antwerp: Garant.

Finlay, L. (2005), "'Reflexive Embodied Empathy:' A Phenomenology of Participant-researcher Intersubjectivity," *The Humanistic Psychologist* 33 (4): 271–92.

Gray, D. B., M. Gould, and J. E. Bickenbach (2003), "Environmental Barriers and Disability," *Journal of Architectural and Planning Research* 20 (1): 29–37.

Heylighen, A., and M. Bianchin (2018), "Building Justice: How to Overcome the Inclusive Design Paradox?," *Built Environment* 44 (1): 23–35.

Heylighen, A., J. Schijlen, V. Van der Linden, D. Meulenijzer, and P. Vermeersch (2016), "Socially Innovating Architectural Design Practice by Mobilizing Disability Experience," *Architectural Engineering and Design Management* 12 (4): 253–65.

Heylighen, A., V. Van der Linden, and I. Van Steenwinkel (2017), "Ten Questions Concerning Inclusive Design of the Built Environment," *Building and Environment* 114: 507–17.

Latour, B. (2004), "How to Talk about the Body? The Normative Dimension of Science Studies," *Body Society* 10 (2/3): 205–29.

Ostroff, E. (1997), "Mining Our Natural Resources," *Innovation* 16 (1): 33–5.

Pallasmaa, J. (2005), *The Eyes of the Skin*, UK: John Wiley.

Pérez-Liebergesell, N., P.W. Vermeersch, and A. Heylighen (forthcoming), "Fixing Meets Expressing: Design by Designers with Disability Experience," in E. Guffey (ed.), *After Universal Design: The Disability Design Revolution*, 35–49, London: Bloomsbury.

Sanders, E. B. N., and P. J. Stappers (2008), "Co-creation and the New Landscapes of Design," *CoDesign* 4 (1): 5–18.

Stueber, K. (2018), "Empathy," in E. N. Zalta (ed.), *The Stanford Encyclopedia of Philosophy,* spring edn, Stanford: Metaphysics Research Lab, Stanford University. Available online: https://plato.stanford.edu/entries/empathy/ (accessed June 30, 2021).

Vermeersch, P. W., J. Schijlen, and A. Heylighen (2018), "Designing from Disability Experience: Space for Multi-sensoriality," in *Proceedings of the 15th Participatory Design Conference: Short Papers, Situated Actions, Workshops and Tutorial-Volume 2*: 1–5.

Vermeersch, P. W., and A. Heylighen, sup. (2013), *"Less Vision, More Senses. Towards a More Multisensory Design Approach in Architecture,"* PhD diss, KU Leuven, Leuven.

Vermeersch, P. W., and A. Heylighen (2015), "Mobilizing Disability Experience to Inform Architectural Practice," *Journal of Research Practice* 11 (2): Article M3.

Vermeersch, P. W., and A. Heylighen (2021), "Involving Blind User/Experts in Architectural Design: Conception and Use of More-than-Visual Design Artifacts," *CoDesign* 17 (1): 50–69.

Case Study

14 The Politics of Friction: Designing a Sex Toy for Every Body

DAVID SERLIN

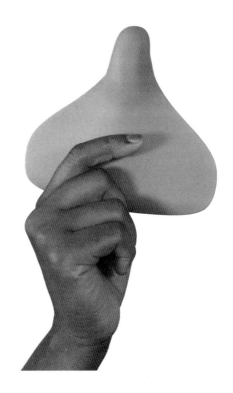

Figure 13 The Enby 2, released in 2021 in pastel blue. Image courtesy of Nick Boyajian and published with permission.

Some forms of sexual pleasure fly under the radar. They stand—or sit, or lay—outside of recognizable conventions of physical intimacy because they do not coalesce around practices attributable to what scholars like Lenore Tiefer call sexual scripts: the focus on penetration, for instance, or the achievement of orgasm.[1] Like the practice of frottage, or erotic touch, or other types of self or mutual stimulation that may or may not result in orgasm, some forms of sexual pleasure are sui generis—as unique as one's fingerprint, as particular as one's sense of smell, as subjective as what makes one ticklish.

The Enby—an alliteration of the acronym "nb" or "N/B," oft-used shorthand to communicate about people who identify as nonbinary—is a sex toy that was created to address and, in some ways, embellish forms of pleasure that exist outside of conventional sexual scripts. Designed in 2018 by engineer and entrepreneur Nick Boyajian, the Enby—now in its second edition—is sold by Wild Flower, a company established and operated in Brooklyn by Boyajian and his partner, Amy. The Enby, shaped like a retro bicycle seat or, perhaps, like a streamlined manta ray, is manufactured from a lightweight silicone and powered by a long-lasting internal battery. Soft, pliable, and comfortable to touch, the body and the "wings" of the manta ray can be twisted, scrunched, rolled, and smushed in any number of ways, directions, and orientations. Using either/both its internal vibration technology or deploying its unconventional shape, the Enby can be held by appendage or appliance, or else slipped inside clothing (such as underwear) or between bodies (such as between two stomachs) to produce a desirable friction. It can be used in tandem with familiar sexual habits but also help facilitate new forms of erotic exploration that have nothing to do with the habits circumscribed by genital- or orifice-shaped sex toys. For people who identify as nonbinary or trans or genderqueer, such a toy is more than just an ally of pleasure. It is an ally in new productions of sexual subjectivity.

We often associate the term *assistive device* with technology-based extensions of the body, such as a prosthetic or a wheelchair, that enable a user to accomplish a goal or facilitate function. Why are sex toys not included in that mix? Even at the level of their materials, sex toys are part of the same multibillion-dollar nexus of industrial production that includes assistive devices like hearing aids, prosthetic arms, portable ventilators, and medical-delivery systems via smart phone apps, all of which are made possible by synthetics like silicone and rubber, miniaturized electronic components, and the tiny batteries that power them all. In their study of the culture of the designers of sex toys, Jeffrey and Shaowen Bardzell have described objects deliberately manufactured to provide their intended customer(s) with user-centered forms of control and autonomy. For many of these designers, access to pleasure is a "birthright" akin to access to education or voting (Bardzell 2011) And yet, despite this emphatic call to pleasure through a democratic ethos of access (and vice versa), the pairing of the phrases "sex toys" and "assistive devices" still remains for many a nonstarter, like siblings separated at birth who share the same DNA but no language to communicate with one another.

The Enby's intended goal forges a common bond between sex toys and assistive devices and all the possible hybrid permutations endowed by those terms. By avoiding a representative shape like that of a phallus or vagina, for example, the Enby addresses nonbinary expressions of gender and sexuality that may well be "sexual" in a conventional sense but which exceed our language for what constitutes "sexual" since they may bear no relationship to conventional codes of gender.[2] In original advertisements for the Enby in 2019, for instance, the device was presented in proximity to gender-neutral images of stomachs and thighs but never to breasts or crotches; hands feature tapered fingers with black nail varnish and silver Goth jewelry, an aesthetic which was carried over into the two colors in which the Enby was first available, *ash* (dark gray) and *plum* (dark purplish-brown). These were colors that not only eschewed gender coding but, like fetish or bondage gear, had no ambition to realism. The Enby 2 is now available in a single color—a nearly nostalgic midcentury pastel blue—that is certainly less edgy than the original Goth tones but still maintains a distinction from sex toys in garish colors like patent-leather black and hen-party pink.

Boyajian explains that the Enby 2's color choice was an attempt at being "brighter and happier" at the height of the global pandemic while also trying to maintain the product's unique gender-resistant identity (Boyajian 2021). But Boyajian's approach to color, like other material aspects of the Enby, challenges not only binaries of gender but other types of either/or binaries that are presumptively embedded in conventional sex toy design. Loosely associated with the global "maker movement" that began to take shape in urban entrepreneurial zones in areas like Brooklyn in the late 1990s, Boyajian created the prototype for the Enby at his kitchen table, using 3D CAD software and a 3D printer to make different molds. After eventually deciding on a final version, he used these molds to cast prototypes in silicone. Boyajian then offered early iterations of the Enby to friends and colleagues who agreed to serve as test subjects. In many cases, Boyajian chose individuals whose relationship to a device used for sexual pleasure was inherently complex: some identified as nonbinary, of course, whereas others identified as gender-normative but sexually queer, and still others identified as physically or cognitively disabled but publicly recognized as cisgender and heteronormative. the Enby clearly taps into the gestalt of the current moment by designing for incipient communities of potential users across a wide spectrum of physical and social needs. Boyajian acknowledged in 2020 that because he had not patented the Enby or sought out intellectual property protection for his design, there were already "three or four" knock-off versions available online. He remains sanguine about this decision, stressing its accessibility as a form of empowerment. "If people want to enjoy my design," he points out, "then more power to them" (Boyajian 2020).

Boyajian's original design for the Enby was clearly uninterested in the idea of training or expecting its user to follow or maintain any kind of physical or social script, sexual or otherwise. It intentionally eschewed either a formal shape (such as that of a phallus or vagina) or a formal orientation (such as an in-out or up-down motion). Among the initial requests from test users were a device for male-to-female trans women who wanted a comfortable toy after their surgeries, a device for a nonbinary person with a vulva who wanted to hump and grind without penetration, a device for a cisgender man with mobility impairments who wanted to stimulate his perineum, and a device for individuals and partners who identified as disabled but who had no experience with sex toys at all. The updated Enby 2 goes one step further by incorporating design elements inspired by feedback from users with physical impairments such as rheumatoid arthritis. Boyajian was able to source a flexible silicon-based material for Enby 2 with an inherent "stickiness" to it without itself being sticky that maintains its shape for people who have a difficult time holding or manipulating the toy with their hands. As with other designs intended for increased accessibility, such as the famed Oxo "good grip" can opener, the low effort option is always the popular option.

The Enby proves that pleasure should never be the exclusive domain of those who can manipulate a toy according to familiar physical routines of habitual use. As a sex toy, the Enby occupies a vibrant intersection of political and design activism that puts the user rather than the expert—be they industrial, psychological, or commercial—in charge of crafting new approaches to social interaction for which the sex toy is both a medium and a barometer. And as an assistive device, it makes possible forms of embodied sexuality that are typically rendered invisible by the privileges of ablebodiedness.

One could think of the Enby as an important descendent of interventions from the social movements of the 1960s and early 1970s that included various forms of mutual caregiving as well as equity in sexual pleasure.[3] In 1975, for example, author Sue Bregman published *Sexuality and the Spinal Cord Injured Woman*, a landmark handbook focused on disabled women's sexuality, with funding from the University of Minnesota Medical School and the US Department of Health, Education, and Welfare. Such a revolutionary approach to the sexuality of disabled women was unique in the era, though the period in question may be remembered for mainstream films like *Coming Home* (dir. Hal Ashby, 1978) or documentaries like *The Skin Horse* (dir. Nigel Evans and John Samson, 1983), better-known works that represent "raw" examples of the sexual lives of people with disabilities, regarding both their material experiences as well as their ambitions and frustrations. Through quantitative data, oral histories, and earnest line drawings, Bregman's book advocated for the untapped potential among disabled women to experience sexual pleasure. While Bregman assiduously avoids heterosexualizing her informants, most of the erotic encounters she describes, whether mutual acts with a partner or else private acts like masturbation, are orgasm-oriented. Only in one brief passage—one woman declares, "I enjoy skin against skin, feeling the full weight of my partner's body above me" even if she "cannot feel all over"—does Bregman address a form of erotic practice that may be unrecognizable as a conventional form of sexuality but which, for people with disabilities, may compete with or even replace sexual scripts focused on penetration or orgasm while also ascending to the heights of subjective sexual pleasure (9).

One can also see the Enby as part of the explosive growth of internet-based retail boutique sites that sell clothing and accessories, often by their own in-house product designers and makers, that were started or at least crowdsourced by female consumers who were disheartened by available (and male-dominated) options. This includes sex-positive feminist lifestyle brands such as Babeland (formerly known as Toys in Babeland), Dame, and Maude as well as clothing companies such as Slick Chicks, Play Out, and Urbody, whose websites feature everything from nonbinary athletic gear to side-fastening underwear. Like their feminist forbearers in the 1970s, these are companies that are seeking ways to offer sexual freedom and economic autonomy to people who have struggled historically to find their own needs or desires reflected in the mainstream marketplace. Importantly, however, these new products are not simply retrograde gestures that harken back to what was once called "unisex" design (e.g., jeans and T-shirts) that emerged during the gender and sexual liberation movements of the 1970s. The concept of unisex, radical in its day, was used to challenge gender hierarchies in much the same way that wheelchair ramps and curb cuts in sidewalks installed during the same era were used to promote a more inclusion vision of the built environment.

For many twenty-first-century designers and entrepreneurs, the political promise of the heyday of unisex left many design conventions (e.g., buttons and zippers) and measurement standards (e.g., increasingly diminutive sizes as an industry "norm") more or less intact, an especially disappointing result for those with differently abled or gender-noncompliant bodies. Contemporary approaches to diversity and accessibility thus call out the unisex design conventions of the 1970s: not just at the level of gender presentation and sizing but also at the level of flexible materials (e.g., elastic, spandex), tactile comfort (e.g., bamboo, mesh), sustainability and environmental responsibility (e.g., recycled goods, low water use), and a queer sensibility that resists anything that indexes gender-normative or ableist design (e.g., shoulder holsters rather than purses or messenger bags).

While the impulse to assign a singular meaning to the Enby is as seductive as the imminent ripples of pleasure potentially produced by the toy itself, any project to explicate or interpret an object like the Enby requires taking stock of its intended use as well as the histories (and futures) suggested by that use. In creating a product that is so flexible, the Enby essentially allows users to co-create experiences with an object rather than adhere to the expectations and demands of a particular object, such as that of a vibrator or a penis pump, which may be lightweight but are burdened by specific instructions and/or finite settings. And by avoiding a conventional appearance—except, perhaps, its manta ray-like shape that invokes the promise of interspecies sexuality—the Enby is both unrecognizable and also capable of creating new forms of recognition produced either subjectively by a single user or intersubjectively by two or more users. In doing so, it not only produces unique forms of pleasure but also challenges how we conceive the category of assistive devices. Like nonbinary underwear or side-fastening pants for people who use wheelchairs, the Enby is a product that illustrates how designing for every body is not merely a gesture of goodwill but an opportunity for innovation that embraces varieties of embodied experience rather than shutting them down.

Notes

1. See Tiefer 1995.
2. See "Meet the Disruptors," Authority (May 21, 2021) at https://medium.com/authority-magazine/meet-the-disruptors-nick-and-amy-boyajian-of-wild-flower-on-the-three-things-you-need-to-shake-up-9a7cf59de951 (last accessed July 26, 2021).
3. See Serlin 2012.

References

Bardzell, J., and S. Bardzell (2011), "'Pleasure Is Your Birthright': Digitally Enabled Designer Sex Toys as a Case of Third-Wave HCI." Paper Presented at Annual Conference on Computer-Human Interaction (CHI), May 7–12, 2011, Vancouver, BC, Canada.

Boyajian, N. (2020), interview by Author, January 16.

Boyajian, N. (2021), Interview by Author, October 12.

Bregman, S. (1975), *Sexuality and the Spinal Cord Injured Woman*, Minneapolis: Sister Kenny Institute.

Serlin, D. (2012), "Carney Landis and the Psychosexual Landscape of Touch in Mid-20th-Century America," *History of Psychology* 15 (3): 209–16.

Tiefer, L. (1995), *Sex is Not a Natural Act and Other Essays*, New York and London: Routledge.

Case Study

15 The Face-Based Pain Scale: A Tool for Whom?

GABI SCHAFFZIN

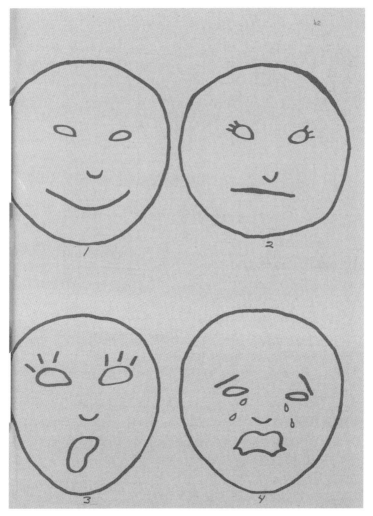

Figure 14 Bertha Alyea, "The Four Face Tool," 1978. This work is licensed under a Creative Commons Attribution-NonCommercial-NoDerivs 3.0 License.

The face-based pain scale aids in the evaluation and measurement of a patient's felt physical pain in the clinical and laboratory context. The history of face-based pain scales begins with a 1974 master's thesis by Jo Eland, "Children's Communication of Pain." Eland asked children to relate to images of a dog in varying states of pain after observing that young children are incapable of communicating their pain—both due to their own lack of vocabulary and the inability of their caretakers to properly interpret what little range of emotional expression children have. She argued that nurses were ill-equipped at the time to handle the assessment, active intervention, and evaluation of their patients' conditions. A projective instrument, wherein children could hopefully identify their own conditions in the graphically represented situations of others, could help. A few years later, in 1978, another nursing student, Bertha Alyea, used a similarly projective technique, though this time by showing patients stick-figure drawings of children with varied facial expressions. Notably, Alyea writes that the drawings she made for the tests "have no age, sex, or race—giving them universality," a condition she regards as an "advantage" (Alyea 1978).

In 1981, Donna Wong and Connie Baker launched their research into a new pediatric pain scale while both working at the Hillcrest Medical Center in Tulsa, Oklahoma. Wong, a nurse and professor in child development, and Baker, a child life specialist, felt that their patients, who were primarily pediatric burn victims, did not have an adequate tool with which to communicate the intensity of their pain. The team used stickers as rewards when working with children and noticed that many came with facial expressions. Baker eventually began asking patients to fill in blank circles with illustrations representative of the way they felt. Composites of the drawings were made for further testing before a professional illustrator was hired to produce the final product (Wong and Baker 2000).

The Wong-Baker FACES scale, the most widely used and familiar scale (Tomlinson et al. 2010), is a horizontally oriented set of cartoon faces representing varied states of affect. On the left, a broadly smiling face has wide circular eyes and arching eyebrows, suggestive of a cheerful countenance. Under the circular drawing is a zero, along with the label, "No Hurt." Looking to the right of this initial, painless figure, the smile gradually turns down to become a frown, the eyes and eyebrows drop, and eventually the figure begins to cry. The six numerals skip by two and end at ten and the labels read "Hurts Little Bit," "Hurts Little More," "Hurts Even More," "Hurts Whole Lot," and "Hurts Worst." In 1988, Wong and Baker tested their scale against five other graphic tools for pain assessment in a study with pediatric patients meant to determine the validity, reliability, and preference of each scale (FACES won in the last category; the other two were inconclusive). Just about every study introducing a new scale, Eland's work included, has attempted to prove the *validity* of that tool—that the information being collected can be considered valuable for the task at hand.[1] Further, each scale's designer chose the human face to engage with their young subjects. A face can be the site of compassion, fear, anguish, anxiety, and more. It is where we look when we need confirmation from someone we trust that everything will be alright. These nurses interacted with young faces in pain on a regular basis and then were tasked with deciding whether those faces required relief from that pain. And yet, it should be noted that the scales always relate pain back to the body, erasing the possibility that pain affect exists beyond it. In so doing, then, the scale fails to provide equity in our understanding and treatment of pain.

Virginia Jarratt uses the metaphor of "keyholder" to illustrate the immense responsibility placed on the nurse in the monitoring and care of patients, though the term extends beyond metaphor, as holding the keys to the pharmaceutical cabinet was an important part of the nurse's job starting in the latter part of the twentieth century (Jarratt 1965). Thanks to rapid corporatization in the medical field—this was the era of the rise of the HMO—intense pressure was being placed on hospital staff to become more "efficient." As such, nurses—who had to this point been primarily treated as highly dependent near-bystanders—were suddenly given a level of agency "unthinkable a decade earlier" (Malka 2007). For the nurse to make an evaluation of pain and its treatment without hesitation, however, was not simply a matter of caring for a child expediently. Hyper-specialization also was put to the service of the new health management organization systems' pervasive concerns about how to keep down costs. Efficient evaluation and treatment meant that nurses were expected to see more patients, generate more revenue, and increase income margins (Sherman 1984).

Enter, then, the face-based pain scale for children, most of which were created by nurses; women who faced pediatric patients in pain on a regular basis and at an increasingly rapid rate through the 1980s, and who, most likely inspired by the burgeoning feminist self-health movement to encourage patients to show and tell their symptoms and experiences, were also newly granted increased autonomy in diagnosis. The scales that existed to this point—primarily based on numeric or color-based measurements of intensity—were not right for these young patients who, per Eland's research, could not comprehend the concept of pain, let alone its measurement. Fed up, perhaps, by a medical industry that ignored these children's pain, perhaps even inspired by the Boston Women's Health Collective, whose *Our Bodies Ourselves* saw wide distribution and multiple updates throughout the latter years of the twentieth century, these nurses took matters into their own hands. They commissioned illustrators or photographers, applied—and were often rejected—for funding for major studies, and sought out licensing agreements to protect their work from misuse or unauthorized distribution.[2]

We might look at the origin narratives surrounding these scales and argue that it was a participatory project; not only were the *users* of the tools (the nurses) directly involved in their creation but so were the subjects being measured (pediatric patients). I wish to complicate this account, however, by questioning what sort of effect centering the goals of the measurer—in this case, universality and validity—has on the subject. Wong and Baker chose the cartoon face because "it avoids gender, age, and racial biases" (2000), but the attempt to universalize the iconography of the face in these scales is betrayed by the necessity to choose defaults for the sake of efficiency and applicability. Further, these scales reify those pain tropes which represent normative pain expression: contorting the face, furrowing the brow, tears, opening the mouth. The Wong-Baker FACES scale can problematize pain evaluation (Tomlinson et al. 2010), as subjects are being conditioned to limit their understanding of pain through a very specific visual representation of that pain (e.g., "If tears exist for a pain score of 10, and I do not cry, then I must not feel a 10").

The simple line drawings of the pain scales do little to inspire the necessarily complex narratives that accompany pain, and this benefits the caretaker or researcher who must record and either act on or move on from the pain measurement. By paring down the details on the face scale, the designer signals to the viewer that their answer should be stark as well. This in turn reinforces the efficient nature of the scales and makes them even more valuable in medical and pharmaceutical fields demanding higher throughput of their practitioners in the same decades during which the scales' use proliferated. And yet these simple line drawings can still be understood as having material implications on the ways that the pained patient is heard, trusted, and treated.

As a caregiver evaluates a subject's pain via the graphic pain scale, the patient's pain traverses a multitude of transactional points (McCosker 2012). First, the patient must feel the pain with an initiation of the pain sensation—a needle, for example, inserted through the skin. The patient grimaces, pulls away, cries, exclaims, or expresses a combination of some or none of these. Whether present at the time of injury or not, the caretaker attempts to understand the pain by looking at and listening to the patient. A graphic scale mediates this understanding and configures the caretaker's reference point. The observer acts or empathizes accordingly.

By arguing that the best way to mediate the transfer of the affective force of pain is through the image of the face, the designers of face-based scales are conditioning both the observers and subjects using the scale to concentrate on the face as the primary locus for this affect. We might extend the image of the face to represent the body in general; any patient who has been asked to walk around an examination room while the caretaker observes their gait should understand the ways that the visible demonstration of pain is privileged in the biomedical context. This, in turn, diminishes the focus on non-bodily expressions of pain, thus erasing the possibility that the individual who does not visibly grimace or limp is not, in fact, in pain. By conditioning the subject and observer to relate pain back to the body, we are erasing the possibility that pain affect exists elsewhere within these assemblages. This erasure fails to provide equity in our consideration and identification of pain.

The Wong-Baker FACES scale has been translated into over fifty languages and still sees widespread distribution. It, and other scales like it, emerged at a time when the efficiency with which a practitioner could evaluate pain for both validity and intensity was made a (profit-motivated) priority. The pain scales discussed in this chapter were designed with care in mind, but ultimately make demands of their users. The proliferation of the face-based scale came at a time when hospitals, increasingly privatizing under conglomerate healthcare providers, and under pressure from the government, prioritized speed, efficiency, and proof over what might have been an otherwise more caring governance. The faces on the scales played into this shift, conditioning our understanding of pain as present on the body, not something that might exist in an assemblage of affect and empathy, ultimately betraying the sorts of subjects who participated in their design.

Notes

1. In addition to Wong and Baker 2009, see Kuttner and LePage 1983, McGrath et al. 1984, Beyer et al. 2009, Bieri et al. 1990.
2. See, for example, Wong and Baker 2000.

References

Alyea, B. C. (1978), "Child Pain Rating after Injection Preparation," [PhD or MA?] diss., University of Missouri, Columbia, Missouri. Available online: https://mospace.umsystem.edu/xmlui/handle/10355/69121.

Baker, C. M. (2009), "Wong-Baker FACES® History—Wong-Baker FACES Foundation," 2009. Available online: http://wongbakerfaces.org/us/wong-baker-faces-history/.

Beyer, J. E., A. M. Villarruel, and M. J. Denyes (2009), "The Oucher: User's Manual and Technical Report," September 18. Available online: https://sites.nursing.upenn.edu/oucher/wp-content/uploads/sites/12/2019/07/2009_Users_Manual.pdf.

Bieri, D., R. A. Reeve, G. D. Champion, L. Addicoat, and J. B. Ziegler (1990), "The Faces Pain Scale for the Self-Assessment of the Severity of Pain Experienced by Children: Development, Initial Validation, and Preliminary Investigation for Ratio Scale Properties," *Pain* 41 (2): 139–50.

Boston Women's Health Collective (1970), *Our Bodies, Ourselves*, Boston: Boston Women's Health Collective. Available online: https://www.ourbodiesourselves.org/cms/assets/uploads/2014/04/Women-and-Their-Bodies-1970.pdf.

Eland, J. M. (1974), "Children's Communication of Pain," PhD diss., University of Iowa, Iowa City, Iowa.

Jarratt, V. (1965), "The Keeper of the Keys," *The American Journal of Nursing* 65 (7): 68–70. Available online: https://doi.org/10.2307/3453262.

Kuttner, L., and T. LePage (1983), "The Development of Pictorial Self-Report Scales of Pain and Anxiety for Children," unpublished manuscript.

Malka, S. G. (2007), *Daring to Care: American Nursing and Second-Wave Feminism*, Champaign, IL: University of Illinois Press.

McCosker, A. (2012), "Pain Sense: Nociception, Affect and the Visual Encounter," *Transformations* 22.

McGrath, P. A., L. L. de Veber, and M. T. Hearn (1984), "Multi-Dimensional Pain Assessment in Children," *PAIN*, Paper presented at Fourth World Congress on Pain of the International Association for the Study of Pain, January 18. Available online: https://doi.org/10.1016/0304-3959(84)90172-6.

Sherman, H. D. (1984), "Hospital Efficiency Measurement and Evaluation: Empirical Test of a New Technique," *Medical Care* 22 (10): 922–38.

Tomlinson, D., C. L. von Baeyer, J. N. Stinson, and L. Sung (2010), "A Systematic Review of Faces Scales for the Self-Report of Pain Intensity in Children," *Pediatrics* 126 (5): e1168–98. Available online: https://doi.org/10.1542/peds.2010-1609.

Wong, D. L., and C. M. Baker (2000), *Reference Manual for the Wong-Baker FACES Pain Rating Scale*, Oklahoma: City of Hope Pain Resource Center.

Case Study

16 Next Practice: Toward Equalities Design

NATASHA TROTMAN

Figure 15 Natasha Trotman, *Parallels*, 2018. Image courtesy of Natasha Trotman.

I consider myself a designer of equalities. My journey started with an undergraduate degree in graphic and media design, and this led me to advanced studies in information and experience design. In my practice, I have always believed that I am mining the unknown but doing this has revealed deeper inequalities; I began to realize that the design challenge was not in the data, the experiences, or the graphics alone; the real design challenge was and is the inequalities in the profession itself.

My thinking around the need to design for equity and equalities started to emerge as a consequence of the events of the 2020 pandemic and the murder of George Floyd. This was not just my observing other people's inequalities but was also a life-long experience of inequality as a neurodivergent woman from the African diaspora.

These profound and challenging realities reveal the dueling positionalities of the various aspects of design; my own lived experience and desire to begin "designing out" deficits came to the fore. How best to strike the balance to ensure the change being designed is sustainable? The pandemic and the pervasive events highlighting social and racial inequality forced the world to contend with difficult concepts and gave rise to uncomfortable questions across society, among which is: How might design address the root causes of inequality and its legacies? But some sectors were not and are not ready to redefine everything that they thought was "normal." Designers must be willing to ask fundamental questions concerning how inclusive and diverse the field truly was, is, and can be. We must be willing to consider more (inclusive) embedded sustainable solutions.

Potency and Power: Inequalities, By Design

In the 2018 UK Design Council report titled "The Design Economy," I first found evidence that confirmed what my years of experience as a Black disabled woman in the design world already suggested: UK government statistics found that only 5.1 percent of small and medium-sized businesses in the UK were led by a majority of people from an ethnic minority (2018). The Design Economy report also found that in the UK design sector 78 percent of designers identified as male and only 13 percent as from Black, Asian, and minority ethnic backgrounds.[1] This left me with the question: where are all the disabled, diverse genders, and ethnically diverse designers?

Gender

The UK's design workforce is primarily male, and the 78 percent figure far exceeds the wider workforce in the UK, which is 53 percent male in contrast. Women generally form the minority in six of the eight design subsectors focused on in the Design Council report; this is all the more significant if we bear in mind that women make up 63 percent of students studying creative arts and design at university level. The report also revealed that women were in an extremely low percentage of senior roles (2018).

Race and Ethnicity

The design sector employs a slightly higher proportion of ethnically diverse people than the wider UK economy—13 percent in comparison to 11 percent of the wider UK workforce (Design Council 2018). But again, racially diverse designers are least likely to be in senior roles, accounting for only 12 percent of all design managers.

Disability and Neurodiversity

Significantly, designers who identify as disabled and/or neurodivergent are not measured or reported in the UK Design Council's 2018 report. Disability in all its permutations has not been accounted for. More generally, the gaps between perception and lived experience have fostered the creation of well-intentioned surveys on inclusivity and the sponsoring of diversity moments with events and other efforts. However, the lived realities around race and gender, to say nothing of disability, should be acknowledged. The need for such experiences, authored by those who identify as disabled and neurodivergent designers, remains significant.

I have long wondered where a person like myself, with multiple identities and challenges, stands within these scaffolds. In *Black Feminist Thought*, sociologist Patricia Hill Collins unpacks this challenge by describing what she calls the "matrix of domination" (Collins 2000). Most initiatives only speak to a part of and not the entirety of my own experiences. These fall within the matrix of domination defined by Collins, such as being working class, neurodivergent, (racialized as) Black, and a woman. By acknowledging the dueling positionalities of people like me and encouraging them to work in the field, we can start to develop true equalities within design itself.

But, along with access, diversity, and inclusion, ableism has a place in this discussion. Indeed, activist Talia Lewis argues that ableism is "a system that places value on people's bodies and minds based on societally constructed ideas of normalcy, intelligence, excellence and productivity." Ultimately, TL argues, it is part of a series of "constructed ideas" that are all "deeply rooted in anti-Blackness, eugenics, colonialism and capitalism" (Lewis 2020). These forms of systemic oppression lead people and society to determine who is valuable and worthy based on a person's language, appearance, religion, and/or their ability to satisfactorily (re)produce, excel, and behave. You do not have to be disabled to experience ableism, but also, even if you do fall into the mainstream, you are what I would term as a temporarily abled person (TAB). Indeed, people do age and our circumstances do change. Ability and disability make up a continuum of sorts.

The social model of disability identifies systemic barriers, attitudinal barriers, and social barriers that create difficult or impossible terrain for individuals with disabilities to navigate. But systemic barriers within design extend to the larger profession and the way it is structured. In *Design Justice*, Sasha Costanza-Chock asks the reader to consider how design simultaneously distributes both benefits and harms or penalties and privilege. This, of course, is based on our location within an interlocking system of oppression (2020). This can change. If this distribution has been configured into the field of design, a task for twenty-first-century designers is to design them out. Recruitment, retention, access, and fostering a sense of belonging are all key ingredients for redesigning for positive future outcomes. Intersectional analysis is required within a twenty-first-century designer's suite of skills.

Person Focused Methods in Design Research and Engines of Curiosity and Discovery

But how can these systemic problems be designed out in a manner that includes change management? And how can this cover aspects of institutional or professional "defenses" against change? These questions need deep thought, consideration, and a willingness to sit with the discomfort of these various, simultaneously occurring realities and challenges. Now is the time to explore the notions I discussed above and begin to design better, more nuanced outcomes. Using the lens of Equalities Design—and true equality in design—is more than a far-off ambition. We need real examples of marginalized and racialized groups represented in the field, to examine the way that design is structured and their impact on the design processes. This ranges from the selection of who sits on teams of designers and researchers to who makes choices and delivers outputs based on the choices of those belonging to marginalized groups.

Already, designers like myself, who exist at the intersection of the African diaspora, the working class, and neurodivergence, witnessed the great (Covid-19) pivot with shock and awe as the world "opened up." Adjustment requests and accommodations that were previously refused and labeled unfeasible and too complex—or costly—were rolled out within a matter of weeks. Everything from clinical health appointments to digital work could be done remotely. This could have enabled the pivot to accessible design practices years ago; now it promises multi-modal and fully integrated hybrid practices in today's design landscape, allowing people with disabilities to be fully present in the field. While the pivot to digital work and engagement is not a "fix all," it is a step toward a much needed change. With the aim of illuminating anomalies, previously unmeasured voices, the unheard, and underserved in practicing design research, it is important to acknowledge different modalities and methods.

There are visible peaks of what I call the iceberg of inequalities. But I want to venture into the submerged "unseen" areas and gaps by looking at data and experiences alongside mapping the existing parameters. Equitable practices do not involve neuro-segregation and the separation of neurodivergent or disabled persons from neurotypical/non-disabled people. Separate streams of entry to work positions may be well intentioned. However, these practices fail to facilitate or embed the type of integrated change that instills a sense of belonging. Instead, by opting to separate those who identify as neurodivergent and disabled from the mainstream, this creates a dynamic where people have to "out" themselves to get support or adjustments or these individuals must struggle in the mainstream, it is also worth noting that access to a health professional and/or gaining a diagnosis is not available/an option to all for social and economic reasons (with women and girls being overlooked or mis-diagnosed concerning neurodivergence, another barrier to diagnosis for all is where access to health care has a financial component). The option of customization is key, as separate does not always equate to equal. Not every person feels safe to disclose confidential medical information—due to the risk of real-world social and material penalties—nor should they have to. How can we design in dignity, equipping people and enabling them to thrive without having to share confidential data about themselves?

To tackle this and design in transparent, equalized spaces means more than equity,; it requires equalities. If the objects, services, and places we access and use are adaptable, they will be made for a broader range of people. The hope is that no declarations will be required in the future, designing in dignity, kindness, and access; in short, this means re-worlding with equalities at the very core.

Note

1. The findings from Design Economy 2021 are still being unpacked and to some extent collected via the three-year live research program. Design Economy (2021) will be a growing cross-sector resource. Due to the pandemic, there have been significant changes to the work landscape across sectors. As mentioned in the UK Parliaments Public Accounts Committee published report unemployment among young Black people surges to 41.6 percent in the pandemic and unemployment in young white people increased from 10.1 percent to 12.4 percent in the UK. The Design Sector in the UK the Design Council's 2018 Design Economy report showed that 78 percent of designers are male and that people from Black, Asian, and minority ethnic groups are underrepresented at the leadership level in the field and subsectors. It will be interesting to see research findings throughout the three-year journey and whether there is any correlation to the wider workforce statistics.

References

Collins, P. H. (2000), *Black Feminist Thought*, London: Routledge. Available online: https://books.google.co.uk/books?id=cdtYsU3zR14C&newbks=1&newbks_redir=0&hl=en&redir_esc=y (accessed September 8, 2021).

Costanza-Chock, S. (2020), *Design Justice: Community-led Practices to Build the Worlds We Need* [ebook]. The MIT Press. Available at https://design-justice.pubpub.org/ (also added to chapter).

Design Council (2018), "Does Design Have a Diversity Issue?" [Video], Vimeo, September 18. Available online: https://vimeo.com/291498463 (accessed June 11, 2021).

Design Council (2018), *The Design Economy 2018*. Available online: https://www.designcouncil.org.uk/resources/report/design-economy-2018(accessed June 11, 2021).

Design Council (2021), *Design Economy 2021.* Available online: https://designeconomy.co.uk/ (accessed September 8, 2021).

Emergent Divergence [website]. Available online: https://emergentdivergence.com/2021/10/24/autistic-people-and-police-brutality-in-the-uk-baron-cohen-the-aggressor/ (accessed October 6, 2021).

GOV.UK (2020), "Ethnicity Facts and Figures," November 16. Available online: https://www.ethnicity-facts-figures.service.gov.uk/workforce-and-business/business/leadership-of-small-and-medium-enterprises/latest (accessed September 8, 2021).

Lewis, T. (2020), "Ableism 2020: An Updated Definition," *talilalewis.com* (blog). Available online: https://www.talilalewis.com/blog/ableism-2020-an-updated-definition (accessed June 11, 2021).

UK Parliament Committee (2021), "DWP Unable to Explain 'Shocking Inequality' as Unemployment among Young Black People Surges to 41.6% in Pandemic," September 8. Available online: https://committees.parliament.uk/committee/127/public-accounts-committee/news/157314/dwp-unable-to-explain-shocking-inequality-as-unemployment-among-young-black-people-surges-to-416-in-pandemic/ (accessed September 8, 2021).

Section 3 Speculation

Introduction

Speculative interventions complicate our understanding of design as primarily functional. In the case of disability design they also introduce types of use (and nonuse) that present disability access, pride, and culture. In so doing, they can move our understandings beyond what is possible in capitalist commodity culture, helping us conceive new directions for design or even worlds where disability might be conceived differently

Fantasy and speculation are sometimes misunderstood as the opposite of action and especially activism. But speculation, whether it exists as critical design or interrogative design, presents opportunities for friction and productive contestation. In so doing, speculation allows designers to move beyond design's role as problem-solver, making it into a question-instigator. Speculative or critical design can also be freeing, allowing us to imagine new meanings in older forms or even propose novel and as yet unrecognized options for design. Critiques can introduce conceptions of different, radical futures.

In so doing, we might find critiques of the status quo, as well as evidence—if only just a glimpse—of a repaired world. Sara Hendren notes how speculative disability design can help move design beyond strictly conventional definitions. By returning to scientist Carl Sagan's call for a science of wonder and skepticism and applying it to design, Hendren imagines new vistas for the field. When disability meets speculative design, she argues, pressing and matter-of-fact questions of day-to-day access can mingle with other more open-ended, probing, "what-if questions."

In "Speculating on Upstanding Norms," Ashley Shew contemplates norms and standards, describing how they can shape design. But she also notes the problem of speculative design propositions that are made for and not by disabled people. Shew examines critically the fixation that many technologists still have with wheelchairs that bring users to the eye level of people who stand upright. But even more broadly, she also calls attention to who *still* imagines what kinds of assistive technologies exist, and for whom and for what reasons.

As Lindsey D. Felt observes in "M Eifler's Prosthetic Memory as Speculative Archive," some of this design forces us to rethink ideas of assistance. Constructing a digital repository of moments from their life, the "Prosthetic Memory" allows Eifler, who experienced a traumatic brain injury that left them with long-term amnesia, to explore the limits of recollection and personal identity. In this case, Eifler's memory becomes a surprisingly communal site of imaginative possibility. But in so doing, they extend the idea of prosthesis beyond bodily support and blur the human and Artificial Intelligence.

The activist roots of speculative design allow Carline Cardus to explore lived disability experience in The Way Ahead, a collaborative design project. By co-opting the authoritative power of official road signage, Cardus finds an unusual platform to bring attention to disabled people's voices. Cardus initially created the project as an activist project, asking disabled members of the public a simple question: "If you had to think about changing the way something in the world about the way you access something in the world, how would you say it, via an instruction, a direction, a warning, or a danger or danger sign?" Placing their missives on signs that retain the shapes and symbols associated with official messaging, she gives new authority to their often overlooked observations, unexpressed feelings and demands.

In "Customizing Reading: Harvey Lauer's 'Reading Machine of the Future'," Mara Mills makes clear the gaps that still exist in technologies for vision-impaired people by introducing the speculative design wish of the late "father" of modified electronic devices for the blind Harvey Lauer(1933–2019). Mills explains his vision for a "multimodal reading aid" while introducing an essay Lauer wrote in 1994. Still remarkably apt, Lauer speculated on the power of a design that could be a computerized, disability-centered tool with braille, tonal, vibratory, and speech outputs for translating text and graphics. In material terms, Emily Watlington makes similar demands, asking us to imagine a dream world better suited for persons who are arthritic like herself. In "A Squishy House," Watlington pictures for us a living space made of soft, squishy material. Watlington uses disability design to introduce conceptions of radical fantasies for the future. In so doing, she also speculates on the "access loop," questioning whether meeting her own access needs will create a barrier for others.

Thinking further about others' access, Louise Hickman explores captioning for film and video as an expressive and complex "practice of care." Where conventional film making includes captioning as an after-thought, Hickman describes the processes she and artist Shannon Finnegan used to create the short film "Captioning on Captioning" (2020). Where mainstream filmmaking works to render these processes invisible, Finnegan and Hickman edited the film to show the interdependence that normally takes place behind the scenes in such productions. In so doing, they reveal such access giving as suffused with care, vulnerability, and intimacy.

Working on projects like the Soul of Neurodiversity Manifesto and the Black Disabled Lives Matter symbol, Jennifer White Johnson speculates on how design creativity can focus on Black bodies with disabilities. Imagining both design and mothering as acts of resistance, White Johnson's "CripJoy: Black Disabled Joy as an Act of Resistance" aligns with the disability justice movement, using the lens of design to examine the potent compound of disability and racism. In so doing, she ultimately argues that new design frameworks are needed and even necessary if we as a society are going to move forward.

Key Points

- Thinking creatively about disability allows designers can create personal objects that productively disrupt our notions of personhood, independence and autonomy.

- Speculative disability design can help us ask and suspend questions about how the bodymind functions.

- The highly pragmatic language of design often carries authority and power; co-opting its forms can give voice and authority to the life experiences and narratives of marginalized people.

- Accessibility is a creative engagement between body, community, and world, but that it's not treated that way. It's often treated as some sort of mechanical, almost punitive thing that comes on afterwards.

- Engaging disability as a creative practice means questioning norms of many kinds, including what we think we know.

- Disability experience can create new narratives and produce unconventional knowledge; speculating on this can prod us to see even the most commonly accepted materials and practices with new eyes.

- The lens of speculative design can highlight the intersection of disability and visibility of marginalized populations, or even the compound of disability and racism.

17 Speculative Making

SARA HENDREN

Science involves a seemingly self-contradictory mix of attitudes. On the one hand, it requires an almost complete openness to all ideas no matter how bizarre and weird they sound, a propensity to wonder … But at the same time, science requires the most vigorous and uncompromising skepticism, because the vast majority of ideas are simply wrong, and the only way you can distinguish the right from the wrong is by critical experiment and analysis. Too much openness, and you accept every notion, idea, and hypothesis—which is tantamount to knowing nothing. Too much skepticism—especially rejection of the ideas before they're adequately tested—and you're closed to the advance of science.

—Carl Sagan "Wonder and Skepticism"

Carl Sagan—beloved public thinker in astronomy and host of the massive PBS hit television series *Cosmos*—wrote these words about wonder and skepticism in the domains of science. He was speaking to imagined readers in the space of the laboratory, the realm of experiment and analysis and control variables, asking his fellow scientists to inhabit two distinctive and even polarized habits of mind. Sagan championed *wonder*, a playfulness and almost willful naïveté about the possible questions that science might take up, alongside *skepticism*, an exacting and clear-eyed ability to cut through ideas that have no merit, no matter how long one has spent pursuing them. Many thinkers can deploy *one* of these virtues well; very few can practice and expertly inhabit both of them, and even fewer can leap between those two dispositions with agility and grace.

Just as Sagan called for wonder and skepticism in the sciences, the best designers juxtapose these qualities as intellectual virtues, with one requiring the other. Moreover, wonder and skepticism might be the most succinct and plainspoken way to characterize what's called *speculative design*, a concept that can be especially generative in the high-stakes politics of disability and the built world. In this chapter, I borrow Sagan's "seemingly self-contradictory mix of attitudes, (Sagan 1995: 30)" but I use wonder and skepticism to speculate on the places where design and disability meet.

Speculative design—or perhaps *interrogative* design, or *critical* design—has its own deep field of scholarship and practices.[1] For introductory purposes, we might say that it broadly belongs to the pole of design practice that's nearer to art than to engineering. Its work is primarily cultural and symbolic, often operating in the mode of what we might call *wonder*. These enigmatic artifacts, encounters, or environments invent possibilities that aren't quite real; they sketch worlds that suggest an *otherwise* future, whether desirable or undesirable.[2] Our wonder is activated by a set of *what if* questions made vividly real. If we accept John Heskett's definition of design as an alloy of utility and significance, we might say that speculative design leans more heavily in the direction of the latter, foregrounding significance via expressive qualities in a designed object (Heskett 2005). Much like artworks, speculative designs surprise an audience with a re-enchanted or estranged or inverted sensory world, jogging viewers' perceptions *awake* in a new way. These designs are things-to-think-with; they enlarge our imagination about the future, even as they seem at home in our everyday ecosystems. Instead of abstract rhetorical language for possible sociopolitical and cultural futures, speculative design builds its questions into tangible forms. They are concrete ways to gather social groups around an idea. Together, we can kick its (literal or figurative) tires, and make sense of how more democratic, peaceful, and/or just worlds might be created.

Perhaps such speculation sounds indistinguishable from artmaking. In speculative *design*, however, artifacts are not purely experimental, contemplative objects. Where the experience of estrangement or enchantment is expected in the context of a gallery or stage, works of speculative design are different. Because they are grounded in the pragmatic and everyday things that populate our worlds, they enchant through the very utility also present in their features. Speculative culture-makers like Fiona Raby and Anthony Dunne, Pedro Reyes, Natalie Jeremijenko, Rick Lowe, or the German collective RaumLabor mix wonder and skepticism; they help us reconsider our own worlds with a combination of fantastical *and* pragmatic forms. However playful their initial packaging, they build prototypes that engage our *wonder* about the way the world might be. But with an unmistakable bite of critique, they also invite *skepticism* about the way things are. In the strongest works, both wonder and skepticism are held suspended, unresolved, each suggesting the other in turn.

Jeremijenko's *AgBag* project, for example, is a foldable, suspendible bag for growing plants; it's made from Tyvek, with a counterweighted structure to hang as a "container garden" in places with little or no architectural footprint. The *AgBag* is a useful design, a purchasable product for people to tend in very small urban spaces. Users can grow pollinator plants, for example, from tiny balcony railings, adding to the local biodiversity of cities where green space is scarce. But the source for the *AgBags* project is Jeremijenko's Environmental Health Clinic—a laboratory-studio as "hospital" for helping its audiences think through their own role in climate change. Jeremijenko has said that her work aims to address the "crisis of agency" that many people feel in the face of systems-level intransigence for remediating the climate crisis.[3] The *AgBags* are both a design to use and a design-to-think-with: they take on greater meaning in the larger discourse around Jeremijenko's work. They are available for purchase but not subject to the laws of mass production and persuasive advertising. And most importantly, they provide a boundary object for individual citizens to grapple with the conundrum of self-as-agent in the face of systemic complexity.[4]

The *AgBags*' power lies in their ability to engage our wonder and skepticism, together and in tandem. The ingenuity of "found" container space—hanging bags instead of laying garden beds—activates our wonder. Why must we wait for large plots of land to expand our green spaces? How might cities create agricultural systems that build *up* instead of *out*, as in traditional farming? And where might the facade of a building become a makeshift garden, as Jeremijenko's group did around the Postmasters Gallery in New York City in 2011? If a building's normative structures could be so easily manipulated, what else might be possible? But the project simultaneously helps us summon our skepticism: Do our tiny incremental choices matter in the future of the planet? What would an aggregate of individual actions look like? What would it take for a city to invest in urban agriculture without claiming that the land for it doesn't exist? The project does its speculative work by mixing utility and significance, by invoking our wonder and our skepticism, by refusing to settle on easy directives, simplistic moralizing, or earnestness that is devoid of play. Instead, the design helps us keep the complexity at stake, but it does so with a joyous spectacle and a clever reframing of extant resources: a powerful invitation to stay connected to the most serious issues in our lives.

The *AgBag* project carries instructive parallels for thinking about disability, designed objects, and the socio-technical ecosystems that show up where bodies meet the built world. The role of speculation might seem, at first glance, to be a luxury, a diversion into play and symbolism that leaves aside urgent issues of basic accessibility. But assistive technologies and inclusive environments, built in a speculative vein, might provide very practical and urgent means of everyday access while also pointing outward from themselves to a larger cultural milieu. Moreover, even a brief examination of contemporary issues in assistive technologies and environments shows us the thorny complexity of any design practice where it meets disability. These designs solve problems, where warranted, but they also hold questions up for examination, and they let questions live indefinitely—practical things that are also things-to-think-with. Designing this way is far easier to affirm than to enact, but works like the *AgBag*, among so many others, demonstrate that it is indeed possible. What might a mix of wonder and skepticism in speculative design offer when it comes to disability and the built world, especially with an eye toward design practices that might be "post-universal"?

If designers and engineers are interested in deafness, for example, they might direct their work toward hearing-restoration technologies such as cochlear implants. But they might also, or instead, investigate the design principles and practices of DeafSpace architecture at Gallaudet University. Here the built environment is conceived not to restore hearing but to accommodate and indeed *accentuate* the experiences and needs and pleasures of deafness. One is a wearable technology working to "cure," and one is at the scale of architecture, building rooms and hallways for enacting life and work.[5] Choosing one or the other endeavor need not be oppositional for engineers and designers, but the choices do proceed from different logical foundations. Each begs us to consider the possibilities offered by deep wonder ("how might architecture deliver somatic signals, instead of acoustic ones?"), *and* for cultivating the discipline of skepticism ("who is driving the development of cochlear implants, and how would we measure their success as technology?").[6] Speculative design builds these habits of mind into its very artifacts. The playful, joyous environments of DeafSpace insist that we *wonder* at the human sensorium, rather than rushing above all to fix its needs. We might then hold that wonder while also bringing the most rigorous scrutiny and skepticism to the delicate engineering work of cochlear implants—their technological specifications, their cost, their distribution, and their various and even contradictory social functions in hearing and deaf communities. We might, too, bring our deepest wonder to some of the very best examples of restorative hearing technologies—including advances in ordinary hearing aids for mild hearing loss that comes with aging. And we might extend our skepticism in every direction, holding up the mirror to our own assumptions, activating our deep curiosity about people and their many worlds. Wonder and skepticism are habits of mind, practices that serve us in their distinctive but complementary mindsets. Each is its own discipline. Each offers its own insights and is constrained necessarily by its limitations.

Autism spectrum conditions occupy a similarly contested social and medical conundrum for engineers and designers. On the one hand, there's a flourishing series of research and development efforts in laboratory settings for creating "rehabilitative" technologies for autism: software and hardware that teaches skills for recognizing verbal cues, facial expressions, and other social and relational signals. These tools may well be desirable and useful to people who want them. But there are other efforts that proceed outside this rehabilitative logic: adaptive workplace arrangements like information technology firms whose human resources are specifically designed to recruit and train workers on the autism spectrum.[7] These firms are organized with the commonplace cognitive strengths of many autistic people in mind, and they are set up to help workers flourish, and to deliver a competitive set of services. From rehabilitation to accommodation, inside and outside the demands of the market—again, these efforts need not be seen as incompatible. But their very different structures and scales should give any designer or engineer pause—a productive, generative pause—in deciding which lines of research to take up.

Works like Jeremijenko's *AgBag* invite us to look at socio-technical ideas of health and repair when it comes to the natural environment—matters of individual agency and matters of the common good. Ideas in disability beg for a similar multi-scale treatment, addressing individuals as they meet their larger systems, inviting us to more and more *varied* approaches to design for a meaningfully accessible world. We might activate our wonder and our skepticism by design choices that are alternately playful, pragmatic, utopian or dystopian, confrontational or friendly, stark and clinical, or warm and organic. We might grapple with the various and competing goods of restoration, cure, accommodation, and provocation. The possibilities *grow* alongside the urgency of the issues. Indeed, their very urgency demands multiplicity, not foreclosure. Speculation offers evocative tools for making questions visible and for prototyping useful everyday futures.

My own design practice was galvanized by an enigmatic object called the "Squeeze Chair": the bespoke technology designed by engineer and autistic self-advocate Temple Grandin, and its later speculative variation designed in partnership with artist Wendy Jacob. Grandin built herself a customized chair as a climb-in chamber for relaxing after work, an object that became highly publicized in a *New Yorker* profile by the neuroscientist and writer Oliver Sacks.[8] Grandin's chair is built of wood, with wrap-around sides that provide mechanical touch, a form of pleasurable deep sensory pressure, to the sitter. It's a form of self-designed prosthetic furniture, built for sensory stimulation and delivered by an object rather than by human contact. But the object is also a provocation for critical designers: What other functions could a chair really bring to the human body? Grandin's insight into the atypical sensory processing conditions that often come with autism breaks open our wonder about the body and about household furniture as well. Could seating, in some strange and happy future, also give affection? After some conversation with Grandin in 1995, Jacob launched the Squeeze Chair project. The research and design resulted in several other models of compression-style squeeze chairs, with the resulting furniture taking on the look and feel of ordinary club chairs much like you might see in a household living room. But the newer chairs offer a deep squeeze by the upholstered arms, delivered via a foot pump that is operated by someone else. It's a chair that is partly therapeutically useful, partly critical object, partly social exchange, and partly sheer wonderment. These objects have been exhibited in gallery settings—squeeze chairs sometimes shown alongside Grandin's architectural and engineering designs—but have also (briefly) entered schools as useful objects present in ordinary classrooms.

Grandin and Jacob's speculative design work, replete with wonder and skepticism, elasticized my perceptions and practices when I set out to work in disability, an artist-researcher working in engineering, and inhabitant of a hybrid laboratory-studio. It helped to elasticize the very definition of disability, the array of potential tools or techniques outside the mainstream, the constellation of needs and wishes held by atypical people seeking recognizable human flourishing. It did so by offering a mix of wonder and skepticism in the form of artifacts—helping to sharpen my observations and more patiently form my questions for the work of building accessible worlds. Instead of rendering the subjects of design and disability as purely medical or technological, speculative design allows us all to see the dimensional, unresolved, socio-technical, and utterly human nature of disability experience.

The "alter-podium," a laboratory collaboration I began at Olin College as a co-design project with art historian and curator Amanda Cachia, is a work of speculative design in this vein. Amanda has a form of dwarfism; the world is not designed for a body at her scale. She spends much of her day accommodating to the shapes and sizes of average human height, whether in cafeterias or cars, while reaching for light switches or finding an accessible chair. She came to my lab at Olin College of Engineering to produce *a lectern*, tailor-made for Amanda's short stature and her

5. For the affordances and limitations of what Alison Kafer calls the "curative imaginary," see Kafer 2013.
6. See more on DeafSpace in Byrd 2017.
7. See the complexities of this burgeoning effort in, e.g., Vogus and Taylor 2018.
8. See Sacks, "An Anthropologist on Mars," the *New Yorker*, December 27, 1993.

References

Byrd, T. (2017), "Deaf Space," in J. Boys (ed.), *Disability, Space, Architecture: A Reader*, 241–6, New York: Routledge.

Cachia, A. (2016), "The Alterpodium: A Performative Design and Disability Intervention," *Design and Culture: The Journal of the Design Studies Forum* 8 (3): Fall 2016.

Dunne, A., and F. Raby (2013), *Speculative Everything: Design, Fiction, and Social Dreaming*, Cambridge, MA: MIT Press.

Forlano, Laura, and Anijo Mathew (2014), "From Design Fiction to Design Friction: Speculative and Participatory Design of Values-Embedded Urban Technology," *Journal of Urban Technology* 21 (4): 7–24.

Greene, M. (2001), "Thinking of Things as if They Could Be Otherwise: the Arts and Intimations of a Better Social Order," in M. Greene (ed.), *Variations on a Blue Guitar: The Lincoln Center Institute Lectures on Aesthetic Education*, 116–21, New York: Teachers College Press.

Heskett, J. (2005), *Design: A Very Short Introduction*, Oxford: Oxford University Press.

Kafer, A. (2013), *Feminist, Queer, Crip*, Bloomington, IN: Indiana University Press.

Pullin, G. (2010), *Design Meets Disability*, Cambridge, MA: MIT Press.

Ratto, M., and M. Boler, eds (2014), *DIY Citizenship: Critical Making and Social Media*, Cambridge, MA: MIT Press.

Sagan, C. (1995), "Wonder and Skepticism," *Skeptical Inquirer*, February 24–30.

Taylor, S. (2017), *Beasts of Burden: Animal and Disability Liberation*, New York: The New Press.

Vogus, T. and J. L. Taylor (July 2018), "Flipping the Script: Bringing an Organization Perspective to the Study of Autism at Work," *Autism* 22 (5): 514–16.

Wodiczko, K. (1999), *Critical Vehicles: Writings, Projects, Interviews*, Cambridge, MA: MIT Press.

18 Speculating on Upstanding Norms

ASHLEY SHEW

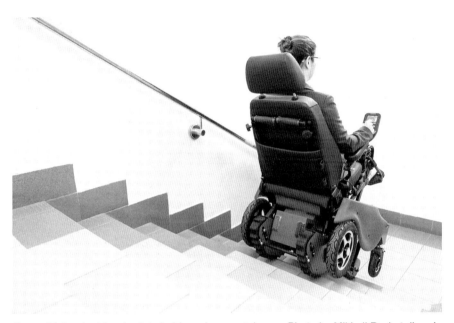

Figure 17 An electric wheelchair drives down a staircase. Photo by Mikhail Reshetnikov / EyeEm via Getty Images.

In 2021 the American Bionics Project assumed the tagline "Striving to Make Wheelchairs Obsolete by 2035." Aiming to "stimulate the development of revolutionary technologies for people with lower-limb disabilities," the nonprofit focuses on developing state of the art prosthetics, exo-skeletons, and a host of new mobility solutions (American Bionics Project 2021). *But imagine seeing the wheelchair, a relatively simple device that is often viewed as a neutral or useful technology and used by millions of people today, as something to strive to make obsolete.* Such speculative designs often open many questions as they appear to answer. Many people take their own wheelchair use as a positive aspect of their lives and mobility. Activist Lawrence Carter-Long calls them "chariots of independence" (2018). Scholar Elizabeth Guffey calls them "the chair that changed the world" (2017). Often enough, wheelchairs are heralded as a great and long-established, enduring technology.

Much has been built around our ideas about standing and walking; moreover, these assumptions often get shoved into what we think is good for people. These ideas can make people seem virtuous or good, especially when we talk of upstanding citizens and moral uprightness. And in the realm of disability, the "ritualized ideal" of wheelchair users standing and walking is deeply ingrained into our narratives about disablement, impairment and technology (Peace 2015).

It has already been keenly observed that technologies are culturally embedded throughout history (Oldenziel 2004; Schaffer and Simon 1985). We shouldn't expect that disability technologies should be any different: the cultural meaning and context of technological development matters. Raman Srinivasan details one such embedding with the prosthetic Jaipur foot in India (2002: 327–47). He calls this technology "culturally appropriate" as the Jaipur foot allows for squatting, sitting cross-legged, and generally participating in Indian life. Most prosthetic feet found on the market in the United States and Europe have very little range of ankle motion: as someone who uses a prosthetic just like this, I cannot fully squat in any foot that I've been fitted with. In general, this is not a problem for any of the activities I do as someone living in the United States. How we move our bodies can indeed be culturally dependent, shaped by differences in how we design our toilets, tables, chairs, etc. I consider in this chapter the example of wheelchairs in order to explore the relationship between how things are built and the disability technologies that get heralded.

Disabled people never get to have neutral technological choices. Everything we use fits into speculative narratives over which we have no control. And in these stories, designers are supposed to save us; it is often their guiding narrative about us. It means that we get a lot of technology we don't want—or that we might want—but the circumstances are not right for it. Designers often know little about the infrastructure they are working in, the systems of billing and insurance we try to live within, the systems of denials that tell us we aren't disabled enough to deserve a device, the hassles we encounter in the built environment, and the expectations about our tech use that we do not necessarily share.

While speculation can be highly imaginative, it can also mean taking assumptions to be true when, in fact, there can be insufficient evidence for their truth. In this chapter I specifically address agency (who makes what) and design speculation (for what reasons) in terms of disability technologies. My immediate object of study is wheelchairs that lift users up and place them higher in a visual range, as well as exoskeletons that also are meant to put users "at eye-level." But much like standing and not standing, many normative notions taken for granted in design are based on misguided understanding and unfounded speculation; furthermore, these can ultimately detract from disabled peoples' own functionality and self-determination. Speculative designs often set the limits of public discourse and disabled agency.

Upright Solutions

By suggesting that we speculate on design's "upstanding norms," I want to examine the environmental obstacles and designs that shape how we think about bodies and technologies, as well as what we take as "solutions" for life's activities. In popular speech, the word *norms* often refers to a standard or pattern, defining ideas or things that are typical or usual. But norms can also refer to a subset of people. First developed by disability studies theorist Rosemarie Garland-Thomson, the term *normate* describes nondisabled people (1997; see also Hamraie 2017). For Garland-Thomson, the normate is an imaginary everyman who embodies self-determination, health, sturdiness, and independence in mainstream culture; the normate is everything that disabled people are not. But there is also a colloquial use to the word among the disabled community; here we might refer to nondisabled others as norms. Thus, I might say to my disabled co-conspirator that "we don't want to freak out the norms" when we plan disability-centered programming (although maybe we do). In this way, I also refer to upstanding norms as nondisabled people who stand up.

But upstanding norms also suggest how standing and posture are encoded in the English language. We hear talk of *upright* or *upstanding* citizens as those who are morally good or model in behavior. Those who *stand tall* have dignity. And, of course, *lame* is used as a negative. *Crippled*, for many, substitutes in our language as someone or something that is being held back, substantially hurt, or broken down. In the English language, the word *invalid* can indicate the opposite of valid, but is also an outmoded term once used to designate disabled.

But many words that were once about disability are still used in English to indicate negative things or to put other people down as general insults: spaz, hysterical, dumb, feebleminded, moron, idiot, r*tarded, blind to …, paralyzed by …, etc.[1] These words and many others reflect the continuing bias against disability often termed ableism. This ableism may appear even when people aren't employing them specifically about disability at a given time. These words give a window into casual cultural attitudes about disability and suggest how nondisabled ways of being are presented as morally better categories. Who wouldn't want to be upright, stand tall, and stand up for what they believe in?

This chapter is not primarily about words. We need only reflect on how we talk about what it is to be good or moral to have a sense of how things are normed. Of course, the norming—making things normal, normalizing—takes place in how we build infrastructure and how nondisabled people conceive technologies for disability.

Exo-ctly What We Don't Need

In her 2005 memoir *Too Late to Die Young*, activist Harriett McBryde Johnson describes how she was introduced to these attitudes, first learning how wheelchairs have come to be understood by the public when she came across the fundraising campaigns for the Muscular Dystrophy Association in her youth. When *Parade* magazine featured an article profiling comedian Jerry Lewis, the host of the long-running MDA telethons, she learned what he imagined it would be like to have muscular dystrophy. Lewis describes how he "would put myself in that chair … that steel imprisonment that long has been deemed the dystrophic child's plight."

As a young wheelchair user herself, Johnson recalls reading this description and her immediate, visceral reaction:

I am stunned. Sitting here in my steel imprisonment ... I can't believe it, and it gets worse. Lewis says if you go to a restaurant in a wheelchair, "Ninety percent of the pasta winds up on your lap!" He waxes miserable about the "indignities" of getting help with bathing and dressing ... He piles them on, the incidents, the outrageous insults, the stereotypes. Then comes the moral of the story: "I just have to learn to try to be good at being a half person ... and get on with my life. I may be a full human being in my heart and soul, yet I am still a half person."

(2005)

As Johnson will learn, most of what the public has absorbed about using wheelchairs is that they are a terrible plight. We see this in how people talk about being "wheelchair bound," as if the chairs didn't have wheels and cannot go places. Of course, this mindset is exacerbated because the symbol of disability is most often a wheelchair; those of us who are not wheelchair users still often follow the paths, use the parking, and find restrooms that are marked with a wheelchair symbol. Wheelchairs seem like easy pickings: so many people see disability and think wheelchair, and they see wheelchair and think tragedy. This may explain the attitude behind the American Bionics Project and their desire to make wheelchairs obsolete by 2035. It also helps us understand the questionable development of newer, more speculative types of wheelchairs and cutting-edge exoskeletons.

The broader public's assumptions may explain why so many wheelchair projects that can climb stairs continue to make news. Every few months, it seems, a news story breaks about some new wheelchair, usually made at a university by a team of humanitarian engineers, that can climb stairs (Jackson 2019). These devices, which can traverse staircases with systems that typically send a wheelchair user up a case of stairs backwards, are interesting in their public presentation and reception: they get a lot more attention in the press than actual interest from wheelchair users.

One would think that, if wheelchairs with the capability to climb staircases are desirable, these speculative designs would be welcomed within the disability community. But it matters who is doing the speculating. As journalist Andrew Pulrang writes, "It's interesting and possibly significant that non-disabled people seem overall to be more interested in stair-climbing wheelchairs than actual wheelchair users" (2019). These prototype wheelchairs are often slow, have the perception of being dangerous—what happens if you get stuck mid-staircase?—and look cumbersome; what happens if you get tipped? If this is a personal mobility alternative meant to replace ramps and elevators, then most wheelchair users aren't interested. When it comes to many of the fancy wheelchairs we continue to see written about and *freely advertised as news (though most are PR)*, we are often reading stories written for nondisabled people about "hope for disabled people" (Pulrang 2019).

Much like the stair climbing wheelchair, it's hard to make sense of exoskeleton development. A zoological term, an exoskeleton provides both support and protection by covering the exterior bodies of some invertebrate animals. Redefined in human terms, wearable exoskeletons designed for strength and mobility have emerged as a potential alternative to wheelchairs. Ultimately, there are many good uses for exoskeletons, including those developed for farming applications and in-patient stroke rehabilitation. However, the broader conversation, especially in popular news and entertainment, is limited. Our understanding of exoskeletons features two main approaches: applications for wheelchair users and military uses meant to create super-soldiers. While I focus on the wheelchair user case here, the two groups are not unrelated: many of these projects are military-funded, and focus on disabled veterans in testing and use.

Often enough these speculative technologies are publicly lauded but sometimes also understood out of context. Furthermore, this can happen in a way that degrades wheelchair use and wheelchair users. Writing on the *Bad Cripple* blog, Bill Peace explains the need for more context in discussions about exoskeleton:

> Your typical bipedal person exposed to a barrage of misleading news stories is led to believe all paralyzed people share one goal in life—walking. Please cue the soaring inspirational music accompanied by the brave and noble young man or woman, struggling to walk surrounded by health care professionals, computer scientists, and engineers who share the same ritualized ideal.
>
> (2015)

Such hidden assumptions and norms may overrate walking, but most of our conversations about exoskeletons also equate wheelchair use with lower limb paralysis. In fact, many people use wheelchairs for other reasons. Standing up itself can be a risk for disabled people when it comes to disabilities like POTS (Postural orthostatic tachycardia syndrome) and EDS (Ehlers-Danlos syndrome).

Because a culture of ignorance around the experience of disability generally shapes these speculative conversations about exoskeletons, some very basic questions still need to be asked. In one of my classes a student impetuously responded to an image of an exoskeleton projected on an overhead screen and asked, "How do people poop in that?" Indeed, the design in question had a bar placed securely across the buttocks; taking off pants would be hard, if not impossible, while geared up in the suit. In the end, the user would need to take the exoskeleton completely off in order to go sit on a toilet.[2]

Certainly some technologies have made demonstrable differences in wheelchair design. For example, many wheelchair users laud elevated lifts that use hydraulics to move the seat of the wheelchair up, placing the user higher, and value the features that these technologies provide. Many power chairs that have lift functionality are generally appreciated and often sought by disabled users. Crip scholar Bethany Stevens has written evocatively about her transitions between different devices for mobility but singles out her use of Svetlana, her power wheelchair with lift capability. As she notes, the functionalities are different between Svetlana and her earlier manual chairs. At the same time, she has also observed her use of the power wheelchair with lift changes the perception of others and how she is viewed, as she explains:

I have never felt this supported by a wheelchair. In my home, I move between using my manual chair and power chair. But I find Svetlana's twelve-inch elevated lift useful in the kitchen and the power wheelchair overall more comfortable than my office chair. With the beauty of movement with different devices comes a balance of costs and benefits from each. While Svetlana has offered speed, power, and height (which I have often longed for as a little woman), I traded off the ability to slow dance with my wife. This is a loss in my life, but learning to find more gains is part of the adaptive nature of being disabled and creative.

(Nelson, Shew, and Stevens 2019: 7)

While wheelchairs that aid users in "standing" or in being elevated to eye-height can be helpful to disabled people, in marketing material directed at disabled consumers they are often cast as "solving" particular social and built-world problems. That is, they are presented as helping people not deal so much with impairments, but rather logistics problems that disabled people have around interaction and infrastructure. This component is often emphasized by such names for wheelchairs of this type like the "iLevel." In addition to touting stability and safety features, the Quantum iLevel advertising is particularly telling. As its marketing explains, "the world is not designed around seated height" (iLevel Powerchairs 2021). To disabled consumers, the technology is not cast as solving a problem of body, but the practical working around of the inconvenient ways in which the world is built.

If we may step back: why do wheelchairs even need a lift? Why is "eye-level" a cultivated norm? It dominates aspects of the world as it has been designed around us. Invariably, libraries and grocery stores stack and display their goods much higher than a seated person can reach. Even more puzzling is the recent proliferation of bar-height furniture. No longer found simply in bars anymore, raised height or "bar seating" has been on trend the past few years; bar-height tables and bar seating, standing tables, lecterns at a "standard" height, which not only excludes chair users but also defaults toward taller people, reception desks, bank teller counters, airport desks, medical office, and check-in windows have become ubiquitous. Furthermore, as these raised furnishings proliferate, it becomes harder to find available seating at standard height in many restaurants, dining halls and, of course, bars.[3]

Whether raised height seating or tall library stack shelving, designed environments often systematically put chair users at a disadvantage.[4] But we rarely acknowledge how these features must be contextualized as part of a system that has been set up in ways that can be hostile to shorter, mobility disabled, and wheelchair-using consumers. One account from popular media heralded a stand-up wheelchair that lets a user adjust themselves to standing while in the device. Noting the innovation, viewers are told that John Christensen, a man who used a wheelchair for twenty years, was able to reach a book on a high shelf without assistance when he tested the chair. "Makes life a little easier," John told CBS News, "You don't have to ask anybody to do something for you" (Mattern 2016).

The need to ask others for help adds a social aspect to the desire for "eye-level" devices. Wheelchair users have written powerfully about being left out of social conversations, being ignored by staff in restaurants and other businesses, and even having nondisabled people standing near them mistaken as caregivers. In many ways, chairs with the ability to elevate the user allow the user to change perceptions. Certainly, one should recognize that these perceptions are often rooted in unconscious ableist bias that excludes those below a certain height. But these assumptions can also shape the types of technologies made for—not with—disabled people.

It's Rude to Stair: Dongles and Speculation

In many ways, stair-climbing wheelchairs and exoskeletons have been designed and developed in order to meet a series of social norms. In her book *Staring*, Rosemarie Garland-Thomson writes about the ways in which arm amputees use prosthetic limbs to camouflage disability or redirect starers. "A mechanical hand answers the needs of its wearer," she notes, "whereas a cosmetic hand answers the needs of its starer" (2009: 129). Rather than use mechanical hands like hooks that serve for greater function in terms of use, Garland-Thomson details the ways in which wearers may use cosmetic arms to avoid the intrusive gaze of strangers. We might think about another form of assistive technology, for example wheelchairs with elevated lifts and manual wheelchairs with "stand-up" capability, as sometimes doing this as well. Indeed, stair-climbing wheelchairs, exoskeletons and other high-tech devices of questionable use to most disabled people are cast as "disability dongles" a term coined by disabled design critic Liz Jackson and shared by other disabled design critics and historians on Twitter, like Alex Hagaard, Bess Williamson, Jaipreet Virdi, and more. Disability dongles often draw from theoretical knowledge, often constructed by nondisabled people and extrapolated into real-world situations. They might also be considered a form of speculation gone wrong.

Dongles, in their usual meaning, are small pieces of computer hardware used to connect devices and enable increased functionality. But, while dongles seem to offer technology solutions by piecing laptops, headphones, monitors, and other devices together, they aren't as easy or effortless as they seem (Morgan 2019). According to Jackson, disability dongles extend this conundrum still further. The disability dongle, she insists, is "a well-intended, elegant, yet useless solution to a problem we never knew we had" (Jackson 2019). In social media, Jackson's hashtag #DisabilityDongle has been highlighting these cases and not only is affixed to stair-climbing wheelchairs and exoskeletons but also includes sign language gloves and haptic navigation systems for blind people. But the name gained broader circulation in 2019 after an online design blog began heavily publicizing a stair-climbing wheelchair. When a promotional video was launched and social media promoters announced that "These students just blew minds with their wheelchair prototype," Jackson began a grassroots campaign in response (2019). Collecting social media replies from disabled people, Jackson quickly gained traction for the idea behind this term (2019). Disability activist Alice Wong summarized the problematic introduction of such technologies and the uncritical press coverage that often accompanies them. In some cases, misleading "Stories like this," Wong notes, "'blow minds' because enthusiasm for tech trumps advancements in accessible infrastructure & polic[i]es" (2019).

But ultimately, Jackson suggests, the narratives woven around disability dongles seem to grant a technologically-assisted redemption of disabled people. In this way, they make us worthy, normalized, "includeable," or even just more palatable or legible to a public (Shew 2019; Titchkosky 2011).

Disability dongles like stair-climbing wheelchairs present a number of other technical and conceptual problems. Often they are produced as singular experiments or are one-offs designed by engineering student teams; many of these devices are never meant to be commercially viable. Indeed, the costs for such new equipment, should they be commercialized, are almost always prohibitively expensive. But the makers of dongles often also forget to design for maintenance. Indeed, the difficulty in keeping even relatively simple wheelchairs maintained and in good repair is well known. This is often highlighted by wheelchair users, who detail the weeks and months of degrading experience it takes for repair (Coffey 2021; McBride 2021; Peace 2019). During this time, of course, wheelchair users are "without their legs," having lost their mobility. The social, economic, and emotional toll this exacts from daily living is clear; the lack of good, timely systems of maintenance, repair, and replacement is hard to overestimate. And this is for the things we have now. Disability dongles, like stair-climbing chairs, pose even greater challenges to these systems, especially in one-off designs created by engineering teams who aren't thinking about use, users, and the context in which disabled life takes place.

Not only do disability dongles invoke long-standing and growing frustration around the failures of affordability in high disability tech, but these complex technological devices only highlight the ignorance and unlawful failures in construction and planning around ramps, elevators and other environmental features required by the 1990 Americans with Disabilities Act. As journalist s.e. smith suggests, "Stair-climbing wheelchairs are an excellent example of the overlapping problems with disability dongles; people with mobility impairments know that there's a problem (stairs), and they've repeatedly articulated solutions. But those solutions are not new gadgets …" Instead, smith argues that "most built environments rely heavily on stairs, and … while elevators and ramps both exist, many designers choose not to use them" (2019). Effectively, these technical developments also hinge on biases ingrained in social institutions and design expectations about what users should desire. Extra value placed on standing and ambulating elevates the development of technological fixes, instead of addressing poor planning and designs that serve to exclude such as entrances around the back for a ramp, elevator outages, unmarked routes, and unnecessary stairs or stairways privileged by architects. But smith detects a darker undercurrent here as well. "There is," smith avers, "an inherently segregational nature to new access-oriented technologies like this …" (2019).

Ultimately, the kind of speculation behind these dongles points to a phenomenon I call "technoableism" (Shew 2020). Technoableism is particular type of ableism whereby disability technologies are heralded as life-changing, empowering, and redemptive; almost inevitably they are part of a narrative about technology that emphasizes how terrible being disabled must be. It also implies that technology is needed to make disabled people worthy or "includeable" (Titchkowsky 2011) in society as a whole. Only with devices designed and developed by others can people with bodily impairments become super-able to "overcome" disability.

But technoableism also involves questions of self-determination and personal agency. It is an approach to design and development whereby nondisabled helpers are themselves elevated as *enabling* freedom to disability disabled people. In this case they offer liberation through devices and technologies. Conversely, through technoableism, disabled people are expected be grateful to the people who want to help, whether it is "help" we want or not. We disabled people are both seen and also completely unseen in these encounters. While we are expected to be good test pilots for tech, we are uncompensated for our labor and design, with the expectation that we are grateful to be consulted. Significantly, the disabled people who collaborate in testing and developing these technologies are rarely named in patent applications, scientific publications, and news stories. At best, if we are named at all, we might be presented as brand ambassadors. *We are the center but never central to these narratives and norms.*

Dis-Orientation

Several years ago, I made inquiries about attending an amputee peer support group in my region. When I spoke on the phone with a fellow amputee, I was quizzed about how well I walked and what tech I was using. I was then told that my attendance would be good at these gatherings because there are some older men in the group who won't even try. But is it a question of trying, or have chosen differently?

Discussions about disability and assistive technologies often ignore the cost, physical and time-wise, to getting fit and learning how to walk and changes to the tech and our bodies over time. I didn't go to that support group because I was seeking support and community, and not to shame other amputees into being better amputees, better at performing their disabilities, making what are perceived as better device (and therefore life) choices. Disabled people shouldn't be pitted against one another for technological, and therefore moral, superiority. That I was quizzed about how I walk in order to hang out with other disabled people really speaks to the layers of ableism, lateral, societal, internalized, and more, that disabled people have to contend with. What's more, many people believe there actually exists a *right* technology, and here's where the crux lies. We need to become dis-oriented, shaken from the orientation we often take to designing, using, and understanding disability technologies.

The negotiations we face when confronted with these technologies inevitably take place against the backdrop of a world that asks us to stand and walk with a good gait too. Activist Donna Walton summed up the problem, and how she resolved it for herself in acceptance:

> I worked so hard to build and maintain self-esteem and confidence that I almost risked losing it when I decided that I had to walk "normal" again in order to attain society's ideal for physical attractiveness. My gimpy gait is mine, and it is very "normal" to me. I feel now that I have evolved into my own reality consistent with being a woman, an African American, and subsequently an amputee, with each level of my survival affording me enough clay to mold a self-assured persona unique to my struggles. … Just being able to walk or to get where we want to go, whether it is with a cane or in a wheelchair, is the point, isn't it?
>
> (2011)

When we talk about design, broadly, we often focus on individual devices without the context of people who might want the device. So much of our cultural understanding of disability is shaped by negative stereotypes; almost inevitably we believe that disabled bodies are calling out for intervention. This kind of understanding, what scholar Rua Williams calls an "interventional logic" (2019), is still easy to observe around us.

Being able to go places or to participate in community, whether with a cane or wheelchair or prosthetic leg, should be the point. But too often we are told there are right ways to be disabled and correct technologies to use. The technological is tied to the moral here. Disability access and inclusion should not be premised on tech. And upstanding norms, embedded into technological design and the speculation of designers, work against the normalization of disability within society. Agency in disability design means that our perspectives matter. What many of us want are places and spaces that allow for more ways of being in the world, no matter how we roll or stroll.

Acknowledgments

This material is based on work supported by the National Science Foundation under Award No. 1750260. Any opinions, findings, and conclusions or recommendations expressed in this material are those of the author and do not necessarily reflect the views of the National Science Foundation.

Notes

1. In the philosophy of technology, the multistability of objects describes objects that have a number of stable functions, but might not have one sole function. Our smartphones have become an example of that phenomenon, but even something as simple as an iron that is used often as a doorstop may qualify here. When I talk about speculative design as limiting discourse and agency, I mean that we disabled users are given actually less determination in the multifunctions we often find for our tools, and, in public discourse,

we also see how certain functionalities—standing and walking, in what I will share here—are prized and reified and made "the" goal or function of the tools we use in the minds of designers.

2. Lydia X.Z. Brown updates a page on Ableist Language here: https://www.autistichoya.com/p/ableist-words-and-terms-to-avoid.html.

3. Given that one of the few disability-led hack-a-thon tech events focused on hoist lifts to help wheelchair-using women get on toilets (Farr 2014), the functionality of a rig to help paralyzed wheelchair users have more private toilet access is something desired. Even this event, though, felt like "everything about it presumed that the disabled person was the object. And I want to say in parentheses of pity because that was how it was framed," according to disability rights legend Corbett O'Toole, who participated in the event (Critical Design Lab 2020).

4. Parts of my university went wild for bar-height tables in the past decade, with random study tables in this height sprinkled through new buildings. And there are but two tables I can comfortably sit at, as an amputee, in the fancy new dining hall nearest to my university office. Furthermore, they are almost always occupied. It feels like they wanted to make the campus more hostile to disabled people, though I suspect they just forgot we exist.

References

American Bionics Project (2021), "Groundbreaking Solutions for People with Physical Disabilities: Striving to Make Wheelchairs Obsolete by 2035," *American Bionics Project*. Available online: https://www.americanbionics.org/ (accessed October 27, 2021).

Brown, L. X. Z. (2012), "Ableism/Language," *Autistic Hoya*. Available online: https://www.autistichoya.com/p/ableist-words-and-terms-to-avoid.html (accessed August 14, 2021).

Carter-Long, L. (2018), *Why the Way We Talk about Disability Matters*, [Radio program] Wisconsin Public Radio, March 19. Available online: https://www.wpr.org/shows/why-way-we-talk-about-disability-matters (accessed March 30, 2021).

Coffey, H. (2021), "'This is My Life': Woman Accuses Airline of Breaking Her Wheelchair in Viral Video," *Independent*, May 27. Available online: https://www.independent.co.uk/travel/news-and-advice/delta-broken-wheelchair-tiktok-disabled-b1854960.html (May 27, 2021).

Critical Design Lab (2020), "Contra* Making (2) with Corbett O'Toole," *Contra Podcast*, 27 April 2020. Available online: https://www.mapping-access.com/podcast/2020/4/27/contra-podcast-episode-28-contramaking-2-with-corbett-otoole.

Garland-Thomson, R. (1997), *Extraordinary Bodies*, New York: Columbia University Press.

Garland-Thomson, R. (2009), *Staring: How We Look*, New York: Oxford University Press.

Guffey, E. (2017), *Designing Disability*, London: Bloomsbury.

Hamraie, A. (2017), *Building Access*, Minneapolis: University of Minnesota Press.

Farr, C (2015), "Techies and People with Disabilities Team Up for 'Makeathon'," *KQED*, September 14. Available online: https://www.kqed.org/futureofyou/39078/techies-and-people-with-disabilities-team-up-for-makeathon (accessed March 30, 2021).

Jackson, L. (2019), "A Community Response to #DisabilityDongle," *Medium*, April 22. Available online: https://medium.com/@eejackson/a-community-response-to-a-disabilitydongle-d0a37703d7c2 (accessed April 22, 2019).

Johnson, H. M. (2005), *Too Late to Die Young: Nearly True Tales from a Life*, New York: Macmillan Publishing.

Longmore, P. K. (2016), *Telethons: Spectacle, Disability, and the Business of Charity*, New York: Oxford University Press.

Manning, L. (2009), "The Magic Wand," *International Journal of Inclusive Education* 13 (7): 785. Available online: https://www.tandfonline.com/doi/full/10.1080/136031109030 46069.

Mattern, J. L. (2016), "This Standing Wheelchair Could be a Game Changer," *Woman's Day*, September 16. Available online: https://www.womansday.com/health-fitness/a56312/standing-wheelchair/.

McBride, S. (2021), "An Airline Damaged Her Wheelchair so Disabled Social Media Took Care of It," *New Mobility*, May 26. Available online: https://newmobility.com/airline-damaged-wheelchair/. (accessed June 15, 2021).

Morgan, C. (2019), "Apple Dongle Problem Isn't Getting any Better," *Business Insider*, February 22. Available online: https://www.businessinsider.com/apple-dongle-problem-iphone-issues-everything-wrong-2019-2.

Nario-Redmond, M., D. Gospodinov, and A. Cobb (2017), "Crip for a Day: The Unintended Negative Consequences of Disability Simulations," *Rehabilitation Psychology* 62 (3): 324–33. Available online: https://pubmed.ncbi.nlm.nih.gov/28287757/.

Nelson, M. K., A Shew, and B. Stevens (2019), "Transmobility: Possibilities in Cyborg (Cripborg) Bodies," *Catalyst: Feminism, Theory, Technoscience* 5 (1). Available online: https://catalystjournal.org/index.php/catalyst/article/view/29617.

Oldenziel, R. (2004), *Making Technology Masculine: Men, Women, and Modern Machines in America, 1870–1945*, Amsterdam, NLD: Amsterdam University Press.

Peace, B. (2015), "Obsession with Walking," *Bad Cripple* (blog), January 7. http://badcripple.blogspot.com/2015/01/obsession-with-walking.html.

Peace, B. (2019), "Airline Statistics on Destruction of Wheelchairs Placed in Cargo Hold," *Bad Cripple* (blog), May 2. Available online: http://badcripple.blogspot.com/2019/05/airline-statistics-on-destruction-of.html.

Pulrang, A. (2019), "Not so Brilliant Maybe?" *Disability Thinking* (blog), September 1. Available online: https://disabilitythinking.com/disabilitythinking/2019/9/1/not-so-brilliant.

Quantum (2021), "How Can iLevel Power Chairs Benefit Me?" Available online: https://www.quantumrehab.com/ilevel-power-chairs/how-can-ilevel-power-chairs-benefit-me.asp.

Shapin, S, and Simon Schaffer (1985), *Leviathan and the Air-Pump: Hobbes, Boyle, and the Experimental Life*, Princeton, NJ: Princeton University Press.

Shew, A. (2019), "Stop Depicting Technology as Redeeming Disabled People," *Nursing Clio*, April 23. Available online: https://nursingclio.org/2019/04/23/stop-depicting-technology-as-redeeming-disabled-people/.

Shew, A. (2020), "Ableism, Technoableism, and Future AI," *IEEE Technology and Society Magazine*, 39 (1): 40–85. March 2020. Available online: https://ieeexplore.ieee.org/document/9035527 (accessed October 27, 2021).

Silverman, A. (2017), "Disability Simulations: What Does the Research Say?" *Braille Monitor* 60 (6). Available online: https://nfb.org//sites/default/files/images/nfb/publications/bm/bm17/bm1706/bm170602.htm.

Smith, S. E. (2019), "Disabled People Don't Need so Many Fancy New Gadgets. We Just Need More Ramps," *Vox*. Available online: https://www.vox.com/first-person/2019/4/30/18523006/disabled-wheelchair-access-ramps-stair-climbing. (accessed January 15, 2021).

Srinivasan, R. (2002), "Technology Sits Cross Legged," in K. Ott, D. Serlin, and S. Mihm (eds), *Artificial Parts, Practical Lives*, 327–47, New York: New York University Press.

Titchkosky, T. (2011), *The Question of Access: Disability, Space, Meaning*, Toronto: University of Toronto Press.

Walton, D. (2011), "What's a Leg Got to Do with It?: Black, Female, and Disabled in America," *Center for Women Policy Studies*, February. Available online: http://www.peacewomen.org/sites/default/files/whatsaleggottodowithit_blackfemaleanddisabledinamerica_donnarwalton_0.pdf.

Williams, R. M. (2019), "Metaeugenics and Metaresistance: From Manufacturing the 'Includable Body' to Walking away from the Broom Closet," *Canadian Journal of Children's Rights / Revue canadienne des droits des enfants* 6 (1): 60–77.

Williamson, B., and E. Guffey, eds (2020), *Making Disability Modern: Design Histories*, London: Bloomsbury.

Wong, A. Twitter, April 21, 2019. Available online: https://twitter.com/SFdirewolf/status/1120174873244889090.

Case Study

19 M Eifler's *Prosthetic Memory* as Speculative Archive

LINDSEY D. FELT

Figure 18 M Eifler aka BlinkPopShift in collaboration with Steve Sedlmayr, *Prosthetic Memory*, 2020.

Prosthetic Memory could be described as a speculative archive in its clear orientation toward the future. A digital repository of moments in artist-researcher M Eifler's life, the archive includes videos that are sorted and called up by a machine learning algorithm. Nearly every video begins with the interpellation, "Hey future self." It stages a conversation between the artist in the present and the artist in the future, straining to shape and anticipate the moods and mental states of Eifler at some near or distant date. In one video, Eifler sits in the car, leans forward with their chin resting on the steering wheel, and says, "Instead of driving home, I am talking to you. How are you? How are you feeling?" (BlinkPopShift 2019a) As a speculative archive, *Prosthetic Memory* moves beyond the function of an archive as a site of critical knowledge production, and becomes one focused on holistic well-being, intervention, and narrative transformation. When M has the opportunity to boot up the full system at home, it provides them with an overwhelming sense of comfort and warmth, flooding them with nostalgia for a past self they cannot naturally remember.

These videos index a searchable memory bank of M Eifler, aka BlinkPopShift, a disabled, nonbinary, queer artist based in San Francisco. *Prosthetic Memory* curates an archival database for the artist who cannot form long-term memories. Eifler's creative practice blooms out of a longing to understand their bodymind's ecosystem—in particular its neurological pathways of chronic pain and memory dysregulation—through constellating systems of self-care, archive-building, machine prosthetics, and algorithmic simulations. A senior design researcher at Microsoft who is embedded in the company's internal innovation incubator, Eifler occupies a liminal position as a user of the designs they create and an expert agitating for disability design justice within Silicon Valley.

The Human in the AI

In early childhood, Eifler experienced a traumatic brain injury that left them with long-term amnesia. After Eifler learned they were in the fifth percentile for functioning memory in a neuropsychological evaluation, they developed a daily journaling practice for an autodidactical research project on their memory disability. In an effort to organize and make meaning of these private archives through an integrated arts-research lens, Eifler began building a bespoke artificial intelligence using a machine learning algorithm called YOLO (an algorithm that can run on a live camera feed) to recognize and sort these artifacts. The AI training took place in their home on a custom dual Intel Xeon workstation, a high-performance processor for data-intensive applications. The training process generated so much energy that it heated up Eifler's home studio to balmy eighty degrees in the winter months. Ultimately, Eifler finessed the AI to retrieve objects, events, people, and even moods, much like the multiplicitous neural pathways human memory encodes. Running a powerful GTX 970 graphics card typically used for serious gaming on an HP Envy system that was housed under a desk in a lockbox for its San Francisco exhibition, *Prosthetic Memory* could recall a video within five seconds or less of being introduced to a new image. The human interaction component of the AI became a crucial feature: the system only performed when a person visiting Eifler's installation turned a page in the journal.

In its initial conception, *Prosthetic Memory* was intended to be a computational prosthesis to enhance Eifler's memory recall for personal use. The design is unique in this respect as it is not a technological approximation of a neurotypical person's mental processes. Though it is in dialogue with artistic documentations of the self like Lynn Hershman Leeson's *The Electronic Diaries* (1984–2019), *Prosthetic Memory* represents the next generation of this impulse to explore the slippage between the artist's real and virtual self. It articulates a powerful example of crip aesthetics in which Eifler, a multiply-disabled artist-designer, hacked and reimagined corporate machine learning tools frequently used for surveillance and racial profiling to be responsive to the needs of one user. As a public-facing installation, the work also extended an invitation for others to join the artist's process of discovery and recollection. *Prosthetic Memory* remains a work in progress too, much like our own memories: it continues to iterate and evolve in complexity.

Intimate Data and CripTech

Eifler's piece asks, how do we understand AI when it is created and maintained within one's own home? And how can one person use machine learning for such individualized needs? "We hear a lot about AI," Eifler muses, "but there's very few direct experiences of people using AI in intimate situations, with intimate data to craft their own tools and prostheses using this technology" (BlinkPopShift 2020).

First publicly presented at "Recoding CripTech" at SOMArts Cultural Center in San Francisco in January 2020, Eifler and programming collaborator Steve Sedlmayr crafted *Prosthetic Memory* to help us see the possibilities for a home-grown, human-centered AI designed for self-care, comfort, and mutual aid rather than corporate surveillance. Installed as a white desk, a nondescript chair, and a binder splayed open that holds laminated pages of colorful drawings, handwritten notes, and collages, *Prosthetic Memory* is deceptive. This is no simple workspace. A large video projection on the desk's surface unspools footage of artist M Eifler from their bed. The camera pans from a scruffy cat curled up in a nest of blankets to Eifler speaking: "Hey future self," Eifler says and yawns, slowly rubbing their eyes. "Um, I'm tired, I was up at 4:30—I just couldn't sleep through the pain anymore, so we have officially broken our three day streak of good days." Eifler yawns again, subdued. "See if I can get my brain to do any work today. I don't know. Come on brain, you can do it," exhorts Eifler (BlinkPopShift 2019b).

A handwritten Post-It instructs visitors to turn the pages of the binder. A video camera linked to an artificial intelligence program scans the image, prompting a new video to play. In another clip, Eifler is face-down with their forehead resting on a yoga block speaking into the camera; other scenes show M in the car reflecting on the serpentine coils of chronic pain, taking a jaunty stroll in the neighborhood, riding the BART train, gleefully celebrating progress on the work of uploading and tagging videos that day.

The material staging of this installation—from a sunflower-yellow painted wall and a sweatshirt hanging from a shelf to a bulletin board dotted with Post-It notes and a cat's cradle of string—recreates the artist's studio space to rehome the AI's computer processor. The Post-It notes document an analog story of M's organizational logic behind the piece, with grids of numerical tags corresponding to dates. The physical design of the installation animates the profoundly personal nature of this data, where it originated and lives, and informs how both the artist and visitors engage with it.

If we explore this example as one that embodies a "design for one" or user-initiated design, we quickly realize that M's work defies easy categorization. M's corporate research explores the fringes of immersive virtual media systems; this work also bleeds into their evolving arts practice that is uniquely attuned to their own needs in personal spaces. But what I find telling is that in spite of being ensconced within a technology company that mass-produces computer products and electronics, Eifler is anti-universal design. They believe that a universal model of design cannot functionally or realistically cater to each person's individual disabilities and needs. This sensibility shines through in *Prosthetic Memory,* which captures highly idiosyncratic, intimate data—the artist's bio-rhythms, moods, behaviors, and everyday habits—for future temporal reference.

Just like M tends to their own memory like a garden, planting the seeds with new videos and journal entries that take on the shape of the artist's life—or a computational refraction of a life—*Prosthetic Memory* encodes its creator's diligent practice of self-care. This theme runs throughout the video logs, as Eifler often documents reflections in bed with heating pads during their chronic pain flare-ups, or discusses the merits and inadequacies of techniques and positions for mitigating pain. These moments of human fallibility are uncannily expressed in the AI's functionality too. *Prosthetic Memory* experienced performance issues in its first run, and Eifler assessed that its detection accuracy rate was roughly 80 percent. Through the four weeks of the exhibition, Eifler and their partner Steve Sedlmayr frequently visited the installation to tweak its operations or the positioning of the camera. While exhibiting Eifler's work, my co-curator Vanessa Chang and I notified them when the system crashed, but Eifler and Sedlmayr monitored it from a home computer that enabled them to fix the system on the fly without having to visit the gallery space. In this way, *Prosthetic Memory* grew beyond the scope of the artist's care: it asked of us and those who engaged with the installation to participate in communal caretaking.

At the same time, by addressing Eifler's "future self," *Prosthetic Memory* is also reminiscent of scholar Alison Kafer's concept of "crip futurity" (2013). Kafer notes how disabled people are stripped of agency to both imagine and occupy their own futures. Kafer's crip futurity yearns for a world where disability is not only welcome but where disabled people's experiences, practices, and ways of knowing might shape future structures. In one video titled "Tyranny of the Remembering Self," M thinks aloud about the purpose of their video diaries. This project feels different from "just vacation photos," Eifler says, or the "narcissistic exploration of the good times in my life" that social media platforms like Instagram enable. The archival work is processual rather than product-oriented, as it allows Eifler "to see myself thinking and to explore my thinking in a very day-to-day accumulatory way" (BlinkPopShift 2019b). *Prosthetic Memory* allows Eifler to explore the limits of their memory as a surprisingly communal site of imaginative possibility. It maps out a new way of approaching crip futurity and world-building through computational systems. In so doing, it not only preserves disabled narratives but also suggests how we might build new networks out of these stories and foster new forms of communal connectivity.

References

BlinkPopShift (2019a), "Pain Is a Greenhouse Gas," video filmed January 18.
Available online: https://www.youtube.com/watch?v=3O06xU8X9Qk&t=198s
(accessed October 21, 2021).

BlinkPopShift (2019b), "Tyranny of the Remembering Self," video filmed January 29.
Available online: https://www.youtube.com/watch?v=EPc7P8vA_MU (accessed on
21 October 2021).

BlinkPopShift (2020), "Prosthetic Memory," video filmed February 19. Available online:
https://www.youtube.com/watch?v=HEEQC6d-4e8 (accessed October 18, 2021).

Eifler, M. (2020), *Prosthetic Memory*, multimedia AI installation, SOMArts Cultural Center,
San Francisco, CA.

Eifler, M. (2021), email message to author, November 2.

Kafer, A. (2013), *Feminist Queer Crip*, Indianapolis, IN: University of Indiana Press.

Case Study

20 The Way Ahead

CAROLINE CARDUS

Figure 19 Caroline Cardus,
Don't Touch My Chair,
from *The Way Ahead* 2021
edition. © Caroline Cardus.

I was browsing magazines in a newsagent one day when I suddenly felt my wheelchair pulled sharply backward. Without a word of apology or glance in my direction, someone stepped into the space I had been occupying and casually proceeded to take a magazine off the shelf.

As a wheelchair user, I am well aware that people sometimes see me as an obstacle, a fire hazard, or incompetent in some way. I also know how often people seem to think of my wheelchair as a thing, and forget that it is a part of me. The knowledge of how my wheelchair—with me in it—has been moved as if it were just another piece of furniture is only one of the incidents that shaped *The Way Ahead*. Conceived as a simple, direct, and humorous action, this is a collaborative design project that uses familiar road sign symbols and formats to illustrate and convey the experiences of disabled people. By illustrating the barriers they face at home, work, and in the community, it contains and expresses this knowledge. This group of signs uses the clarity and legibility of government road signage to present disabled people's point of view, reflecting the issues they wish government and society were better at addressing.

Being a well-established visual system and carrying considerable authority, simple road signs seemed a good starting point for a project that could be easily understood but also offer a subversive way of highlighting disabled people's voices. Most people understand road signs and see them every day. Information on these signs is easily communicated simply using shapes, symbols, and colors. There are signs that give orders, signs that warn, signs that give information, and signs that give direction. By making up blank signs and then bringing them to workshops of fellow disabled people, I asked, "If you had to think about changing the way you access something in the world, how would you say it via an instruction, a direction, a warning, or a danger sign?" The final result was a collaborative design project that has toured throughout the UK since 2004. After seventeen years it has become an ongoing project with new tours and signs planned from 2021 onward.

Designed collaboratively with other disabled residents of Milton Keynes, the project includes an array of road and wayfinding signs. Within this format are a variety of schematic, official-looking diagrams accompanied by slogans. One stylized pictogram, for example, shows a crowd of standing stick figures and is accompanied by a sign reading "may contain hidden disabilities." And, remembering my incident with the stranger who moved me and my wheelchair as if we were a piece of discarded furniture, another depicts two stick figures, one standing behind another sitting in a wheelchair. With an exclamation point hovering over the pair, a printed message reads "don't touch my chair." *The Way Ahead* aims to uncover less discussed issues of disablement, equality, and access.

Certainly access was foremost on my mind when I moved to Milton Keynes in 2004. As a newly built town, it was designed for "easy movement and access" (The Plan for Milton Keynes 1970). Attracted by modern public buildings and shops with better access than older English towns, many physically disabled people moved there and continue to do so. As a visual artist born with a genetic condition which began affecting my mobility during the third year of my art degree, I have moved in and out of ambulant and immobile states. I myself moved to Milton Keynes for its unprecedented access, but I also have a healthy appreciation of the UK Disability Rights Movement, whose activism in changing building codes has prompted such things to happen (The British Council of Organizations of Disabled People 1997). I decided to focus on attitudes around this kind of access when I began an artist residency with Inter-Action MK, a community arts organization in Milton Keynes in 2004. *The Way Ahead* was initially funded by this group and expected to run for six months—a common time frame for community arts projects. But the project also worked with disabled people in Milton Keynes, sharing our awareness that we live somewhere where life had become easier, yet with the speculative insight there was much more to do before disabled people experience true equality.

In order to begin *The Way Ahead*, I visited groups of disabled people in Milton Keynes, and also took the project to some training sessions run by Disability Rights activists. Perhaps because disabled people experience inaccessibility so often, participants accepted the concept readily. The ideas evolved quickly, often with many people in the group joining in a conversation. One sign, *Trip City Roundabout*, began when a group of blind and partially sighted people started talking about common obstacles on pavements. When things like dog mess, bollards, A-frame boards, and garbage bins are left on pathways and sidewalks, they all become obstacles to vision-impaired people. Milton Keynes is known for its roundabouts. This group-designed sign places a person with a probing cane at the schematic entrance to one such roundabout that has exits to all those hazards.

While many groups designed together, sometimes individuals like artist Adam Reynolds shaped powerful images on their own.[1] Always an innovator in disability arts, Reynolds did things his own way—like opening his own gallery when nobody wanted to show work by disabled artists. His positive instruction sign in a blue circle shows many arrows of different shapes and sizes all radiating outward. Calling his sign *Forwards in Every Direction/Be Diverse*, Reynolds's design was meant to visualize what disability rights should be doing on a wider scale. The large bold arrows, small arrows, and one with a slight detour all work for me as a metaphor for progress in life.

But more immediately, we found that this signage is especially effective because people do not question *who* is giving the orders on a road sign. They just obey it and the format comes with authority built in. Subverting that voice of authority by adding the voices of disabled people to it appealed to my own sense of mischief. But it also gained a particular power when elaborated on by people like Disability Action Network (DAN) founder Barbara Lisicki.[2] She made a red triangular warning sign with a plate beneath it that reads "Stroppy Crips Ahead." Lisicki organized and has been at the forefront of some historic disability rights protests in the UK. Having chained herself to a bus to protest access issues, Lisicki's drawing presented a wheelchair user involved in a similar action. Moreover, her scrappy slogan plays on slang—the disability rights movement co-opted the word *crip* as a term of empowerment and *stroppy* expresses a British slang for an ornery or cantankerous person. "Stroppy Crips Ahead" sums up her uncompromising attitude on discrimination with a mischievous punk spirit.

In these ways, *The Way Ahead* also embodies the very real concerns of the disability rights movement. The original 2004 project was framed against new legislation giving disabled people more rights to access facilities and services including shops and public buildings. In contrast, UK disability rights activists argued that this legislation did not go far enough. This was—and still is—a rich seam for an artist activist to mine. The project expresses all the different ways disabled people still had very *little* access. It serves as a good rebuke to those who feel that disability access is an issue soon to be resolved. There is not only a breadth of practical information to impart about rights and access but a depth to the human experience when the appropriate access is not present. The account should come from the individual who has experienced it, as authenticity is so important—and sometimes lacking—when others continue to represent what disabled people want. We should not allow others to move our experiences aside like inconvenient obstacles. Recording these experiences culturally in my work continues to be *The Way Ahead*.

Notes

1. See Adam Reynolds' profile 1. https://the-ndaca.org/the-people/adam-reynolds/.
2. See Barbara Lisicki's profile https://the-ndaca.org/the-people/barbara-lisicki/.

References

The British Council of Organizations of Disabled People (1997), *The Disabled People's Movement: Book Four*, Somercotes, Derbyshire: Bailey & Sons Ltd. Available online: https://disability-studies.leeds.ac.uk/wp-content/uploads/sites/40/library/BCODP-workbook4.pdf.
Milton Keynes Development Corporation (1970), *Milton Keynes Master Plan*. Available online: https://theplanformiltonkeynes.co.uk.
Trades Union Congress (2004), "October 2004: the Disability Discrimination Act and Your Business," *TUC*, May 25. Available online: https://www.tuc.org.uk/research-analysis/reports/october-2004-disability-discrimination-act-and-your-business#a1.

Case Study

21 Customizing Reading: Harvey Lauer's "Reading Machine of the Future"

MARA MILLS AND HARVEY LAUER

Figure 20 Harvey Lauer with his Kurzweil Reading Machine, 1977. From the collection of Lauer / Mills.

This chapter is a revised and expanded version of a blog post originally titled "Other Electronic Books: Print Disability and Reading Machines," published on the conference page for *Unbound: Speculations on the Future of the Book*, Massachusetts Institute of Technology, April 30, 2012, https://futurebook.mit.edu/2012/04/other-electronic-books-print-disability-and-reading-machines/. The authors are grateful for the opportunity to preserve Lauer's text in this volume.

If today we distinguish between e-books and p-books, the "p" standing for print, already by the early twentieth century blind people and blindness researchers had partitioned "the book" and reading into an assortment of formats and practices. These include conventional ink print as well as raised print, braille, musical print, and talking books. In addition to the creation of alternate reading formats, blind people demanded access to print via tools that would ultimately transform the ink print book. Electrical and electronic reading machines—actual and speculative—that convert text into tones, speech, or vibrations helped bring about the e-book through their techniques for scanning, document digitization, and optical character recognition (OCR).

The first such reading machine, the Optophone, was designed in London by Edmund Fournier d'Albe in 1913 (Chan, Mills and Sayers 2018; Mills 2015). A "direct translator," it scanned print and generated a corresponding pattern of tones. Vladimir Zworykin, largely remembered for his work on television, visited Fournier d'Albe in London in the 1910s and saw a demonstration of the Optophone. At RCA in the 1940s, he built a reading machine that operated on the same principles, followed by an early OCR device that spelled out words letter-by-letter using a pre-recorded voice on magnetic tape. In 1963, John Linvill began working on an *optical-to-tactile* converter—the Optacon—partly as an aid for his blind daughter (Mills 2015). Linvill soon became chair of the electrical engineering department at Stanford, and the Optacon project became central to early microelectronics research at the university (Lécuyer 2005: 138, 250). Linvill and his collaborator, Jim Bliss, believed that a tactile code was easier to learn than an audible one, because the analogy between visible and vibratory print was more direct, both formats being two-dimensional. Extending the technique of character recognition (rather than direct translation), in 1973 Raymond Kurzweil launched the Kurzweil Reading Machine for the Blind, a text-to-speech device with multi-font OCR. As he recalls in *The Age of Spiritual Machines*, "We subsequently applied the scanning and omni-font OCR to commercial uses such as entering data into data bases and into the emerging word processing computers. New information services, such as Lexis, an on-line legal research service, and Nexis, a news service, were built using the Kurzweil Data Entry Machine to scan and recognize written documents"(Kurzweil 1999). Despite the publicity surrounding the Kurzweil machine, it was prohibitively costly for most individual use and it was not truly "omni-font," reading only limited printed materials.

Harvey Lauer (1933–2019), the blind rehabilitation and technology transfer specialist at the Hines VA Hospital for over thirty years, was one of the foremost experts on twentieth-century reading machines. Colleagues Robert Gockman and Stephen Miagawa called him "the 'father' of modified electronic devices for the blind and the 'Bionic Man' of the Central Blind Rehabilitation Center" (Miagawa 1996). Lauer attended the Janesville State School for the Blind, where he studied music and tinkered with electronics and audio components (Mills and Sterne 2020). He earned his BA in Sociology from the University of Wisconsin-Milwaukee in 1956 and his MS in Vocational Counseling from Hunter College the following year. Throughout his career, Lauer argued that "one medium isn't enough" when it comes to reading and communication, because the blind community is internally diverse: blindness is an "umbrella" category rather than a single identity. People themselves change over time, not to mention the formats, opportunities, and environments for reading (Lauer 1989).

A few years before his retirement from the VA in 1997, Lauer wrote a speculative paper on the "Reading Machine of the Future." By that time, personal computers were common and flatbed scanners were becoming affordable for home use. Text-to-speech software was beginning to replace the standalone reading machine. But the increasing complexity of graphical user interfaces inhibited blind computer users, and a conservative approach to reading (e.g., tying print to speech alone) was embedded in commercial OCR software. Since the days of Alan Turing, digital computers have been called "universal machines" for their "general purpose" ability to process all sorts of data—however, this should not be confused with universal design (Turing 1936). Each generation of computer hardware has created its own physical accessibility barriers, and even the customization and personalization enabled by software tend to presume a nondisabled user.

Lauer advocated a computerized, disability-centered "multi-modal reading aid" with braille, tonal, vibratory, and speech outputs for translating text and graphics according to reading material, situation, and individual inclination. With his permission, I've excerpted a selection from an unpublished article he wrote in 1994—the year Tim Berners-Lee founded W3C (The International World Wide Web Consortium) and the early days of the Web's new information ecology. In "Reading Machine of the Future but the Future Won't Just Happen," Harvey speaks from his three decades of experience with experimental reading machines, as well as his newfound frustration with the ableism of personal computing, graphical interfaces, and the emerging visual culture of the internet.[1]

Reading Machine of the Future but the Future Won't Just Happen

Harvey Lauer

September 12, 1994

From 1964 to the present, I have used, tested, and taught fourteen reading machines and many more devices for accessing computers. Working for the Department of Veterans Affairs, formerly the Veterans Administration, I saw much progress and several lessons forgotten.

The system I feel we really need will have a choice of modalities—speech, Braille, large print, and dynamic graphic displays. It will be configurable according to the user's needs and abilities. It will scan pages into its memory, process them as best it can, and then allow us to read them in our choice of medium. Automatic sequencing would be our first choice for easily scanned letters, articles, and books. But it will also let us examine them with a keyboard, a tablet, a mouse, or perhaps tools from Virtual Reality. It will offer us any combination of speech, refreshable braille, or large print as well as a verbal description of the format or layout. Because we will be able to use that description to locate what we want to read, it will be easier to use than current OCR machines, but not larger. When we also need to examine shapes, we will switch on tonal and/or vibratory (graphical) outputs. Examining the shape of a character or icon is far easier than reading with such an output.

In short, the system will offer a three-level approach to reading. The first choice is to have a page or screenful of text recognized and presented either as a stream of data or as data formatted by the machine. We can now do that with OCR machines. At the second level, we can choose to have the machine describe items found on pages or screen displays and their locations. We can have either brief descriptions or descriptions in "excruciating detail." We can then choose items by name or characteristics. That won't always be sufficient, so we will have a third choice. We can choose to examine portions of the page or individual items found by the machine, using speech, braille characters, a display of tones, an array of vibrators, a graphic braille-dot display, or magnified and enhanced images. Once the basic system is developed, it will constitute a "platform" for people like us to test its practical values and for researchers to test new ideas for presenting information to humans.

It's 1997. You place a page on your scanner. It could be a recipe, a page from a textbook, or part of a manual. You direct the machine to scan it into memory. You suspect that it isn't straight text, so you don't first direct the machine to present it in speech or braille. You request a description of the format and learn that the machine found two columns of text at the top, a table, and a picture with a caption. It also noted there were some tiny unidentified shapes, possibly fractions.

You then turn to your mouse (or other tracking device) which you move on an X/Y tablet. (This concept of a tablet was best articulated by Noel Runyan of Personal Data Systems in Sunnyvale, California.) You switch to freehand tracking and examine the rest of the page for gross features, without zooming. You find the table, plus what appears to be a diagram and some more text. With the mouse at the top of that text, you switch to assisted tracking. Now the system either corrects for mis-tracking or the mouse offers resistance in one or the other direction, depending upon your choices. As you scan manually, the text is spoken to you. After reading the block of text, you read the caption and examine the table. You find that some of the information needs to be read across columns, and some makes sense only when read as columns. You are thankful that you don't have an old-fashioned OCR, screen reader, and Optacon to tackle this job.

Then you find a longer piece of data you want to copy, so you "block and copy" it to a file. In examining the diagram, you find tiny print you want to read, but the OCR can't recognize it, so you zoom in (magnify) and switch to the mode in which shapes can be examined. Depending on your equipment and your abilities, you can have them presented as vibrating patterns on an Optacon array, as tone patterns, as a graphic, dot image on a rapidly refreshing array of braille dots, or as a combination of those modalities. You may or may not have the skill to read in this way; few people make the effort to develop it nowadays. What you do is examine the characters slowly and trace the lines of drawings in which you are interested.

With the new instrument, we won't have to give up nearly as often and seek sighted assistance. Optacon users will no longer have to remove the page and search about with camera in hand as if reading a map through a straw. Computer users will still have our screen access software. OCR users will still have their convenient, automatic features. However, when you use a current OCR machine to scan a page with a complex format, the data is frequently rearranged to the point where it's unusable. Such items as titles, captions, and dollar amounts are frequently scrambled together. It makes me feel as if I am eating food that someone else has first chewed. With the proposed system, when its automatic features scramble or mangle our data, we can examine it as I have described.

The exciting point is this: The proposed integrated system with several optional modules would harness available technology to allow us to apply the wide gamut of human abilities among us to a wide gamut of reading tasks. In 1980, I presented this idea in a paltry one-page document added to an article about reading machines. I then called it the Multi-dimensional Page Memory System. I've given it a new name—the Multi-modal Reading Aid.

Note

1. In 2017, shortly before his death, Lauer revisited the topic of reading machines—past and prospective—in preparation for an episode of the *Field Noise* podcast produced by Craig Eley. This episode, "Harvey's Alphabet," includes an interview by Eley with Lauer, as well as archival recordings of historical reading machine output collected from Lauer and digitized by Mills. Listen to the episode at *Field Noise*, https://fieldnoise.com/harvey.

References

Chan, T., M. Mills, and J. Sayers (2018), "Optophonic Reading, Prototyping Optophones," *Amodern* 8 (January). Available online: http://amodern.net/article/optophonic-reading/.

Kurzweil, R. (1999), *The Age of Spiritual Machines: When Computers Exceed Human Intelligence*, New York: Penguin: 175.

Lauer, H. (1989), "Why One Medium Isn't Enough," *OCLC Micro* 5 (6) (December): 22–5.

Lécuyer, C. (2005), *Making Silicon Valley: Innovation and the Growth of High Tech, 1930–1970*, Cambridge, MA: MIT Press: 138, 250.

Miagawa, S. (1996), "Bionic Man of CBC," typescript (retirement messages from colleagues) in Mills's possession, September 30.

Mills, M. (2015), "Optophones and Musical Print," *Sounding Out!*, January 5, 2015. Available online: https://soundstudiesblog.com/2015/01/05/optophones-and-musical-print/.

Mills, M., and J. Sterne (2020), "Aural Speed Reading: Some Historical Bookmarks," *PMLA* 135 (2) (March): 401–11.

Turing, A. (1936), "On Computable Numbers, with an Application to the Entscheidungsproblem," *Proceedings of the London Mathematical Society* 2 (42): 230–65.

Case Study

22 "Captioning on Captioning" with Shannon Finnegan

LOUISE HICKMAN

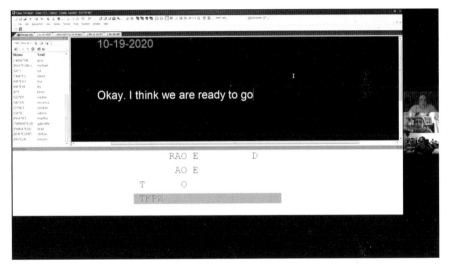

Figure 21 Still from *Captioning on Captioning*, 2020. Image courtesy of Louise Hickman and Shannon Finnegan.

Captioning on Captioning (2020) opens up with a shared view of a computer screen, which depicts the personal desktop of the real-time writer featured in this film, "Jennifer." Captions appear on screen: "Okay. I think we are ready to go." It is here where we first encounter speech-to-text transcription under real-time conditions—which is in this opening scene. Elsewhere on screen, the desktop view is divided into three distinct areas (from left to right): the first depicting the captioner's dictionary of steno briefs, including the names of frequent speakers; the second, centrally placed, are the captions described above; and the third area, occupying much of the lower screen, is perhaps the most perplexing operation for unfamiliar viewers. It is the raw data—steno briefs—of spoken speech transcribed by Jennifer into her stenographic software. The steno briefs' fleeting appearance, scrolling upward on the screen, gives viewers a portal into the real-time transcription of raw data into readable texts. In this film the internal mechanisms of real-time writing are rendered visible to show the intimate knowledge involved in captioning, producing, and caring for the other, all of which are required to procure access for D/deaf and Hard of Hearing readers (Hickman 2018).

Just over seven minutes long, this film by Louise Hickman (London, UK) and Shannon Finnegan (New York City, US) was made in collaboration with the real-time writer Jennifer (San Diego, US). The film was conceived as a way to document, celebrate, and speculate on the failure of speech-to-text transcription work, and to find patterns of spoken speech that cease to exist in the stenographer's dictionary software. These also marked the ephemeral encounters that escape the academic and social discourse spoken around the seminar table. The ephemeral nature of this notation gives insight into the process of "producing access," glimpsing a fleeting moment of queer and crip sociality. The impulse of this film is to document and construct an archive of transgressive speech acts.

The group's three members met for four meetings in late 2020 to utilize the share-screen function in a Zoom meeting room. We can now recognize this as a cultural artifact of pandemic mediations in our collective domestic and working spaces. The collapse of these spaces—home and work, public, and private—leads the group to focus on the complex "practice of care" instead of foregrounding the captioner's speech-to-text latency, or the delay between the recording of audio and its transcription into text. By inverting the invisibility of real-time writing, Shannon collaborated with Louise to edit the film in such a way as to show discrete moments of care, vulnerability, and intimacy. The showing of these moments is motivated by an imperative of disability justice: the documenting and editing of the film's production process is itself a political act that renders the invisible or fleeting visible—this editing process itself, however, being one to which viewers don't have access. It was during editing that we began to question the impulse to edit out our own speech, or to "tidy up" the dialogue between Shannon, Louise, and Jennifer. In turn, we grappled with multiple jarring encounters between the collaborators, including sentimental and affectionate utterances shared by Louise and the captioner that transgress the professional distance between service "user" and "provider," and more broadly, between colloquial speech and academic work. Who and why do we maintain these boundaries in our collective work? The answer does not resolve itself in the film but points toward the intersections between spoken speech, the signifier, the practice of real-time writing, phonetic data, and the familiarity with academic discourse, which all merge to produce "captions" as a sociotechnical text. To make sense of potential socio-technical transgressions, Mara Mills refers to the French psychoanalyst Jacques Lacan and his seminars on cybernetics. Mills accounts for Lacan's work pertaining to "the message" and the potential "jamming" of speech brought about by technology, namely the telephone. It is in these sites that speech can encounter "failure, interruption, and misinformation." (2010: 36) Mills writes further: "Speech could be broken into bits, much like 'the subject'—which, Lacan had earlier announced, 'is no one. It is decomposed, in pieces. And it is jammed'" (36). Mills then concludes: "Jamming, in [communication engineers'] discourse, referred to outside attacks on communication that interfered with reception, such as the deliberate addition of noise to a signal. In the name of efficiency, engineers worked to eliminate jams and accidental line noise from transmissions—as well as the 'irrelevant' and 'redundant' material that suddenly seemed to be intrinsic to speech" (2010). The same dynamic is at play in the transcription process. Engineers and stenographers may attempt to eliminate jams (which can extend in this case to automated captions). But this means that they must find an ideological horizon where efficiency and profitability meet. A "positivist" turn toward documenting these very mistakes—like speech-to-text latency and other socio technical transgressions—in many ways inspired the origins of this project, in which the speech excessive to (yet fundamental to the process of) official documentation is foregrounded. The measuring of words-per-minutes, too, serves as an empirical benchmark for assessing both the successes and failures of captioning.

In many ways this speculation allows us to rethink normative timekeeping in terms of the critique provided by "crip time." The latter term seeks to represent different modes of temporality that regimes of homogeneous and measured time subsume. Crip time is also a separatist project, one that clashes with the principle of real-time work, which demands captioning to be literally "on-time." The tension between being *on-time* and *opting out* of normative timekeeping is at the core of this project, which draws attention to the antagonisms inherent in an *understanding of access as a means of production*. It is the mistakes, transgressions, and latency, rather than the achievement of the perfect reproduction of mechanical text (one that mimics the reproduction of indifferent speech), that characterize the production of access. Knowing that these normatively defined failures are essential and intrinsic to the realization of captioning, how do we best preserve the future of access work (captioning among other types transcriptive work) when stenographers and their labor are often measured against the impossible conditions determined by speech, discourse, technological innovation, and the scalability of free software?

References

Hickman, L. (2018), "Access Workers, Transcription Machines, and Other Intimate Colleagues: Disability, Technology and Labor Practices in the Production of Knowledge," PhD diss., University of California San Diego, San Diego.

Mills, M. (2010), "Deaf Jam: From Inscription to Reproduction to Information," *Social Text* 28 (1): 35–58.

Case Study

23 A Squishy House

EMILY WATLINGTON

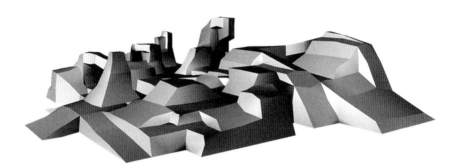

Figure 22 Architectural drawing of the Squishy House designed by Gabriel Cira. Courtesy of ARCH CIRA.

When I walk to the grocery store from my apartment in Cambridge, I always go out of my way to cut through a neighborhood playground that has this rubber material. It's not a shortcut: I go out of my way to experience the few moments of relief afforded by the surface that softens the inevitable blow of my ankles hitting the ground. In many ways, I'm so used to the pain that I'm most likely to remember it in those few moments of relief. That's also why aerial yoga is my favorite form of exercise; I'm not especially athletic, but it feels fantastic to take a break from the ground or surfaces that push back and to suspend my body in a swath of fabric. In my fantasy world, I wouldn't have to take "scenic" routes to experience this feeling but, instead, I'd live in a squishy house. I've been imagining the design of this building for a number of years.

My dream house—or really my dream world—would be lined with that squishy rubber flooring you sometimes find on playgrounds, designed to buffer the falls that inevitably occur when children climb jungle gyms. As an arthritic person, the feeling that occurs when my bones collide with hard pavement as I walk is a daily source of pain. I often have nightmares about it. Shoes with thick, bouncy soles are a way of carrying this material around on my body, and I'm thankful that fashionable sneakers are having a moment, as historically, most orthopedic shoes have been designed for elderly people. There's nothing wrong with those sorts of shoes—I've worn them before—but it's so nice to have options. Wearing this material on my soles, however, doesn't eliminate the sensation, it just dampens it.

Maybe this design is not so fantastical. Wanting to see if and how it might play out in real space, I asked architect Gabriel Cira to collaborate on the design of a squishy house. During the design process, we discovered a number of issues that surprised both of us. Our speculative design is not a whole house but more of a living room-type space, for leisure and for socializing. Cira pointed out that the material might make comfortable furniture as well—soft enough to sit on, hard enough to be a table that supports a glass of water (though if you want to write, you'll need some sort of clipboard). In the design there are shapes that might be used as seating, replete with back support, arm rests, and end tables.

It's hard to say, however, how squishy grounds would intersect with other people's access needs. Sometimes I wish we could line subway stations with rubber flooring, but I suspect it would be hard to use crutches or walkers, for example, when walking across the platform. I haven't tried it myself, but often these devices are used to stabilize and bear weight, which means that they rely on the hardness of the ground. If I had a house with squishy floors, I wonder, would it be hard to have a friend using crutches come over for dinner? Or what if I became injured and needed crutches myself? This sort of questioning—asking whether meeting my own access needs will create a barrier for someone else—is called an access loop.

I admit that I myself had a hard time imagining the aesthetics of this house. Usually this sort of material is made to look like asphalt or applied with bright colors we associate with childhood and play. Many materials intended for access or comfort are designed for children or for elderly people; from our teenage years through middle age, we are largely expected to be independent, nondisabled, and capable of taking care of our own needs without the support of objects or others. But I am also excited about the aesthetic prompt this material elicits. I enjoy bright colors, but I resent the implied infantilization and ageist assumptions about impairment.

I find that my imagination is often colored by the built work of the New York-based conceptual art and architecture duo Madeline Gins and Shusaku Arakawa. In their most speculative work, the pair used bright colors and alternative flooring for precisely the opposite purpose. Instead of designing for comfort, Arakawa and Gins intended with their "Reversible Destiny" projects to create domestic environments that were difficult to walk around, that deliberately induced physical exertion (2002). If everyday activities are turned into opportunities for exercise, according to Arakawa and Gins, users could become fit and healthy, and ideally stave off death.

In the end, the squishy house reminds me of a *Seinfeld* episode where a character named Kramer announces he is going to rid his apartment of furniture and replace it all with "levels." He considered the width of the aisles and the slopes of ramps, and there are no stairs. One could, conceivably, climb over some of the forms. Even though the shapes were set in place and not exactly adjustable, they could be used in many different ways by many different bodies. Predictably, Kramer's friends laugh off his design. Of course, his vision had little to do with access, and perhaps was even inaccessible. But in one's own home, we all ought to be liberated to configure a space intended for our own unique needs instead of being pressured to conform to design norms. Kramer's total irreverence toward arbitrary norms might seem laughable, but his vision resonates with my fantasy for a squishy house, encapsulating something that is badly needed in design today—a new and even radical spirit of accessibility.

References

Drawing by Gabriel Cira

Gins, M., and S. Arakawa (2002), *Architectural Body*, Tuscaloosa: University of Alabama Press.

Case Study

24 Black Disabled Joy as an Act of Resistance

JEN WHITE-JOHNSON

Figure 23 Seven-year-old Black and autistic boy holding "Black Disabled
Lives Matter" poster, 2020. Image courtesy of Jen White-Johnson.

More than half of Black/brown bodies in the United States with disabilities will be arrested by the time they reach their late twenties. Black disabled people are a direct target among them. They are stigmatized and misunderstood at higher rates. We often don't hear or read about them until after they are taken from us. We don't see many positive stories or acts of #AutisticJoy and #BlackDisabledJoy among Black/brown bodies because they don't make headlines.

Inspired by radical feminism, revolutionary mothering,[1] and the activism of Fannie Lou Hamer and other disabled people of color, my design and artistic practice reexamines the role of a socially engaged practitioner, educator, and mother all the while amplifying narratives from the disability community. In both my personal and academic work, I have explored pedagogical approaches for implementing socially engaged art practice in the curriculum inside and outside of the classroom, all through the lens of creative resistance. When my son was diagnosed as autistic at the age of three, I felt it important to begin redefining my role as a disabled mother of a disabled child. I wanted to explore how my art and design practice could inform a framework for community engagement by advocating for disabled and autistic communities. But in the process, I took up Crip Joy[2] as a design expression that could be an act of resistance, breaking the visual cycle of unjust, ableist, and oppressive stigmas within social and clinical practices. The work continues and as a Disabled Afro-Latina parent to an eight-year-old Black and autistic son, my sole job is to preserve his present so that he can exist in the future.

Design and Mothering as an Act of Resistance

Once I realized that living in my truths held immense power, I began to disclose my disability as a nondiagnosed ADHD woman living with a thyroid disorder and anxiety. My creative design and disability justice work began to transform how Black and brown disabled families are seen in digital media and how allyship between neurodivergent peoples and neurotypical caregivers can create change, shifting stigmas, cultivating a desire to "tell our truths to live," and creating a socially inclusive caregiving approach while amplifying invisible communities.

My definition of mothering as an act of resistance aims to empower and to activate change—encouraging families and communities to engage in conversations about acceptance, starting with how neurodivergent children are treated, seen, and valued. The work became rooted in creating digital and print media about and with my autistic son, but it was also meant to uplift the disability community. Reclaiming visual narratives and breaking the stigma of our disabled and autistic journey, photography and design became a tool to highlight what I often didn't see depicted in the media: aiming to break unjust stigmas, centering and celebrating mothering and carework as a Black disabled woman as a liberatory and revolutionary act.

I knew that my creative practice and parent/child advocacy work had to celebrate the often missing narrative of neurodiversity and autism acceptance/advocacy in

Black and brown families. My first photo zine, *Knox Roxs*, set a personal framework and helped define what autism acceptance can mean for BIPOC families. Autistic Joy became visible, and we knew with this independent format, we could keep ownership of the visual content and narrative. I had no desire to create a photo zine that defined autism in the eyes of clinicians or a "how-to guide" for parenting an autistic child. The zine was a true expression of what love and acceptance can look like if you let it in, truly unmasked. In February 2019, we were honored to see the *KnoxRoxs* photo zine permanently archived on the shelves in the Metropolitan Museum of Art library as artistic research amplifying Black and brown disability culture.

Zines are vital in communicating our artistic visions and ignite change. My work continues to shift the narrative of Black neurodivergent disability visual culture, and I use zines to bridge underserved BIPOC communities both in and out of the classroom. Additionally, the creation process encouraged more work and art direction from my son. This became a way to show families how to create and collaborate with their neurodivergent kids and people in their communities, all the while encouraging them to be more accepting of autism itself. In 2019 the zine prompted a series of community photo and zine workshops, fostering conversation around the practice of design and mothering as an act of resistance, all the while raising disabled children of color. The workshops were led by me and conducted with various community-based organizations. In facilitating these workshops I came to see zine making as a liberatory space and practice, helping to create an immersive and interactive safe space, all the while amplifying experiences and narratives of disabled children and adults. But they also created a dialogue between me and other neurodivergent families and communities.

My community work shifted in 2020, when I was in the middle of an artist-mother studio residency and my photo and design advocacy work suddenly had to continue at home due to the Covid pandemic. My ADHD and anxiety heightened. I was concerned that my desire to create would be stifled by no longer being in a studio. At the same time, however, I know what it is to be disabled. We often must work within limited means and constraints; we still make magic. Being in isolation didn't stop our creativity, and the need to stay active from home during my residency highlighted the need for my design activism to take up permanent residence in our home amidst a nation in continued turmoil. In a photo series entitled *Follow Your Light: Photos of Light & Love Made by a Disabled Mom and Her Autistic Son*, we began to experiment with various elements of liberatory sensory play using light paintings, textiles, and fabrics. With that liberation came the need to create and discover accessible ways for my then seven-year-old autistic son to become engaged and immersed in creativity.

Music is an amazing way that Knox communicates his autistic joy. The curves, swooshes, dips, and bops captured through the lights allowed me to capture the essence of his neurodiverse spirit through photography. We used vibrant lights to amplify, evoking a sense of rhythm, beat, and freedom encouraging self expression.

The project resulted in the *Soul of Neurodiversity*, a statement of self-advocacy in our home and influencing a visual framework that set the tone for our definition of autism acceptance. From it we created a *Soul of Neurodiversity Manifesto*:

1 Break the cycle of assimilation.

2 Break the cycle of unjust stigmas.

3 Activate and infuse the narrative of soul in the lives of neurodivergent peoples within spaces.

After the photo series and artist residency ended, we wanted to continue creating virtual dialogue with our disability community. With this in mind, we organized a Kids Solidarity Virtual Zine Fest, prompting other families to create zines themed around social justice—and joy.

To Be Pro Neurodiversity Is to Be Anti-Racist

Our world was boundless with creativity as Covid continued to take hold in our nation and then as footage of the summer 2020 uprisings around the nation and the world began to flood my social media feeds. I felt emotionally exhausted by the weight of seeing Black and brown bodies murdered by "policies" and "laws" meant to protect us. I felt exhausted knowing that Black bodies with disabilities would be excluded from the conversations. I felt solidarity in support for my disabled son. In virtual protest with my Black disabled community, I felt compelled to use my art to bring visibility to these facts. I felt my joy being compromised by the weight of seeing Black and brown disabled bodies discarded and stolen by state violence. And yet, even while in isolation during the pandemic, my son continued to defy ableist stigmas by showing unbridled Black radical autistic joy. I felt compelled to create a graphic that merged the Black power fist—the historic symbol of solidarity and power, which was used by Black revolutionary disabled activists like Fannie Lou Hamer and Brad Lomax—with the neurodiversity infinity symbol. Together, they could convey the message that Black Disabled Lives Matter. I posted the symbol on social media, writing in the caption, "True advocates and allies please take note: To be Pro Neurodiversity is to be Anti Racist."

After this, I watched in disbelief as the graphic was shared across hundreds of profiles and by disability justice advocates and writers over the span of just a couple of days. Since then, it's taken on a beautiful life of its own. In virtual protest I continued to share the digital graphics and created free printable Black Disabled Lives Matter posters for protesters to print and use at uprisings within their communities. The posters traveled from Baltimore to Washington, DC, to San Francisco to London in less than forty-eight hours.

Black disabled people and their perspectives should be at the forefront of the movement for Black lives. As the mother of a Black autistic son, I know that he will instantly be misunderstood by police and other authorities whether he wants to or not. This is because of his disability. I couldn't help but think of Black lives taken from us as a result of state violence like Eleanor Bumpurs, George Floyd, Korrine Gaines, and Elijah McClain. I still have my son and I'm going to do everything in my power to make sure that I'm going to continue to have him. But it's up to all of us to remind people that disabled adults and kids are not disposable. They deserve the opportunity to exist, and to exist in their own way.

After the symbol and disability solidarity statement began to resonate with the disability community (which is often subjected to ableist media), I felt seen and continued to create graphics in virtual protest. Each day I would ask myself, "What can I do? How does disability justice play a role in my family values and my family's overall expression?" I have a social responsibility to use art to educate and dismantle systems of ableist oppression; it was a natural response to use art to uplift and bring visibility to an underserved and dying community. Much of my design and artwork comes directly from conversations that I have with other disabled folks. I want to infuse just and authentic narratives into my work. If our nation continues to show that our young Black autistic men don't have value, what does that say to our current generation of Black autistic youth? How can the use of art and design create cultural shifts in the lives of Black and brown disabled youth? We need to advocate to save lives, abolishing ableism, and celebrating those who are marginalized and considered disposable.

I want my son's joy to be infinite, existing as its own revolution, not needing anyone's permission to show it. Ableist and racist social constructs continue to steal so much Black disabled joy, erasing our humanity and existence. Protesting and practicing radical joy as an act of resistance will further amplify Black disabled lives. Created by the disability community, I believe that design continues to be instrumental in reigniting much needed dialogue about Black disability justice.

Those that sit and rest in their privilege have always been able to breathe while watching those that exist while being Black and disabled in America can't and won't ever breathe again. There is no standard experience as a disabled person outside of the injustices that so many of us face. As a nation we are still a long way from freedom and justice, but I hope the artwork and organizing with the disability community continue to be a step toward maximized representation and transformation.

Notes

1. For additional context around the term, see Gumbs, Martens, and Williams (2016).
2. CripJoy power-centered coaching by and for mad and disabled people founded by Joshua Halstead, Suliaman Khan, and Aminder Virdee.

Reference

Gumbs, A. P., C. Martens, and M. Williams, eds (2016), *Revolutionary Mothering: Love on the Front Lines*, Oakland, CA: PM Press.

List of Contributors

Alison Kurdock Adams is currently working on a master's degree in modern and contemporary art, criticism, and theory from the State University of New York at Purchase, where she is the Strypemonde writing fellow. She speaks and writes about American postindustrial built environments, artistic production in diasporic communities, and the intersection of performance and avant-garde craft practices.

Émeline Brulé is a designer and lecturer in human-computer interaction at the University of Sussex. Her research broadly focuses on inclusion and technologies, and her PhD (2018) focused on schooling experiences of visually impaired children in France and the use of multisensory technologies in this context.

Caroline Cardus is a UK-based artist whose practice focuses on creative activism. Starting from Cardus's own experiences as a disabled woman, her text-based, subversive, and graphic style practice brings forth frank, darkly humorous, and powerful messages about disability inequality and everyday discrimination.

Elise Co is Associate Professor in the Interaction Design and Graduate Media Design Practices departments at ArtCenter College of Design. Co is a multimedia designer, programmer, and principal of Aeolab, a design+technology consultancy she co-founded with Nikita Pashenkov, and is on the faculty at ArtsCenter College of Design. Co holds an MS degree in media arts and sciences and a BS degree in architecture from the Massachusetts Institute of Technology.

Andrew Cook is Lecturer of Design and Making at Jordanstone College of Art and Design, University of Dundee.

Maitraye Das is a Postdoctoral Fellow at the University of Washington and an incoming Assistant Professor at Northeastern University. Her research in human-computer interaction focuses on making collaborative content production more accessible and equitable in ability-diverse teams. She earned her MS and PhD in technology and social behavior from Northwestern University and BS in computer science and engineering from Bangladesh University of Engineering and Technology.

Robert Dirig is Director of Archives and Special Collections at ArtCenter College of Design. He holds an MLIS from the University of California, Los Angeles, and is a member of the Society of American Archivists. Dirig is Co-Principal Investigator for an IMLS grant titled Reimagining Access: Inclusive Technology Design for Archives and Special Collections, which researches what can be learned from people with disabilities to improve access to digital collections.

Lindsey D. Felt is a lecturer at Stanford University in the Program in Writing and Rhetoric. Her research focuses on the intertwined histories of disability, technology, and communication practices in American culture. She has published "Cyberpunk's Other Hackers: The Girls Who Were Plugged In" (2019) in *Catalyst: Feminism, Theory, Technoscience* and "Cripping Media Ecologies" (2022) in Ground Works. She co-curated the Recoding CripTech exhibition at SOMArts Cultural Center in San Francisco as a 2019–20 Curatorial Fellow. Lindsey is also the Disability and Access Lead for Leonardo/ISAST, where she helps direct Leonardo's CripTech Incubator, an art and technology fellowship for disability innovation.

Kelly Fritsch is Assistant Professor in the Department of Sociology and Anthropology and Director of the Disability Justice and Crip Culture Collaboratory at Carleton University. As a crip theorist and critical disability studies scholar, her research probes the workings of ableist social relations, the neoliberal biopolitics of disability, and anti-assimilationist crip disability culture and politics. She is the co-editor of *Disability Injustice: Confronting Criminalization in Canada* (2022) and *Keywords for Radicals: The Contested Vocabulary of Late-Capitalist Struggle* (2016). She is also the co-author of *We Move Together* (2021), a children's book about ableism, accessibility, and disability justice.

Elizabeth Guffey is Professor of Art and Design History and Co-director of the MA Program in Art History at the State University of New York, Purchase College. She is the author of *Retro: The Culture of Revival* (2006) and *Posters: A Global History* (2015). She is also the co-editor of *Making Disability Modern* (with Bess Williamson, 2020) and author of *Designing Disability* (2018). She is the founding editor of the peer-review journal *Design and Culture*.

Joshua Halstead is Assistant Professor in the Designmatters and Humanities and Sciences department at ArtCenter College of Design. His scholar-activist work centers the body as a subject and object of design knowledge and politics.

Aimi Hamraie is Associate Professor of Medicine, Health, and Society and American Studies at Vanderbilt University and Director of the Critical Design Lab. Their research focuses on accessibility and built environments. Trained as a feminist disability scholar, they contribute to the fields of critical disability studies, science and technology studies, and critical design and urbanism. Hamraie is the author of *Building Access: Universal Design and the Politics of Disability* (2017). They are the host of the Contra* podcast on disability and design and co-curator of #CripRitual, a multi-site disability arts exhibition. Hamraie is also a new member of the U.S. Access Board. Hamraie's research is funded by the National Science Foundation, the Social Science Research Council, the Smithsonian Institution, the Mellon Foundation, the Graham Foundation for Advanced Studies in the Arts, and the National Humanities Alliance.

Sara Hendren is a humanist in tech—a design researcher, writer, and professor at Olin College of Engineering. Her book *What Can a Body Do? How We Meet the Built World* (2020) explores the places where disability shows up in design. It was named one of the Best Books of 2020 by NPR, was a finalist for the Massachusetts Book Award in nonfiction, and won the 2021 Science in Society Journalism book prize. Her art and design works have been widely shown in museum exhibitions and are held in the permanent collections at MoMA and the Cooper Hewitt.

Maggie Hendrie is Professor and Chair of Interaction Design and Graduate Media Design Practices at ArtCenter College of Design. She is the co-director of the NASA/JPL/Caltech/ArtCenter Data to Discovery Visualization Program.

Ann Heylighen is a design researcher with a background in architectural engineering. As a professor of design studies at KU Leuven, Department of Architecture, she co-chairs the multidisciplinary Research[x]Design group. Her work focuses on how human diversity in general and disability experience in particular may expand prevailing ways of understanding and designing space. She studied at KU Leuven and ETH Zürich, holds a PhD from KU Leuven, and conducted postdoctoral research at Harvard and UC Berkeley. She currently holds a Francqui Research Professorship, and she is a Fellow of the Design Research Society and Associate Editor of *Design Studies*.

Louise Hickman is Research Associate at the Minderoo Centre for Technology and Democracy at the University of Cambridge. Louise previously worked as Senior Research Officer at the London School of Economics and Political Science Department of Media and Communications and at Ada Lovelace Institute's JUST-AI Network on Data and AI Ethics. She continues to co-convene the JUST AI's working group on rights, access, and refusal. An academic, artist, and activist, she earned her PhD in communication from the University of California, San Diego, in 2018 and held a postdoctoral position in the Feminist Labor Lab at UC San Diego.

Natalia Pérez Liebergesell is a postdoctoral researcher with a background in architecture (ETSAV-UPC, Spain, 2013). After graduating, she edited and co-authored the handmade book *Four Wheelchair-User Architects*, featuring her and her three peers' final thesis projects. Since 2016, she has been part of the Research[x]Design group, where during her PhD (KU Leuven, Belgium, 2020) she investigated intersections between disability (experience) and (architectural) design. Her current research focuses on exploring ways to improve inclusive designing by looking at shared similarities, instead of at differences, between a diverse population.

Todd Masilko is Associate Professor and Faculty Director in the Interaction Design Department at ArtCenter College of Design. Masilko has over fifteen years experience as an interaction designer and strategic design consultant.

Mara Mills is Associate Professor of Media, Culture, and Communication at New York University, where she co-founded and co-directs the Center for Disability Studies. She is co-founder and editorial board member of the journal *Catalyst: Feminism, Theory, Technoscience*. Most recently, she is the co-editor of *Testing Hearing: The Making of Modern Aurality* (Oxford, 2020) and *Crip Authorship: Disability as Method* (NYU, 2023). More information can be found at maramills.org.

Jessica Ryan-Ndegwa graduated with a BA (Hons) in product and furniture design at Kingston University. She is a product designer, blogger, and founder of Design for Disability. In addition to her design work, she serves as a consultant, speaker, and curator at a variety of cultural organizations, including the Institute for Contemporary Arts in London and the Tate Exchange.

Anne Marie Piper is Associate Professor in Informatics at the University of California, Irvine. Her research in human-computer interaction and accessible computing aims to create more equitable and inclusive digital experiences for people of all ages and abilities. She earned her PhD in cognitive science from the University of California, San Diego, MA in education from Stanford University, and BS in computer science from Georgia Tech.

Graham Pullin is Professor of Design and Disability at DJCAD, the art college at the University of Dundee. Here he co-founded Studio Ordinary, a meeting place for disability studies and design research. He is author of the manifesto *Design Meets Disability* (2009; Japanese edition 2022).

Katya Borgos-Rodriguez earned her PhD in technology and social behavior from Northwestern University and BS in computer engineering from the University of Puerto Rico at Mayaguez. Her research focuses on understanding and designing more accessible environments that support creative work and community-building.

Gabi Schaffzin is Assistant Professor in the Department of Design at York University's School of the Arts, Media, Performance, and Design. His current research project combines design history, disability studies, and a history of computing to trace the history of designed pain scales in the United States throughout the twentieth century. His major publications include "From Efficiency to Pain: A History of the Visual Analog Scale" from *Culture and Medicine: Critical Readings in Medical Humanities* (2023) and "Reclaiming the Margins in the Face of the Quantified Self" in *Review of Disability Studies* (2018).

David Serlin is Associate Professor of Communication and Science Studies, and affiliated faculty in Critical Gender Studies and the Interdisciplinary Group in Cognitive Science, at UC San Diego. He is also an affiliated faculty at the Center for the Study of Social Difference at Columbia University. His books include *Replaceable You: Engineering the Body in Postwar America* (2004); *Artificial Parts, Practical Lives: Modern Histories of Prosthetics* (co-editor; 2002); *Imagining Illness: Public Health and Visual Culture* (editor; 2010); *Keywords for Disability Studies* (co-editor; 2015); and *Window Shopping with Helen Keller: Architecture and Disability in Modern Culture* (forthcoming). He was awarded the 2020–21 Rome Prize in Architecture by the American Academy in Rome.

Ashley Shew is Associate Professor of Science and Technology Studies at Virginia Tech and works on philosophy of technology at its intersection with disability studies, emerging tech, and animal studies. She is the co-editor-in-chief of *Techné*, the journal of the Society for Philosophy and Technology (SPT), as well as the co-editor of three philosophy of technology volumes and sole author of *Animal Constructions and Technological Knowledge* (2017).

Katherine M. Steele is the Albert S. Kobayashi Professor of Mechanical Engineering at the University of Washington. She leads the Ability and Innovation Lab, which integrates dynamic musculoskeletal simulation, motion analysis, medical imaging, and device design to understand and support human mobility. In 2020, she co-founded CREATE (create.uw.edu), the UW Center for Research and Education on Accessible Technology and Experiences, and she serves as its associate director. She is also the co-founder of AccessEngineering (uw.edu/doit/accessing), an NSF-supported program that supports individuals with disabilities to pursue careers in engineering and trains all engineers in principles of universal and ability-based design.

Natasha Trotman is an artist-in-residence at Somerset House (studio 48) and an equalities designer, maker, and researcher. She completed her master's degree in information experience design at the Royal College of Art. Previously she worked as a research associate at the Royal College of Art's Helen Hamlyn Centre for Inclusive Design (HHCD) as well as at the Wellcome Collection Hub on the Wellcome Trust and HHCD Design and the Mind Research project, focusing on engagement and co-creation with neurodiverse groups and neurodivergent individuals and the disabled community. Currently a Design Expert for the Design Council. Natasha has been honoured at 10 and 11 Downing Street; she has been selected as a 10×10 Emerging Artist by the British council, and named on the Shaw Trust Powerlist Top 100 Influential Disabled People in the UK 2019 and 2020.

Peter-Willem Vermeersch works as a visiting professor at KU Leuven and as an engineer-architect at archipelago architects in Leuven/Brussels, Belgium. He obtained his MSc and PhD in Engineering: Architecture from KU Leuven and did his internship at Osar architecten, Antwerp, and (Full) Scale architecten, Leuven. At KU Leuven, he is part of the Research[x]Design group, a multidisciplinary group at the interface of design research and social sciences/humanities that conducts research on how space is designed and experienced and the relation between both. His research focuses on how the lived experience of disabled people can inform architectural design practice.

Jaipreet Virdi is Associate Professor in the Department of History at the University of Delaware, whose research focuses on the ways medicine and technology impact the lived experiences of disabled people. She is the author of *Hearing Happiness: Deafness Cures in History* (2020) and co-editor of *Disability and the Victorians: Attitudes, Legacies, Interventions* (2020). She has published articles on design histories of disability, the medicalization of deafness, and histories of diagnostic technologies.

Emily Watlington is a critic, curator, and assistant editor at Art in America. She writes on topics including art, architecture, disability justice, and feminism. A Fulbright scholar who holds a master's degree in the history, theory, and criticism of architecture and art from MIT, she has held curatorial positions at the MIT List Visual Arts Center and at the MassArt Art Museum.

Jen White-Johnson is Adjunct Faculty at Maryland Institute College of Art in Baltimore, Maryland. She holds an MFA in graphic design from the Maryland Institute College of Art and a BA in visual arts from the University of Maryland Baltimore County. Jen is the author of *KnoxRoxs* (2018), a photo-zine dedicated to the visibility of Black/Latinx Neurodivergent Families, and her activist and advocacy work has been featured in *The Washington Post*, *AfroPunk*, *The New York Times*, and *Teen Vogue*. She was selected as an honoree on the 2020 Diversability's D-30 Disability Impact List.

Bess Williamson is Professor of Art History, Theory, and Criticism at the School of the Art Institute of Chicago. She is the author of *Accessible America: A History of Disability and Design* and a co-editor of *Making Disability Modern* (with Elizabeth Guffey, 2020).

Index